Studies in Sociology

Edited by

PROFESSOR W. M. WILLIAMS
University College, Swansea

11
THE SOCIOLOGY OF WOMEN

STUDIES IN SOCIOLOGY

THE
SOCIOLOGY
OF
WOMEN

An Introduction

Sara Delamont
Senior Lecturer in Sociology, University College, Cardiff

London
GEORGE ALLEN & UNWIN
Boston   Sydney

GEORGE ALLEN & UNWIN LTD
40 Museum Street, London WC1A 1LU

© Sara Delamont, 1980

British Library Cataloguing in Publication Data

Delamont, Sara
  Sociology of women.
  1. Women – Great Britain – Social conditions
  I. Title
  301.41′2′0941   HQ1593
  ISBN 0–04–301119–5
  ISBN 0–04–301120–9 Pbk

Typeset in 10 on 11 point Times by Watford Typesetters
and printed in Great Britain
by Billing & Sons Ltd., Guildford, London and Worcester

Contents

Preface

I have aimed this book at the general reader, and the person who is doing sociology courses on life in modern society, at secondary school, in higher education and on courses for health visitors, medical students, and so on. I have therefore avoided much sociological terminology and the more complicated debates about women within sociology, within Marxism and within the feminist movement. However, for those who want to go further, references to these debates will be found in the Further Reading at the end of the book. The book deals with England, Wales and Scotland, but not Northern Ireland because I am not knowledgeable enough about the special conditions which affect life there.

I have tried, as far as possible, to use published material that readers can follow up via a public or college library. I have tried to avoid unpublished theses or obscure and foreign journals as sources in favour of available books, papers and magazines. I hope that anyone who doubts what I say will follow it up and look for himself or herself at the evidence.

Acknowledgements

Professor W. M. Williams of University College, Swansea, first suggested to me that I should write this book, and I am grateful to him for the advice I have received while it was in preparation. I am indebted to various colleagues at University College, Cardiff, and the University of Leicester for ideas and suggestions, and to the members of women's studies groups at Leicester, Cardiff and elsewhere where many of the themes and ideas have been discussed. Throughout the book I have drawn on ideas, conversations and both published and unpublished work by Lorna Duffin, Olive Banks, Mary Ciarain, Geoff Mungham, Irene Jones, Mandy Llewellyn, Anne Murcott and Rhian Ellis, and I am very grateful for their inspiration and permission to use their material. Much of the research was only possible because of the efficiency of the staff of the inter-library loan desk at University College, Cardiff: Shelagh Pollard and Jean Loosemore. The manuscript was typed at various stages by Jaquie Markie, Margaret Simpson, Myrtle Robbins, Mary Sansom and Llewela Gibbons and I am very grateful to all of them.

Finally I wish to thank Paul Atkinson for his trenchant criticisms of the early drafts and his unstinting support during the rewriting.

Chapter 1

Introduction

Good evening, this is the ten o'clock news and Mary Lyon reading it. First, the news headlines.

The Chancellor of the Exchequer, the Right Honourable Frances Buss, has announced today that there will be a mini-budget on 19 June before the summer recess.

The results of the Democratic presidential primary in Georgia shows Bella Azbrug a clear winner over Shirley Chisholm.

The Derby was won today by Blakeney's Niece at 7 to 4, ridden by Emma Willard, trained by Annie Kenny and owned by Lady Hester Stanhope, the millionaire industrialist.

The Secretary of State for the Environment, Prudence Crandall, announced that the Royal Commission on the Road Haulage Industry is to be chaired by Dame Lucy Larcom, President of the Royal College of Surgeons.

The President of Yorkshire County Cricket Club, Phillippa Fawcett, has made it clear that the club is to discipline Geoff Burkett over the controversial incident at Hove last Sunday.

At Question Time the Prime Minister, Dorothea Beale, faced tough questions from Opposition Leader Rhoda Nunn over the new wages settlement for the airline pilots. Nunn claimed that the settlement was highly inflationary, but this has been denied tonight by Captain Catherine Beecher, leader of BALPA, the pilots' union.

Our Middle East correspondent, Lousia Lumsden, has reported further fighting from the Iraq/Iran border tonight.

The Archbishop of Canterbury's visit to Dover today was disrupted by women demonstrating for the right to be ordained full priests of the Anglican Church.

Finally, good news for consumers. Julia Ward Howe, chief executive of the giant food manufacturers CapCorp, has promised to cut 5p in the kilo off coffee from next Monday.

Imagine those are the news headlines for Derby Day, 1984. While the world portrayed has little to do with Orwell's nightmare vision of totalitarianism, it is not a world like ours today. There has obviously been some kind of revolution, which has changed the power relationships in the world in one fundamental way yet left most features of the political and social system untouched. The fundamental change I am suggesting (and if you have not noticed it, you should read the headlines again) probably seems more bizarre and improbable to you than the science fiction ideas of world governments and inter-planetary wars. Yet all I am imagining is that women might be occupying some of the many social positions for which they are *at present* eligible. I am not suggesting a role-reversal, for men are still fighting the wars and playing professional cricket. A woman *could* be President of the United States, Chancellor of the Exchequer of Britain or lead a large union today but on the whole women do not reach such exalted posts. This book examines the various spheres of social life outlined in those news headlines (finance, politics, sport, mass media, work and religion) where women conventionally do not figure in positions of power, and those spheres in which women *do* figure (education, medicine and the family).

I suggest that most people who read those news headlines will find the world portrayed disquieting and even unnatural. Yet the everyday world in which we live has a power balance between the sexes which is just as one-sided, because all the powerful jobs are held by men. It would be perfectly possible for a similar set of headlines to include only men and their occupations, and no one would even notice this or remark upon it. News readers, Chancellors of the Exchequer, foreign statesmen (*sic*), American presidential candidates, jockeys, trainers and owners, chairmen (*sic*) of Royal Commissions, presidents of the Royal College of Surgeons and of county cricket clubs, prime ministers and opposition leaders in the United Kingdom, trade union secretaries, foreign correspondents and leading industrialists are normally all men. This does not make us feel uneasy or uncomfortable. Yet there is no inherent reason why any of these posts cannot be held by women, and we can tolerate one or two of them being so held. At the time of writing the British Prime Minister is a woman, there are a few women news readers, a woman might own the Derby winner, and both Shirley Chisholm and Bella Azbrug might run for President of the USA. Women are no longer unthinkable in one or two top jobs, but a whole Cabinet, a whole trade union council, university senate or board of directors, is still unbelievable. Margaret Thatcher has no other women in her Cabinet, and the 1979 election saw nearly all the leading women politicians in Britain lose their seats. One Prime Minister makes no difference to the male-dominated power structure, unless she is a conscious feminist. One of the aims of this book is to examine why this is so, by discussing the imbalances between the sexes in all areas of endeavour in modern Britain, and analysing the ways in which they are developed and sustained.

This book can therefore be described as a sociological portrait of the women of Britain, but a portrait which sees the women always in the context of the wider society around them. It is, in fact, a sociological, biographically organised picture of women in modern Britain which draws on research findings and other evidence to present a feminist account of women's situation. All these terms – 'sociological', 'biographically organised', 'modern', 'British' and 'feminist' – need both explanation and justification and so this is provided first. Thus, the introduction explains the ways in which these terms are used to structure the book and then describes the range of contents of the other chapters. Explanations of what is meant by modern, biographically organised and British are offered first, with a description of the book's sociological perspective interwoven, followed by some idea of its feminism.

Modern and Sociological

The book is about women in Britain today although it looks back to the last century for some material. The theoretical perspective is sociological, but as far as possible I have tried to avoid or explain technical terms so that the beginner or non-specialist can read it. The idea behind compiling such a sociological work on women today is a simple one. Most social science books, and most social scientists, ignore women unless they are discussing marriage and motherhood, when they tend to reverse the process and neglect men. This bias reflects the fact that all social sciences are male-dominated occupations and the bodies of theory and research they have accumulated systematically neglect women and their place in the world. This book therefore gathers what is known about women in Britain, highlights the *lacunae* in our knowledge, and reassesses many of the traditional fields of sociological endeavour in the light of their coverage of women.

Biographically Oriented

The book is organised biographically. That is, after this introduction and a short chapter on sex and gender, the material on women is presented according to the age of the women concerned. So the book begins with early childhood and follows women as they grow up, age and die. The format is slightly different from most introductory texts in sociology or on modern Britain. Because this book centres on women, it introduces material from the different sociologies (of medicine, politics, and so on) as they become relevant. There is so little research on women that a chronic shortage of data is revealed whichever strategy is adopted, but the biographical structure makes more coherent reading. An entertaining introduction to sociology (Berger and Berger, 1976) has recently been produced using this formula, and in so far as this book has a model I have followed the Bergers.

British and Sociological

This book is a sociological portrait of women in Britain. This means that material from other social sciences, such as anthropology, psychology, economics, and so on, has been kept to a minimum, except where there are no British data. However, because it is a book about British women and not English ones, there is considerable discussion of Wales and Scotland, and of ethnic and cultural minorities.

Feminism

The book is feminist in its overall perspective. Feminism is a term with multiple usage, both good and bad. Here I follow the definition offered by Kraditor (1968, p. 8) who argues that the distinguishing characteristic of all feminists is a desire that women be recognised 'as individuals in their own right'. In other words, feminism is a desire for female self-determination. This desire for autonomy can be found among the aims of the pioneers in the nineteenth century, and can be traced through women's campaigns up to the present day, when women marching to defend the right to control their own fertility chant:

> Women must decide their fate,
> Not the church and not the state.

In academic terms a belief in feminism means several things: that more women should engage in research and teaching, that research should be conducted into all aspects of women's lives, and that all social science theory and research should be rigorously scrutinised for implicit or explicit assumptions about women. This last point is in effect a call for a more scientific attitude among social scientists: a call for them to ask searching questions about sex differences and similarities rather than taking them for granted as *natural*. Thus a sociology without sexism would be a better sociology.

ABOUT THIS BOOK

This book has nine chapters apart from this introduction. Chapter 2 examines how a sociologist looks at sex and gender, drawing to some extent on anthropology and psychology. Cultures other than our own are considered briefly to show how arbitrary our notions of 'natural' and 'unnatural', 'cultural' and 'social', 'normal' and 'abnormal' are. Also in this chapter is a discussion of the controversy over the biological and social bases of sex and gender differences, and of the issues raised by the rise of the new feminism. This chapter, therefore, offers a theoretical overview of the issues which feature in the rest of the book.

The biographical format begins with the third chapter. Early childhood features in Chapter 3 and adolescence in Chapter 4. Women's lives at home and at school are considered, with emphases on subcultural differences within Britain. Even at these early stages in a woman's life, central issues in all sociological analyses such as class, power and wealth are shown to be operating. In Chapter 4 especially differences in the women's lives are revealed. A similar contrast is equally clear in Chapter 5 where early adulthood is discussed.

Chapters 6 to 9 focus on different aspects of adult life: work, class, community, marriage, parenthood, power, politics, leisure, religion, health and deviance. Throughout these four chapters there are noticeable differences between the analyses presented here and those offered in conventional sociology texts. For example, the section on work deals with both paid and unpaid work – including not only housework but also voluntary work – because so much of women's work is not financially rewarded. Similarly, deviance and ill-health are analysed together in a novel way. The deviance of the non-working man is contrasted with the deviance of the working *mother*, while the relationships between illness and work or non-work for the two sexes are seen in the context of the female complaints that are not illnesses, such as pregnancy and the menopause. The key sociological topics of stratification, class and mobility are discussed, emphasising the serious neglect of women in both theory and research and thus querying the truth and applicability of such writing. Women's lives in various kinds of 'community' are examined, covering a range from rural areas to urban ghettos and sprawling suburbs. Families of all kinds are discussed, from rambling extended groups to single parents and conventional couples to communes. The lives of women outside work, community and family are not neglected. Material is presented on non-work activities: politics, sport, religion and mass media are all considered, with the emphasis on discovering overt and covert sources of woman power in modern Britain.

The ninth chapter focuses on parenthood, the sociology of the family, and covers the final stages of women's lives: retirement, widowhood and old age. The concluding chapter summarises the main points of the argument presented in the book and suggests the chief research and theoretical priorities for the future of sociological research on women.

TOWARDS A NON-SEXIST SOCIOLOGY

The central and recurring theme of the analysis in this book is the importance of understanding how sex and class are interrelated to form one system of stratification throughout Britain, a system which is further complicated by ethnic and regional variations. This analysis differs from most conventional sociological approaches, which traditionally concentrate on class inequalities and neglect sex (e.g. Parkin, 1971). It also differs from several of the feminist analyses which stress sexual stratification and ignore or deny class relations (e.g. Firestone, 1972). Only a few authors have tried to come to terms with both inequalities and combine them into one system of stratification (e.g. Parkin, 1979).

The lives and experiences of women in modern Britain are only comprehensible when their place in this double stratification system is understood. Yet most sociologists have only managed to work with one-dimensional class-based stratification systems, because sociology has not taken sex and gender as important topics for study, but has treated them as normal, natural and unproblematic. In studying stratification, as in other ways, sociology is sexist, like the wider society in which it lives, and has been so since its beginnings in the first half of the nineteenth century. It is sexist because it has adopted uncritically the myths and prejudices of the surrounding society about women rather than behaving or thinking in a truly scholarly manner. The best way to demonstrate this is to contrast the socio-logical treatment of other topics with its treatment of women. If we take any cliché of our society, such as 'trade unions are too power-ful', no social scientist would dream of accepting them as true, as statements of fact, or as anything other than a starting point for research. She would want to know who said such things and who did not, why they said them and when, and what purpose such comments served in the culture of their utterance. That is what social science research is all about – scrutinising the beliefs, customs and organisations of a culture – *not* taking them for granted.

This detached, inquiring attitude is characteristic of all the various theoretical 'schools' of sociology. All sociologists would take a claim like 'we're all middle class now' as the inspiration for a research project. No sociologist would build such a claim into a theory of how society works without examining it thoroughly and researching it. Yet clichés and myths about women as insubstantial and un-substantiated as those I have mentioned above abound in sociology. Almost all the sociologists of the last 150 years have built their theories about society as a whole, and about women, around un-examined myths and beliefs concerning the two sexes common in their own time and culture, rather than subjecting these beliefs to critical scrutiny or engaging in thorough research. Thus, sociologists both distinguished and mediocre have assumed that the family and sex role patterns prevailing in the United States and Western Europe in the last 150 years are natural rather than social, fixed rather than changeable, and beneficial for everybody. The authors have then based theories upon these beliefs without ever examining them properly. Clichés and myths such as 'woman's place is in the home', 'women only work for pin money' and 'women are too emotional, they can't think logically' and even 'the right place for women in the movement is prone' underlie a great many theories in modern sociology. This book will show both how such beliefs are deeply embedded in sociology and also how erroneous they are.

Sociology has been unscholarly and sexist. Unless sociologists subject all beliefs and attitudes about women to critical scrutiny and empirical research without preconceptions they will continue to be guilty of sexism. I shall now proceed to show in more detail how deeply sexism has been embedded in sociology and thus how unscholarly it is. There are three sections to this argument dealing with the history of the subject, then its present state and finally the position of women within the profession.

FOUNDING FATHERS

The discipline of sociology began in the turmoil after the French Revolution while Europe and the United States were changing from rural, agricultural to urban, industrial societies with the attendant social problems. The thinkers who founded and developed the subject were attempting to understand what made the new industrial, urban, irreligious society work without breaking down into revolution, crime and disorder. The central figures generally accepted as the founders of the subject and included in histories of sociology are men. In part, this is a true reflection of intellectual and scholarly life in the nineteenth century. Women were denied any formal education, refused access to universities and would not have been accepted as scholars in any field. Thus to cite only male authors as founders of the new discipline of sociology is not, in itself, sexist, because the subject was largely created by men. However, sexism is clearly present in the accounts of the history of the discipline offered today's students, which shows itself in three ways.

First, although women were denied access to formal education and its institutions, there were scholarly women whose ideas were influential in their own time. Some current sociological ideas stem from such women's writings yet these authors are never mentioned in histories of the subject. For example, Talcott Parsons's ideas about the function of the family, which have dominated sociological writing since 1945, derive either consciously or unconsciously from the writings of Catharine Beecher (sister of the Harriet Beecher

Stowe who wrote *Uncle Tom's Cabin*). Beecher wrote prolifically on domestic morality and her ideas are substantially the same as those which permeate Parsons's work. Yet Beecher's enormous influence in nineteenth-century America and her legacy in sociology are unrecorded. Secondly, those male writers who offered scholarly comment on women and their place in society, such as J. S. Mill and Frederick Engels, are rarely included among the founding fathers, while many men who are included wrote unscientific rubbish about women. Thus, for example, Spencer, whose ideas on women were culture-bound and repressive (Duffin, 1978), is always included as a founder of the subject, while Engels, who offered a refreshingly critical – and thus scholarly – account of the role of women is rarely included among the ancestors. I find it hard to accept that this is coincidental. Thirdly, although the writings of the founding fathers are offered to students as insightful but flawed, and the shortcomings of their works paraded, their culture-bound misconceptions about women are not mentioned in the criticisms but left unchallenged. For example, accounts of Durkheim's ideas about the division of labour criticise it, but do not mention that his ideas on women were equally culture-bound.

Finally, it is worth mentioning that introductions to sociology and to its history never point out that its founders were men and explain why that was so. They take it for granted, and do not regard it as a matter for explanation or comment. It is 'natural' that the founders of the subject were men, and not a matter of interest. These four aspects of sexism in the history of sociology can be seen in any recent publication introducing social science to the general reader or intending students. For example, *New Society* ran a series of articles between 1963 and 1967 which gave readers an introduction of twenty-four 'founding fathers of social science' and then published them as a book (Raison, 1969). Only one woman, Beatrice Webb, was allowed to be a founding father, and she only made it as half an entry with her husband. The choice of the title implies that the ancestral figures in sociology were all men, and the choice of authors suggests that contemporary authorities are all men too; only two of the articles were written by women. The picture has not improved since. A second edition appeared in 1979 with several more 'fathers' added but all the new authors are men and the title has remained unchanged (Barker, 1979).

So it is with *Keywords*, by Raymond Williams, which was published in 1976 to widespread acclaim. The book is 'a vocabulary of culture and society' and contains notes on a series of complex terms significant to Williams. While it is a personal book, and a Marxist one, it also reveals the depth of ingrained sexism in intellectual vocabulary. First, it is noticeable that none of the words with which Williams is concerned is related to feminism or any of its associated issues. That, of course, is perfectly reasonable, because they are a personal selection and there is no reason why he should be personally concerned with feminism. Yet it is odd that the entry on 'The Family' fails to mention feminist criticisms of the link he stresses between the modern use of the word family and the capitalist mode of production in which 'a man works to support a family; the family is supported by his work' (p. 110). In the entry on 'Work', Williams does raise an anomaly which lies at the heart of much recent feminist writing. He states that work has become increasingly specialised to mean paid employment and goes on (p. 282):

This is not exclusive; we speak naturally of working in the garden. But, to take one significant example, an active woman, running a house and bringing up children, is distinguished from a woman who works; that is to say, takes paid employment.

The underlying issue here is important for stratification theory, for Marxism and for women, but Williams does not mention any of the consequences of the point he has raised.

Overall, Williams has not come to terms with any feminist ideas, as he shows clearly in his entry on 'Man'. Here he opens up one of the main ambiguities in the English language. He points out that 'the identity of *man* (human) with man (male) has persisted in English longer than in most European languages' (p. 155). Williams goes on to argue that this is only a problem in so far as 'sexual specialisation' has made the word man 'problematic in some general and philosophical theory (cf. Paine's *Rights of Man* (human) and Wollstonecraft's *Rights of Women* (feminine))' (p. 155). Here Williams is suggesting that the identification of man-human with man-male is *only* a problem for readers of abstruse philosophy. This may well be true for Williams, who is a man. But, to borrow from Byron, ''tis women's whole existence'. The far-reaching problems which follow from the identity of man-human with man-male are beautifully exemplified by Williams's own argument. *Feminine* is not an adequate adjective to describe Wollstonecraft's polemic. Paine's work was a demand for human rights (although it is a debatable point whether he meant to include women in his category 'human'). Wollstonecraft's work was a demand for women's rights, and so was the antithesis of feminine. Indeed, describing the *Rights of Women* as feminine or female destroys the subtlety of Wollstonecraft's point. She knew that the word 'man' in Paine's title *de facto* excluded women. She was, in fact, the first feminist precisely because she highlighted the ambiguous nature of the identity of man-human with man-male and realised its consequences. She knew that the identity and its ambiguity constituted one of the most powerful weapons that male supremacists have to suppress and subdue women. The power of that simple identity between man-human and man-male is as strong as ever it was in Wollstonecraft's day. The belated reawakening to the power it exercises among new feminists has led to several studies of sexism in language which are discussed in Chapter 2 and, at a political level, calls for genuinely more inclusive words, however ugly. The call for the use of chairperson rather than chairman, for personpower not manpower, and so on, is understandable in this light. The words *are* ugly, and this is one reason for wanting them used. Because they are unusual they force people to think. If one insists on the use of 'chairperson' one is forcing people to recognise that the office might be open to women. Williams's insensitivity to this shows how deeply sexism has embedded itself in even creative thinkers of our time. This is not to single Williams out particularly, because any other author of his kind would be just the same; rather I have used *Keywords* to show how fundamental a part of our thought sexism is.

If an innovative writer like Williams cannot eradicate the sexism from his thoughts, it is not surprising that the founding fathers of the discipline of sociology in the last hundred years who lacked a feminist body of thought to which to refer failed to think critically about the position of women but adopted the prejudices of their time. It is, therefore, anachronistic to blame authors such as Durkheim (1859–1917) for lacking a fully formed radical feminist position on women. Johnson (1972) has shown that Durkheim's classic *Suicide* shows very little thought about women, but a good deal of repetition of unthinking myths about them. Durkheim thought with great originality about suicide, religion and social order, but not about sex and gender. Duffin (1978) has produced a similar criticism of the work of Spencer, which shows how he used a set of mutually contradictory beliefs to argue that women should not be educated or enfranchised. The Schwendigers (1971) have examined the writings of the early professors of sociology in the United States and conclude that they were 'sexists to a man'. More criticisms of this kind need to be carried out, and offered to students, but they must not fall into the trap of anachronism.

THE SUBJECT TODAY

So much for the history of the subject. Despite a decade of criticism of the sexism in sociology, the subject is unaffected. A recent collection of scholarly articles on sociology (Millman and Kanter, 1975) offers six fundamental indictments of the current state of the discipline.

(1) Important areas of social inquiry have been overlooked because of the use of certain conventional field-defining models; alternative models can open new areas for examination, about both women and men. (p. ix)

(2) Certain methodologies (frequently quantitative) and research situations (such as having male social scientists studying worlds involving women) may systematically prevent the elicitation of certain kinds of information which may be the most important for explaining the phenomenon being studied. (p. xv)

(3) Sociology has focused on public, official, visible and/or dramatic role players and definitions of the situations, yet unofficial, supportive, less dramatic, private and invisible spheres of social life and organisation may be equally important. (p. x)

(4) Sociology frequently explains the status quo (and therefore helps provide rationalisations for existing power distributions), yet social science should explore needed social transformations and encourage a more just, humane society. (p. xiv)

(5) In several fields of study, sex is not taken into account as a factor in behaviour, yet sex may be among the most important explanatory variables. (p. xiv)

(6) Sociology often assumes a 'single society' with respect to men and women, in which generalisations can be made about all participants, yet men and women may actually inhabit different social worlds, and these must be taken into account. (p. xiii)

Throughout this book, the criticisms of empirical sociology made in these six points will be reinforced again and again. The material on politics in Chapter 8 shows these criticisms well. Political sociology has focused obsessively on the dramatic and the official aspects of the male political world, and neglected or actively denigrated women in politics and the political realities of women's lives. This means both that we have almost *no* knowledge of women in politics, and that many interesting political topics have never been researched. For example, women who share the political beliefs of their husbands are *always* assumed to have been politically led, or educated, by the husband. The ideas of a negotiated political reality, or of women influencing the political ideas of their husbands, are never considered, and hence no data relating to them are ever collected. Similar criticisms to those made by Millman and Kantor can be applied to research on 'youth culture', and especially that part of it which deals with working-class youth, where the perspective of girls is systematically neglected or denigrated by researchers. (Chapter 4 examines this issue.)

Careers and Promotions
The other way in which sociology is sexist is its career structure,

recruitment and promotion patterns. Although the majority of undergraduates are women, the senior, permanent staff of the universities and polytechnics where the teaching and research are done are predominantly male. This means that the female students lack role models – women professional sociologists – and research and publications by and about women. The women in the subject lack sisterhood, the structure of support and patronage (sic) which men have. Also, the power positions – editors of journals, heads of department, chairpeople of grant-giving bodies, organisers of professional bodies – are very likely to be men. The membership register of the British Sociological Association makes this abundantly clear. The 1977 edition lists 1,106 members, and only 15·4 per cent (171) are women. Fifty-eight members said they were professors, and only four of those are female. Assuming that non-membership of the BSA among senior established academics is equally distributed among men and women, this probably means that only 10 per cent of the country's sociology chairs are held by women.

The members of the BSA were invited to list their research interests, and a clear sexual division of labour is apparent from the lists published. Those interested in theory, industrial sociology and stratification are nearly all men, while women are likely to be interested in health and illness, education and women. The BSA officers have been predominantly male since its inception. Barbara Wootton and Sheila Allen have been the only two women presidents. Membership of the executive committee has only been significantly influenced by calls for sex equality in the last two or three years, when the women's caucus and subcommittees have tried to improve women's status in the association. Now there are women on the executive committee, and the subcommittees, and some on the board of Sociology, the official journal of the BSA.

Thus in at least three ways modern sociology is as deeply sexist as the society in which it exists. The practical result of such male domination is a serious neglect of empirical work on women, a lack of clear thought about theoretical issues where gender is important, and a large blank space in almost every textbook where gender stratification, gender relations and gender differences should be considered. All sociologists are concerned about class, and most have neglected sex. This book is an attempt to redress that picture by giving weight to sex and class in modern Britain. There are sex and class inequalities which reinforce each other for, as Westergaard and Resler (1975, p. 101) argued recently, sex inequality accentuates class inequality. For example, at work the difference between male and female pay rates gets greater as one descends the occupational scale: in non-routine white-collar work (Class II of the Registrar General's scale) men earn one-fifth more than women in the same jobs, in routine non-manual work men earn one-third more than women, while in manual occupations men earn twice as much as women.

In the rest of this book various spheres in which sex and class inequality exist will be examined. These will show how necessary a more complex stratification theory is, and some of the social facts it will have to accommodate. The next chapter focuses upon sex and gender to gain greater understanding of them, before the data on life in modern Britain are discussed.

Chapter 2

The Sociology of Sex and Gender

> She's made of sunshine, sugar and spice
> She'll be pert and pretty and awfully nice
> Someday she's bound to change her name
> Now choose the one that will stay the same
>
> The name that polls the winning vote
> The famous name that makes up quotes . . .
> May be the name you name your boy.
> (quoted in Walum, 1977, pp. 38–9)

That rhyme comes from an American book on how to choose a name for a new baby. The assumptions about boys and girls, men and women, which are embodied in it are the subject of this chapter. It deals with the issues of sex and gender, and discusses the ways in which, from birth, children are assigned to one or the other *gender* on the basis, usually, of their external sex organs. Then they are caught up in a torrent of myths, preconceptions and assumptions about what it is 'natural', 'appropriate' and 'normal' for males and females to do. In particular this chapter deals with names, clothes, language and early influences on the newborn child, and with wider issues about gender stereotyping in modern society.

GENDER-TYPING THE BABY

The first piece of labelling which affects the newborn baby is the attribution of *gender*. As Walum (1977, p. 5) puts it:

> From before the cradle to beyond the grave, a person is supposed to be inextricably and forever male or female. A distribution of traits of both sexes within one individual does not appear natural. Indeed, we refer to the sexes as opposite rather than different.

Many people regard this opposition as 'natural', a word which can be used to mean 'biological', or 'God-given', or 'morally correct', or all three. Yet the research published in sociology, social anthropology and psychology suggests that most of the things we associate with being male or female are cultural: that is, they are socially determined, and highly changeable throughout history and across the world. To separate things which are biologically based, such as the hormones, chromosomes, anatomy and physiology, from those which are based on cultural features, such as personality and behaviour, throughout this book I have used sex to refer to the former, and gender to the latter. This is technically correct, although it is muddling because common usage in modern Britain takes sex to refer to both kinds of features. For example, just talking of 'sex roles' implies that differences are biological, when they may not be, so gender role is more accurate, if unfamiliar.

Of course, most of the time a person's sex and his or her gender are 'the same', and for practical everyday purposes the distinction is irrelevant. Probably by the age of 3 and certainly by adulthood most people have learnt that males act one way and are *masculine*, while females act *feminine*, according to the conventions of whatever society they have grown up in. When there are inconsistencies between a person's sex and his or her gender social problems arise. For example, there are people who feel themselves to be the other gender from the one in which they were reared and want to have their sex altered to 'fit' (transexuals). Then there are the sad cases revealed by the 'sex tests' at athletic events, which occasionally reveal someone who has lived all her life as a woman to be chromosomally 'male'. These issues are discussed at the end of the chapter, and the point to be made here is that the gender label attached to the child at birth brings with it a whole range of social apparatus: names, clothes, toys, beliefs, behaviours and values. These play a large part in how a child grows up, and are the focus of this chapter.

Unto Us a Girl Is Born
When a baby is born the most significant labelling which takes place is that of gender. Whether this is the nurse coming out of the labour ward to congratulate the father with the words 'It's a boy', or Terry Wogan's jovial question 'Is it a boy or a child?', the initial gender-typing is almost as important as the safe arrival of the child. There is some evidence that contemporary Western societies value boy babies more than girls. Walum (1977) quotes several pieces of American research to suggest this. Jeffery (1976, p. 97), writing about her research on Pakistani families in Lahore and Bristol, quoted a woman who 'said that the first question asked when a child is born is if it is a boy; if it is a girl, the relatives want to

know if she is fair'. Lightness of complexion is particularly valued because it is equated with beauty and high status by these families.

— Once the sex/gender label is applied, a complex process of labelling begins. The first part of this process is the giving of a name. Naming something is a way of gaining control over it, by fixing it firmly into a system of categories, a classification system, as Mary Douglas (1966) has shown us. The names given to children tell us quite a lot about them, including fixing them into a context, by religion, region and ethnic group. Thus Theresa and Bernadette are probably Catholic and possibly Irish in background; Rhian and Myfanwy are almost certainly Welsh; Morag and Ishbel are Scots; Parween and Ruxana are Pakistani; Stacey and Donna almost certainly have working-class backgrounds, Emma and Cordelia probably do not. Equally important, names are nearly always clearly differentiated by gender, so that you will have recognised most of those I have given as being appropriate for girls, and any you did not almost certainly came from a culture with which you are not familiar. When a name is applied to the wrong gender, ridicule and even hostility result, as in the Johnny Cash song 'A boy named Sue'. Ambiguous names, which are not clearly gender-differentiated, are relatively uncommon, and can cause misery and hostility for their possessors.

Collins Gem Dictionary of First Names, originally published in 1969 and reprinted in 1976, contains 'over 2,000 names'. Each entry labels the name with the symbol 'm' or 'f' and gives other information. This dictionary lists only twenty-four names with the designation 'm or f', so that 98 per cent of the names are only for either men or women. The twenty-four names they mention as available for both genders are Alexis, Averil, Beverly, Christian, Christman, Dagma, Easter, Evelyn, Esme, Faith, Hilary, Hope, Joyce, Julian, Kay, Kim, Lindsey, Morven, Noel, Rene, Valentine, plus Frances/Francis, Leslie/Lesley and Vivian/Vivien. It is noticeable that very few of these are in common use for either sex, and the dictionary points out that Faith, Hope, Kim, Kay, Lindsey and Joyce are all more usual for girls. This makes an important point, for it is less of a stigma for a girl to have a boy's name than vice versa. Just as 'tomboy' is less of an insult than calling a boy a 'sissy' or 'nancy boy', so too a girl called Toni or Peta will suffer less torment than a boy called Lindsey or Kay. The importance of the preconceptions aroused by the names of people and their gender-labelling was the subject of an experiment carried out by Goldberg (1974). He presented identical articles to groups of students, with some identified as being by John T. McKay and some by Joan T. McKay. Students rated the articles higher when they thought they had been 'written' by John McKay than when they had been 'written' by Joan McKay, even in fields like domestic science where women might be thought to be experts.

Most common names are, therefore, unambiguously male or female in usage. In addition, the type of name given to the two genders differs. Walum says that parents are guided to choose important boys' names but pretty girls' ones, and argues that American male names are 'short, hard-hitting, and explosive' while the girls' names are 'longer, more melodic, and softer' (1977, p. 39). Thus she suggests American male names are either short in themselves, like Lance, Mark, John or Carl, or have diminutives which are short and explosive, such as Bill, Bob, Steve, Ken, Josh and Sam. The girls' names are not only longer, Corinna, Lucille, or Deborah, but have softer diminutives, such as Debbie, Lucy and Jessie. To see if this was true for Britain I took the names of 378 girls and 399 boys aged 9–13 in an English town and examined them. These were pupils at two schools with a reasonably balanced intake, including some Asian and West Indian pupils, but few upper-class children. I looked to see if the American argument about short men's names held up, and it did. The most popular boys' names were short and staccato, or had such abbreviations. Thus commonest for boys were Andrew, Paul, Steve, Mark, Dave, Dick or Rick, Ian, John, Bob, Rob, Tim, Darren, Mike, Mick, Mart, Nick, Lee, Stuart, Simon, Phil, Pete, Gary, Jase, Jim, Kevin, Shaun/Sean, Chris, Matt and Neill. The girls' names were longer and more elaborate, and did not shorten to monosyllables very easily. Many of the girls' names were diminutives already – Debbie, Mandy, Julie, Katy – and others like Tracey, Stacey and Lisa are actually diminutives which have become independent names. (Tracey is really Theresa, Stacey an American pet name for Anastasia, and Lisa comes from Elisabeth.) In addition, many of the popular names such as Louisa, Rachel, Alison and Michelle do not have a recognised abbreviation.

Pink for a Girl?

Once a baby's gender is established and securely fixed by an appropriate name, a complex set of gender-type equipment and clothing can be added to emphasise the gender label. Baby clothes and equipment, such as cots, pots and bedding, all come in pink or blue, to label the androgynous baby to the outside world, although an examination of the baby clothes offered in stores and catalogues suggests 'safe' colours such as yellow are also popular. Maybe the situation is more acute in the United States where Walum (1977, p. 42) argues that:

> In a trip through an infant section of any department store . . .
> on the girls' racks are princess dresses, granny gowns, pink satin
> pantsuits, and bikinis; on the boys' . . . are baseball uniforms,

tweed suits . . . astronaut pajamas, and starched white dress shirts. Often the differences in style are more subtle . . . [there are] male and female variants of the same basic romper. The male variant snaps from left to right, has a pointed collar and football motif; the female . . . has a peter pan collar with lace trim and embroidered butterflies.

The position in Britain seems less extreme, although there is a clear gender-differentiation in children's clothes. The Mothercare catalogue for Spring/Summer 1978 is obviously not intended for the very conservative family as Dad is shown, in an apron, bathing the infant, putting it to bed and carrying it on his back, and there are one or two black children and an Asian/Oriental expectant mother. However, there are very traditional attitudes displayed about clothes for the two genders after babyhood. The tiny baby is offered clothing mainly in yellow or white. The crawling stage is still *relatively* un-differentiated, although the trend is clear. Small boys would not be dressed in dresses with a red rose, a pair of hearts, or Little Bo Peep on them and girls would not be bought a romper with 'Monaco' and other symbols of Grand Prix motor racing all over it. Pink appears first for the crawling girl, and there is a separation between 'dresses' and 'rompers'. The only 'genderless' garments are the pyjamas; Mothercare believe that nightdresses are dangerous for small children, and offer only pyjamas with 'neutral' patterns like circus scenes or jungle animals on them.

However, once the child stands up his or her day clothes are clearly separated, and at 5 or so the night clothes too are separated. There are no pyjamas offered for girls over 5, for example. The most noticeable thing about the day clothes is the vastly greater variety of girls' clothes compared with boys, although it is a variety of dresses, not all kinds of clothes. Mothercare do not show any girls wearing clothes suitable for climbing trees or other tough activities. The girls' dungarees have a pretty picture on them while the boys' are sturdy denim. An examination of the children's clothes in other mail order catalogues shows Mothercare to be typical. Perhaps the gender-typing of clothes is best exemplified by tracksuits – probably the nearest thing to a unisex garment available – which are always aimed at small boys. Although adult women athletes such as Sonia Lannerman and Gillian Gilks are seen on television in tracksuits, catalogues and shops make no attempt to sell them to girls.

The clothing of babies has been shown to have – along with their names – a great deal to do with how they are treated by adults. Walum (1977, p. 40) reports a crucial experiment in which mothers were shown Beth, a 6-month-old 'girl' in a frilly pink dress, and Adam, a 6-month-old 'boy' in blue rompers. Beth was viewed as 'sweet', with a 'soft cry', offered a doll to play with and smiled at more often. In fact they were the same baby, with a different name and clothes. In a similar experiment, film of a 6-month-old baby dressed in yellow crying, crawling, smiling, and so on was shown to samples of professionals (e.g. pediatricians, psychologists, nursery nurses) and amateurs (mothers and students). Half of each group of viewers were told that the baby was a boy, half that it was a girl, and all were asked to describe what the baby was doing at each stage of the film. The results were clear. All the professionals, and the students, attributed quite different motives to the same be-haviour, according to the sex of the baby. If they thought it was a boy, they described it as angry when it cried; if a girl, as frightened. Only the mothers did not attribute motives, but merely said that the baby was crying, crawling or whatever.

In part, such attribution of aggression to tiny babies according to their sex reflects a common belief that males are naturally 'aggres-sive'. Yet the evidence on this point is clearly inconclusive, and in one famous study turned out to be untenable. Many American researchers had observed newborn babies to see if there were early signs of sex differences. Study after study reported that little girl babies slept peacefully or lay quietly in their cots, while little boy babies yelled lustily and waved their arms and legs. Researchers concluded that from birth boys are more active and aggressive, and thus, some argued, aggression in males must be sex-linked. So many American studies had shown this 'fact' that it had ceased to be a research question, yet when some researchers in Britain attempted a routine confirmation, they found that the sex difference did not exist among British babies. Boys and girls in maternity hospitals did not behave in distinct ways, but slept or yelled apparently at random. This cultural difference called for some explanation, and the answer turned out to be circumcision. The American boy babies had all been circumcised at birth as a matter of routine, while the British ones had not. Thus the supposed sex difference was in fact a reac-tion to medical treatment. All the American boys were in pain or discomfort from an operation on their genitals while the girls were not.

Of course, the main importance of these studies of *perceived* sex and gender differences is that they lead to differential treatment of the two categories of babies. From very early years girls are talked to and cuddled more, while boys are tossed around more vigorously. Girls are seen as fragile, boys are not. From their earliest hours, boys and girls are brought up in different ways, to reinforce different behaviours, and sanction 'wrong' activities. There is no evidence on how far parents, teachers and others are conscious or unconscious of dividing and segregating the young in this way. Some studies sug-gest that parents claim to treat their children alike, but there is also evidence that they are extremely worried about 'inappropriate' behaviour.

LEARNING TO BE A GIRL

But what is inappropriate behaviour? Roger Brown (1965, p. 161) offers two lovely caricatures of 'real' males and females in the United States:

> a *real* boy climbs trees, disdains girls, dirties his knees, plays with soldiers, and takes blue for his favourite colour . . . real boys prefer manual training, gym and arithmetic. In college the boys smoke pipes, drink beer, and major in engineering or physics; . . . the real boy matures into a 'man's man' who plays poker, goes hunting, drinks brandy and dies in the war. . . . A real girl dresses dolls, jumps rope, plays hopscotch and takes pink for her favourite colour. When they go to school, real girls like English and music . . . [in college] the girls chew Juicy Fruit gum, drink cherry cokes, and major in fine arts . . . the real girl becomes a 'feminine' woman who loves children, embroiders handkerchiefs, drinks weak tea, and 'succumbs' to consumption.

It is not clear *exactly* what the British equivalents of these stereotypes are, but the overall picture is much the same. Little boys get dirty, fight, and play with cars and guns, while little girls are kept clean, exchange verbal insults, and play at being housewives and mothers. The behaviour of the adults is equally stereotyped, and can be translated across the Atlantic quite easily. The majority of the population believe that the behaviour and attitudes of males and females should be very different. Such gender role stereotypes can bear heavily upon average, human men and women, who are unlikely to fit the patterns exactly. Goffman (1968, p. 153) has gone so far as to argue that:

> in an important sense there is only one complete unblushing male in America: a young, married, white, urban, northern, heterosexual Protestant father of college education, fully employed, of good complexion, weight and height and a recent record in sports.

Goffman says that American men judge themselves against this ideal and, inevitably, most feel themselves to fall short of it. It is interesting that Goffman offers no equivalent portrait of the ideal, whole woman, for there could not be such a person. All females are invariably stigmatised as not-men, so that even being young, married, white, urban, northern, heterosexual, Protestant, a graduate, a mother, and of good complexion, weight and height does not help a woman become an ideal American, only a second-class one.

The baby girl has to learn to grow into a stigmatised person who is not male, and one important aspect of this learning is the type of language she acquires. It is to language that the chapter now turns, before a consideration of sex, gender and sexuality which concludes it.

TALKING LIKE A LADY

The last decade has seen American linguists pay considerable attention to gender differences in language use. Thorne and Henley (1975) have assembled much of the work as a collection, which I have used extensively in this section. The central idea has been that just as people from different regions speak different dialects, so too the genders speak different *genderlects*. Most of the work on genderlects has been done in the United States and may not apply to British English, or to the other languages of Britain such as Welsh, Gaelic, Urdu and Greek. Peter Trudgill (1974) and Olwen Elyan (1978) are the only British works currently available. So much of what follows is based on American research and experience, and may not always apply to Britain.

Thorne and Henley (1975) like Robin Lakoff (1973) before them, have argued that the gender stratification in society, in which males dominate women, has resulted in two overlapping language-styles in any subculture, a male language-style and a female language-style. There is a range of popular myths about speech which serve to place women in a 'double bind'. Women are believed both to speak more than men, and to be more skilful with words, but at the same time to have nothing worth saying and annoying voices in which to say it. Thus women are regularly described as gossiping, where a similar male conversation would be dignified as a discussion; women's voices are not considered suitable for mass media appearances as news readers, disc jockeys and announcers, and cartoons regularly blame women for wasting time and money on endless telephone calls. An important part of the linguistic study of genderlects is to sort out the myths about language from the realities; in other words, to examine how far women's speech does have the characteristics ascribed to it.

The research shows considerable gender differences in the language used by women, and that spoken to them by men, compared with language used by and to men. The language women use differs from male speech in at least four ways: the intonation patterns (how the voice rises and falls), the pronunciation of certain words and syllables, the syntax (grammatical structures) and the vocabulary (actual choice of words and phrases). The gender differences in intonation and syntax combine to make women's speech more hesitant and less definite than men's. In particular, women are more likely to add tag questions, such as 'isn't it?', 'don't we?', 'couldn't he?', to their statements, and/or to express their statements as if they were questions by their intonation. This means that women very often express their statements as if they were questions. This is a characteristic of people in subordinate roles, especially common in the speech of pupils answering teachers' questions (see Stubbs, 1976), and expresses the relative lack of power women have. Robin Lakoff (1973) offers several examples of this pattern in female speech, such as the woman who answers the query about what time dinner will be with the *question* 'About half-past six?' which carries the clear rider 'if that's all right with you'. Similarly, women are more likely than men to say, not 'Macmillan was the greatest postwar Prime Minister' (a statement), but 'Macmillan was the greatest post-war Prime minister, wasn't he?' (a question seeking agreement). Of course, no one is arguing that men never add tag questions, or make hesitant statements, merely that these occur much more frequently in women's speech.

Similarly, no one argues that women's pronunciation is totally different from men's, but linguists like Trudgill (1974) have shown that there are differences. Trudgill's data show that in southern England women's pronunciation is closer to the received pronunciation (RP) of English: that is, the pronunciation we associate with the BBC and the upper classes. Women in the working class speak 'better' than the men of that class, in that their speech is closer to that of the upper classes. Linguists do not accept that any one system of pronunciation, vocabulary and grammar is actually better than any other, but every society values certain speech forms more than others because they are associated with elite groups. In so far as their speech is closer to that of their social superiors, therefore, working-class women are seen to speak 'posher', 'nicer' or 'better' than their menfolk.

Trudgill (1974) has suggested that women's greater use of the high-status pronunciations may be explained by their insecure social status, and the association of 'rough' speech with masculinity. Thus he argues that women are judged not by what they do but by how they appear, and therefore care more about maintaining a respectable front. They are, in consequence, more sensitive to subtleties such as pronunciation, and their status is more dependent on their using these subtleties. In addition, the rough working-class speech is associated with masculinity, and so refined working-class women will avoid it, while men will cling to it as part of a self-presentation as a 'real man'. Thus in Norwich working-class men clung to one set of pronunciations which identified them as tough and hard, while working-class women's speech moved nearer to 'standard English'. Olwen Elyan and her collaborators (1978) have recently studied this 'posher' speech by women. They found that the closer women's speech was to RP, the more they were seen by listeners as competent, male-like and feminine. That is, women who spoke RP English were seen androgynously; as having both male and female skills and characteristics.

The most noticeable differences between the genders, however, occur in the area of *vocabulary*. Women's speech is characterised by fewer swear words, jokes, numbers and hostile verbs, and more use of psychological state verbs and expressive intensifiers (so, such). Thus a woman is more likely to say 'It was *so* hot in the dance hall' or 'It was *such* a good party' than a man. Robin Lakoff (1973) has plotted many of these differences in vocabulary for America, especially with adjectives, but it is not clear how far they apply in Britain. She suggests that while both genders can say 'great', 'terrific', 'cool' and 'neat', only women can say 'adorable', 'charming', 'sweet', 'lovely' and 'divine', because for a man to use such adjectives implies he is a homosexual (gay). In addition, Lakoff argues that 'women make far more precise discriminations in naming colours' (1973, p. 8) and lists many colour shades American men cannot use without revealing themselves as 'effeminate'. However, she goes on to suggest (p. 13) that:

> Upper-class British men may use the words listed in the 'women's' column, as well as the specific colour words and others we have categorised as specifically feminine, without raising doubts as to their masculinity among other speakers of the same dialect. (This is not true for lower-class Britons, however.)

Detailed work on vocabulary and usage differences in Britain needs to be carried out.

The genderlect of women is therefore based on greater frequencies of intonations and syntactical usages which express hesitancy and deference, speech which is closer to the 'correct' forms than that of males in the same social class, and speech which is less hostile, violent and abusive, and more concerned with nuances, details and feelings. However, it is not true that women talk more than men. Thorne and Henley (1975) include several papers which show that American men talk more than women in experimental conditions and in mixed groups, and that they interrupt women and ignore their contributions. The proverbs and popular wisdom that women are more talkative are, therefore, not substantiated by the evidence, although still widely believed. Indeed, there is also evidence presented by Thorne and Henley that verbal fluency is seen as an asset in a man, but a disadvantage in a woman. This is reflected in the etiquette books written for young women which counsel them to listen to men and stay quiet themselves.

Women's speech is, therefore, rather different from men's,

although not in the ways that it is always believed to be. The woman is, Lakoff (1973, p. 6) argues,

> damned if she does, damned if she doesn't. If she refuses to talk like a lady, she is ridiculed and subjected to criticism as unfeminine, if she does learn, she is ridiculed as unable to think clearly, unable to take part in a serious discussion, in some sense as less than fully human.

In other words, feminine women use the women's genderlect, but by doing so, confine themselves to certain topics, contexts and ways of thinking. Women who use the male genderlect are despised as unfeminine. Yet by not using, or maybe not knowing, male language, women are excluded from many spheres of life. Indeed, lack of knowledge of male language is one reason given for women's failure to advance in many male-dominated occupations. Roger Smith (1976), in a study of Fleet Street journalists, has shown how women are unaware of many technical terms and other information about newspapers with which equivalent or junior males were familiar, and this leads to their being excluded from possible avenues of advancement. He quotes a man saying 'We had this girl in the office – been here for nearly two years and she still thought that "going on the stone" meant going for a piss'. (It is, in fact, a visit to check the accuracy of the printers' layout.) Similar comments about male languages excluding women were made to Fogarty and his colleagues (1971, p. 195) in their study of the BBC. All the studies of male occupations show that there is an overlap between the male language used (jokes, foul language, and so on) and the actual jargon or technical terminology of the job. Women are frequently excluded from the latter, because they cannot participate in the former.

If the language women can use either confines them to a stereotyped feminine role or forces them to be 'aggressive', 'masculine' and 'formidable', the language used about women is even more limiting. This is true of all kinds of speech and writing, from children's books and nursery rhymes through pop songs and mass media writing to academic articles as well as adult conversations. This is such a large topic that many volumes could be written on it. Germaine Greer (1971) includes an interesting section on how the terms of abuse for women nearly all began as bisexual, but became limited to women only, while Thorne and Henley show how nearly every term for a female has sexual connotations, in a way quite unparalleled for men. Thus, for example, 'master' and 'mistress' cannot be seen as equivalents, for mistress has sexual connotations which make its use in a phrase like 'mistress of her subject' both ambiguous and absurd. The use of 'girl' to describe women of 30 and more, the negative implications of 'spinster' compared with 'bachelor', the differentiation of Mrs and Miss, and the denigration of calling someone a 'lady sculptor' are all examples of the ways in which everyday usage belittles women, denies them adult status, limits their autonomy and ties them to home and family. Academic writing is equally biased. It is common to find male academics referred to by surname only (Smith argues) or as 'Dr' or 'Professor', while women are frequently given their forenames (revealing gender) or referred to as 'Miss' or 'Mrs', *even when they are PhDs or professors*. This has an immediate, negative, effect on the reader. Compare the following sentences:

(1) Hurdle argues that the Black Power movement has revolutionised the role of the mother in the black family.
(2) Professor Hurdle argues that the Black Power movement has revolutionised the role of the mother in the black family.
(3) Dolores Hurdle argues that the Black Power movement has revolutionised the role of the mother in the black family.
(4) Mrs/Miss Hurdle argues that the Black Power movement has revolutionised the role of the mother in the black family.

The fourth of these sounds the least authoritative. The fact that they all quote the same scholar is irrelevant; it sounds more authoritative if the gender is hidden, and particularly feeble when the marital status is given. However, there is a problem for the author who wants to cite research by women. If she writes 'Joan Smith says' readers will regard the research as trivial or biased, but if she writes 'Smith says' the reader will assume the author to be male. I regularly mark essays in which students refer to distinguished women scholars such as Olive Banks as 'he'. In this volume I have used the forenames of women authors to reveal how much research has been carried out by women, but this is done at the risk of the reader systematically discounting much of the data cited. This is a problem which is not easily solved.

The insult to academic women implied in referring to them by their marital status is, however, a minor part of the linguistic subordination of women. It pales into insignificance beside the sexist nature of most so-called humour, for example. If women's speech contains fewer jokes, this may be because there are no male equivalents of the woman driver, the mother-in-law, the nagging wife, the brainless 'secretary' with the large bust employed to sit on the boss's knee, or the woman who never stops talking. If women are less hostile, this may be because they do not wish to think in stereotypes in which all women are bitches, witches or lesbians if they veer even slightly from the straight and narrow path of virginity, motherhood and celibate widowhood. Certainly the tremendous hostility to women expressed in male speech, and the way in which all terms used to refer to women quickly become reduced to sexual insults, suggest considerable male hostility and fear of female sexuality which is quite unparalleled in women's speech and worldview. The relation between sex, gender and sexuality is the subject of the last section of this chapter.

SEX, GENDER AND SEXUALITY

Young men and women grow up labelled by their names, clothes and their language as either male or female. The way they grow up will depend almost entirely on the beliefs about appropriate behaviour for men and women in the subculture in which they live, and it is their culture and subculture which determine their gender roles, not their biology, that is, their sex. Ann Oakley's *Sex, Gender and Society* (1972) offers an excellent coverage of the evidence about sex and gender differences from biology, psychology and anthropology, and there is no need to elaborate her arguments here. However, the *social* nature of gender roles is important for understanding sexuality, and it is central to the rest of the book to separate sexuality from both sex and gender.

Popular belief systems tend to associate lack of adherence to traditional gender roles with 'wrong' sexuality. Thus little boys who do not like fighting or little girls who play with trains arouse fears that they will grow up into homosexuals and lesbians. Yet this completely misunderstands the relations between sex, gender and sexuality. If sex is the biologically based differentiation between men and women (genes, chromosomes and sexual organs), and gender is the cultural parts of male and female roles, sexuality refers to the direction in which the sex drive is aroused. In the ideal pattern of socialisation in Britain, the baby who is biologically male is assigned a male gender role and grows up sexually attracted to women. However, real life does not fit the ideal pattern in sex, gender and sexuality, and there is no necessary reason why it should. Whereas the majority of people have by adolescence learnt their 'correct' gender role complete with its sexual attraction pattern, substantial minorities of people have either failed to learn, or chosen to ignore, the socially approved behaviour, in favour of one of the so-called 'deviant' patterns of sexuality.

Apart from those people whose chromosomal system is at odds with their external sexual organs, there are three groups of people whose sexuality is 'at odds' with their sex and/or their gender: homosexuals, transexuals and transvestites. Transvestites are normally attracted, 'correctly', to the opposite gender, but become sexually aroused by wearing the clothing of that gender. Advice columnists like Marje Proops (1977) say that this is quite a common practice among men, and it has been discussed in an academic paper by Brake (1976). To my knowledge, however, there are no studies of women transvestites: that is, women who are sexually attracted to men, but can only be aroused by wearing male clothing. This may be because such behaviour is not seen as a perversion but rather a chic, sexy way to dress. Hence advertisements showing women in male clothes are common. If transvestitism is a 'perversion' among women it has not been seen as one.

Transexuals are frequently mixed up with transvestites. However, transexuals are people who feel that their biological sex is wrong. That is, they are attached to a gender role different from their biological sex organs and body chemistry. Some transexuals choose to dress up as members of the gender they wish to be, but for quite different reasons from the transvestite. Again, however, there are different values placed on the activity when carried out by 'men' and 'women'. Because men are dominant in society it is considered less reprehensible for a woman to wish to be a man, and therefore less peculiar to choose to dress like a man. Women who 'passed' as males are even treated as heroines in certain contexts, such as Leonore in the opera *Fidelio*, and Sweet Polly Oliver who followed her love to the war and saved his life. The position of the man who wishes to be a woman is very different. Such men are despised and ridiculed. Mike Brake (1976) describes their situation thus:

> Transexuals feel themselves to be trapped in the body of the wrong gender . . . Their genitals are . . . a sign of their oppression. They live as the opposite sex, passing by posing as the opposite gender, finally hoping to cross over to the opposite sex by the use of surgery. Usually they are men seeking to become women.

Certainly the mass media have focused on male transexuals who have received surgery, such as Roberta Cowell, April Ashley and Jan Morris. Academic attention has been focused on both male and female transexuals by Suzanne Kessler and Wendy McKenna (1978).

Transexuals and transvestites are minorities in the population, and apparently mainly men. Neither group is homosexual (gay): that is, sexually attracted to its own gender. Transexuals believe they are actually the opposite sex to the one to which they have been assigned, so they are not gay, and transvestites are mainly attracted to the opposite sex. Both are popularly associated with homosexuality although this is quite erroneous. Gay men and women are clear about their own sex and gender and sexually attracted to the same sex and gender. Traditional British society has condemned homosexuality as a sin, or a vice, and claims to be repelled by it. More recently there has been liberal toleration, exemplified by the legislation of 1967, which treats homosexuality as a personal misfortune or handicap due to hormonal 'upsets' or faulty learning, and tolerates it as a harmless personal tragedy. More recently, a militant homosexual movement has arisen which argues that homosexuality is a valid form of sexuality, which should be as socially accepted as heterosexuality. This is the Gay Liberation movement, and associated campaigns. Jeffery Weeks (1977) and Mike Brake (1976) discuss these changes in the climate regarding gay males but a similar work needs to be written on gay women. (Female homosexuals are usually called lesbians after the Greek island of Lesbos where the supposedly gay woman poet Sappho lived. Her poems were burnt by a mediaeval pope and this was probably the first organised suppression of female homosexuality.)

Homosexuality has always existed in societies of all kinds, and it can probably be considered as 'natural' as heterosexuality. Yet social attitudes have changed dramatically between one culture and another. In Britain female homosexuality has never been illegal, but it has never been socially acceptable, while male homosexuality has been in certain cultures. (Male homosexuality between consenting adults over 21 in private was legalised in England and Wales in 1967, but even this limited expression of love is illegal in the armed services and in Scotland.) There is, however, deep suspicion of both male and female homosexuality, and great ignorance about what it is and how it is caused, as this letter to *Woman's Own* (3 June 1978) shows:

> My problem is how best to control my five-year-old son when taking him out. His mother controls him by holding his hand, but this is clearly too physical a method for me to adopt as being of the same sex such contact could lead to him becoming a homosexual.

Such total ignorance about homosexuality in both genders is probably related to the violence of the feelings expressed about it. Marje Proops (1977, p. 136) recounts how she receives many letters revealing violent reactions from parents to male homosexuals. For example, 'one father who wrote to me describing his twenty-year-old son as an obscene monster, said the only answer for the boy and his "foul lover" was castration'. She goes on, 'Boys have written to tell me their fathers whipped them, punched them, beat them up, threw them out of the house' (p. 138), but that 'the discovery of a lesbian daughter doesn't seem to produce the same violent reaction in parents' (p. 146). However, one lesbian has recently been sacked from a stockbroker's office and another as a bus driver, and the popular press was totally unsympathetic to lesbians who wished to become pregnant by AID. Lesbian mothers are also likely to lose their children in custody cases after divorces. Gay women certainly suffer discrimination and prejudice, and they have also found that gay men are oppressive within the Gay Liberation movement (Brake, 1976).

Gay women do not have a large part of this book because there are few data on them, and because it is a book about people in Britain who have learnt or have adopted the female gender role, irrespective of their biological sex, or their sexuality. This is a book about those aspects of British life which impinge on women, and about how British women construct and manage their lives, and for this purpose 'women' means everyone who is *socially* female. The book is about child-rearing, education, work, social class, illness, politics, power and religion, and those aspects of British life affect gay and straight women alike, because they are socially female. Indeed, for the purposes of this volume the male transexual who 'passes' as a woman is a woman. Biology is not destiny for the women of modern Britain, gender is destiny, and gender is both subjective and objective.

Part One

Childhood and Adolescence

Chapter 3

Childhood - the Years from Birth to 11

Washing machine. 4 Programmes operated by Plastic discs, with reversing washing action just like mummy's. Supplied with funnel for soap powder and one packet of washing powder; and one Red Plastic linen box. Rubber hose at back for emptying water. Battery-operated . . . (£9·99) (Marshall Ward, 1977)

Salter Spy Kit. Hours of fun, excitement and suspense, every boy's passport to intrigue. This kit contains: gun, binoculars, camera with a free film, identity card, fingerprint set, mission routes, magnifying glass, code chart, etc. . . . (£4·88) (Quality Post, 1975)

These two paragraphs are taken from toy catalogues of recent years. They describe two toys clearly differentiated according to the sex of the recipient, a toy washing machine for a girl and a spy kit for a boy. The girl is offered a passive, domestic and essentially boring toy, the boy an active, non-domestic, creative and imaginative one. The boy is stretched, the girl confined.

This chapter looks at the ways in which the experiences of children in our society differ, starting with class variations and then moving on to discuss those of sex. There are two main spheres in which children under 11 operate, the home and the school, and these are treated separately.

THE CHILD AT HOME

Throughout this book evidence will be presented to show how differences of class, region, religion and gender interrelate to affect women's lives. The experiences of children are no exception to this, so that a labourer's child in a rural home in East Anglia lives a very different life from a doctor's child in a northern city. Some of these differences are accentuated by gender, some mean that male and female children have very similar lives. Before concentrating on the gender differences in child-rearing, it is important to stress some of the factors that affect boys and girls equally, especially poverty and class. A high proportion of British children experience poverty and hardship which affect boys and girls equally, and the lives of those not in poverty are equally determined by the class of their families – especially the material circumstances, and particularly housing, health and food. There are large class-based differences in child-rearing practices – over matters such as toilet training, bed-times and lying – which affect both sexes equally. (These are documented in the work of John and Elizabeth Newson, 1965, 1970, 1976 and 1978.) There are also well-defined sex differences in how children are brought up – socialised – some of which cut across class, while others are class-specific or even accentuated by the class differences. This chapter focuses on the home life of young girls, but the class differences must not be forgotten.

A great many children in Britain grow up in conditions of poverty and hardship. In part, this is because large families are often poor and because poor people have the largest families, but it is also because children can plunge their parents into poverty, especially if they are born to unmarried women or to couples where the mother has to stop work. The children growing up in poverty are not distributed equally across Britain, nor across social classes; rather they are concentrated in working-class homes in Wales, Scotland and the north of England. Data from the National Child Development Study (Davie *et al.*, 1972; Fogelman, 1976) and the Nottingham-based study of child-rearing by John and Elizabeth Newson make this point, together with recent work on poverty in Wales (Wilding, 1977) and in Scotland (Levitt, 1975). Wedge and Prosser (1973) re-examined the data from the National Child Development Study (NCDS) and found that over a third of the 10,500 children born in one week in 1958 were in bad housing, and came from a low-income family, or one where there was either a single parent or five or more children. One of these handicaps may not be too crippling but one child in sixteen (6 per cent) of the sample had all three categories of handicap. Wedge and Prosser (1973, p. 17) claim that 'on average it will have been the experience of two children in every British classroom'.

This rather startling claim is not, of course, true. These disadvantaged children are not evenly distributed across Britain. They are concentrated in some schools – and in some regions. They are relatively rare in the south of England, much commoner in Wales, Scotland and the north of England. For instance, on the Western Hailes estate in Edinburgh in 1974 some primary schools had 86 per cent of children *in receipt* of free meals (Cook, 1975) either because of large families or poverty. Wedge and Prosser do mention the grosser regional inequalities – while one child in sixteen was disadvantaged by their three criteria in Britain as a whole, in Wales and northern England it is one child in twelve, while in Scotland it is one in ten. Thus, of those children who were 11 in 1969, 11 per cent were domiciled in Scotland, but 19 per cent of the disadvantaged lived there.

Poverty and disadvantage affect boys and girls alike, and no gender differences would be expected here. Lacking a bath or coming from a single-parent family is a disadvantage for a boy or a girl in modern Britain. A boy or girl whose father is in a working-class job, especially an unskilled job, is more likely to suffer a range of handicaps than a child born into a white-collar or professional home. In addition to any handicaps, there are differences in child-rearing across the social classes which relate to many aspects of the children's lives, as the Newsons (1965, 1970, 1976) have shown so vividly. One example will suffice here, the kind of food children are offered and the atmosphere surrounding meals. The food taken by children is different for the different social classes almost from birth. While nearly all children are breast fed for a few days in hospital, once at home, working-class children are nearly all switched to a bottle, while many middle-class babies are not. This is one of the earliest class differences in child-rearing practices to show itself in the child's life – it cannot be explained by poverty or housing, but by *attitudes* towards modesty, child health and family life. Thus the Newsons quote (1965, p. 37) a bricklayer's wife saying:

> Your clothes never seem clean at all, like – always wet through . . . It's not that I don't reckon its good for babies – it's just that it ties you down a bit, you can't go out. You can't do it in the park, can you? And it was warm last year, we was often down the park, and you could just take a napkin and a bottle with you.

An iron-works labourer's wife said (loc. cit.):

> I don't like it anyway – you know – the kids get older – you know – they notice more, and they think more, and they *say* more. I don't like doing it in front of them.

And a machine operator's wife reported: 'My husband's a bit funny about breast feeding – he says it's dirty, he does' (p. 38). Breast feeding is seen to violate notions of modesty and privacy for some women whereas mothers who persevered with breast feeding emphasised either pleasure in the process or duty to the baby. Class differences continue to show up clearly in the weaning of babies; middle-class babies are weaned earlier, whether breast or bottle fed babies. For instance, many working-class children still had an occasional bottle at 3 or 4 years of age, while this was extremely rare in middle-class families.

The later diet of children also differed considerably across the social classes (although the Newsons only found 0·5 per cent of their sample were getting diets deficient in vitamins *and* protein, and claimed to be pleased with the adequate diets all children were getting). Considerable class differences arose in the timing, form and content of meals. For example, many babies in working-class homes were given 'high tea', when their father got home from work, while middle-class children were not. The Newsons quote a day's food for a toddler in a poor home as follows (1965, p. 63):

Breakfast
  I fried up some potatoes, and then he had a bit of bread and butter and a bottle of tea.
Dinner
  He had chips and some more bread and butter and another bottle of tea.
Tea
  Sausages and Yorkshire pudding and potatoes and cauliflower and turnips and gravy. We have us tea when master comes home, you see. And then he had another bottle of tea, like.

This is quite unlike any diet collected in a middle-class family, and such different eating habits are related to different meal-times and attitudes to food between social classes. For example, among 4-year-olds the Newsons found that a minority of working-class families wanted silence at meal-times such as a porter's wife who said: 'Their father doesn't like them to talk while they're eating, he says they can eat their food and there's plenty of time to talk afterwards' (1970, p. 252) A lorry driver's wife's: 'Well, you don't like them rattling on, do you? I say "Oh shurrup and gerrit down yer!" ' can be contrasted with a middle-class mother's comment: 'But talking I *like* at meal-times, that's one of the times we talk *most* . . . That's what meal-times are *for*' (loc. cit.). Meal-times differed markedly across classes in other ways. The working-class households studied by the Newsons were much more likely to have 'running' meals, with the members of the family fed as they arrive home from work. They say (1965, p. 220):

for the man who works all day cramped at the coal face, in the hot vibrating cab of a heavy vehicle, standing at a clanging machine on the factory floor, or out of doors in all weathers . . .

the wife's first function is to feed him. Whether or not the rest of the family is due for a meal, the manual worker expects his dinner to be ready on the table within a few minutes of his return home . . . If there are grown-up sons living at home, the same treatment will be accorded to them, and, if necessary, the housewife will provide hot meals at regular intervals as the men come in.

These brief examples from the rich data collected by the Newsons show that the early life experiences of children in different classes vary considerably. Apart from class differences there are religious, racial and regional differences in child-rearing which have not been thoroughly researched yet. Then, cutting across those differences, there are gender differences, so that little girls are reared differently from little boys. The Newsons show that boys are given greater physical freedom, while girls are kept closer to home and mother from an early age, a finding researched in more detail by Roger Hart (1979). Hart found not only that boys were allowed a much larger 'territory' than girls, but also that parents tacitly allowed boys to leave their territory to range farther afield, while girls were kept inside theirs. Girls were thus doubly restricted. However, very little is known about gender differences in child-rearing and more research needs to be done. It is clear that children learn gender differences young, and that they grow up in a world where toys, games, the mass media and education offer a more rigid separation and stereotyping of gender roles than parents actually impose. (See J. and E. Newson, 1978.) The stereotyped world of toys will make this point adequately before the child leaves the home for the school.

Toys and Games
Unless a child is growing up in the most extreme poverty, he or she is likely to play with toys. The different social classes probably choose different toys, so while the plain varnished beech wood block is an intellectual middle-class toy, the plastic model of a TV character is probably a working-class one. However, gender differences are probably far more significant than class in determining what toys children are given. Small boys are not usually given dolls' houses or miniature washing machines, small girls are not given toy trains or guns. This is made clear in an American study, conducted in 1972 (Goodman *et al.*, 1974) by participant observation in a large store's toy department for thirty hours in the pre-Christmas peak period. The participant observation produced several interesting, though probably predictable, conclusions. The researchers asked shoppers the age and sex of the children for whom gifts were being bought. They found that children under 2 got very similar presents, mainly cuddly toys, things to develop skills in handling objects, and

learning shapes and colours such as blocks, rings and simple constructions. After the age of 2 sex differentiation set in. The researchers found that the adult toy-buyers had rigid gender role norms about appropriate toys *but* would make exceptions for individual children they knew well with idiosyncratic preferences. In other words, adults did not believe that a train was a suitable present for a girl but would consider buying a train for a girl who had specially asked for one. This reflects the finding reported by the Newsons (1978) about parents' concern to safeguard small idiosyncrasies in their own children.

The observers found that adult shoppers spent longer choosing presents for boys than for girls. The majority bought sex-differentiated toys – for example, in the thirty hours no one bought a scientific toy for a girl. The toys, and the salespeople, were clearly divided to help the adults in choosing sex-differentiated toys. Women sales staff were selling the cheap and simple toys, while men were selling all the expensive items, such as bicycles and electric racing car circuits, and all the technical things, such as microscopes. This differentiation was repeated in the toy packaging – examining 860 boxed toys, the researchers found three out of four chemistry sets only showed boys on the boxes, and a quarter had boys and girls. There were no chemistry sets for girls, or with girls only on the box. Then they found a price difference. Of toys costing under 2 dollars, 50 per cent were for girls and 31 per cent for boys, while of toys costing over 5 dollars only 18 per cent were for girls and 34 per cent for boys.

This suggests an imbalance in the *price* of toys for the two sexes – perhaps paralleled by the finding on presents *received*. The researchers asked forty-two girls and forty-two boys what they had had at Christmas 1972, and found that the two groups had received equal numbers of presents, but whereas 73 per cent of the boys' presents were toys and games, only 57 per cent of the girls' presents were. Girls had received gifts of clothes and furniture, while boys had not.

The researchers were distressed by the findings, especially the lack of scientific toys for girls and the restricted range of adult role models offered by the dressing-up costumes. Boys' costumes included an Indian chief, Superman, a marine, a racing motorist, a highway patrol cop, and an astronaut; while a girl could only be a nurse, bride, ballerina, drum majorette or princess. Then, as they point out, the imagined duties of the roles are very different, so that the boy doctor gets pretend medical instruments in his kit, while the nurse's outfit comes with a tray of food and thus renders the job 'closer to the role of waitress than that of medical practitioner' (Goodman *et al.*, 1974, p. 125).

Similar research has not been undertaken in Britain, although it would make a good project for students, to observe and interview in toy shops and departments. As a substitute I examined the Christmas toys offered in two Habitat catalogues and two mail order catalogues. The Habitat catalogues of 1977 and 1977/8, the Quality Post Christmas catalogue for 1975 and the Marshall Ward catalogue for Autumn/Winter 1977 were studied. The Habitat catalogues were chosen to illustrate 'educational', 'middle-class' toys, the mail order firms the working-class toy market. The Habitat 1977 catalogue has four pages of toys, as does the 1977/8 edition, offering forty-four and forty-six items respectively, many the same in both catalogues. Accordingly, I have concentrated the analysis on the later catalogue. Habitat do not show children playing with the toys, thus avoiding one source of gender-typing. Habitat also seem quite careful to avoid explicit gender-typing of toys. 'Lazy days needlecraft' is described as being 'for aspiring seamstresses', a pastry set 'for mini pastry cooks' and a tool set is 'to encourage young carpenters', which perhaps leaves a boy free to be a seamstress or a pastry cook and a girl free to be a carpenter? Most toys are offered simply 'for children', or in the case of the flower-pressing kit 'for botanists from 5 years upwards' and a skipping rope 'for childish skipping games or the serious keep-fit training of a future Olympic athlete'.

However, there is clear evidence of gender role stereotyping in three areas: pictures on boxes, books and the pictures on the jig-saws. For example, 'ORBIT', a board game, shows four boy astronauts on the box, and 'Hide and Squeak' another board game, shows three boys and a cat. The implication is that girls cannot be astronauts. This stereotyping is repeated in their selections of books. Four 'know-how books' are supposed to 'encourage even the most impractical child to have a go at a host of creative activities'. Yet one book has a home-made football game on the cover, one an airplane and one a steamroller; not things a girl is likely to want to model. The fourth book offers ideas in the area of spycraft – 'lots of secret codes and disguises' – but the cover shows a spy with pipe, bow tie and moustache. Just what the infant Mata Hari is wearing! None of these seems especially likely to encourage the impractical girl to start creating things. Gender-stereotyping is also found among the pictures shown on the wooden puzzles and the giant floor jigsaws. Of eight designs, two show women hanging out washing on a line, and only two other women appear, a mother in a wooden puzzle and a farmer's wife in a floor jigsaw. Men are shown in non-domestic roles such as a soldier, a postman and a farmer.

Thus the parents buying toys and games from Habitat are, *de facto*, offering their children stereotyped gender roles. Little girls are shown adult roles as housewives, while little boys are shown a variety of different, non-domestic roles. This picture is accentuated in the mail order catalogues.

The Marshall Ward and Quality Post catalogues contain much larger selections of toys and games, which can be more realistically compared with the American research, and my findings were similar. Most of the toys are not described explicitly as being for one sex or the other. But although the toys are not shown with only one gender, or described as sex-typed, many *are* clearly gender-differentiated, and the gender roles they offer are all too familiar. Boys would not be found playing the 'Miss World' game, where four swimsuited dolls (one black) compete to win the title. Boys are offered a wide range of roles, while girls are only shown a restricted one. Boys in the two catalogues are offered material to play at being Robin Hood, Count Dracula, a postman, cowboy, Indian, astronaut, several kinds of engineer, policeman, footballer, cricketer, boxer, teacher, artist, sculptor, big game hunter, carpenter, scientist and many military roles – paratrooper, helicopter pilot, tank driver, commando, deep sea diver, frogman and Red Devil parachutist (twenty-four roles). Girls are given props to play teacher, nurse, secretary, make-up artist, jewellery-maker, dress designer, Miss World, ballerina, horse woman, gymnast and the domestic acts of sewing, cooking, cleaning, shopping and mothering – i.e. Mother (eleven roles).

Compare these four descriptions:

Beautifully dressed 18 in. soft-bodied doll with Vinyl head and hands. She actually sucks her thumb when it is put into her mouth. She will be a delight for any little girl. (£7·99) (Marshall Ward)

A kitten design umbrella just like mummy's. Dome shaped in clear plastic with attractive design. (£1·50) (Marshall Ward)

Flower drops. Make hundreds of different coloured flowers. Wires are made into loops and dipped into paint to form delicate films of colour within the loops. Small beads are supplied for special effects like berries and pollen. (£3·10) (Quality Post)

Dolly International. Paint your own national costume dolls of Europe. Six beautifully modelled dolls, complete with accessories . . . A set to delight any girl. (£1·95) (Quality Post)

with these:

Six Million Dollar Man is 13 in. high with moulded flexible limbs and body. He is dressed in his red track suit and shoes. In addition to his bionic eye he has a new bionic grip action in his right hand. Activated by depressing the bionic module in his forearm. He'll actually grip, then lift the orange simulated steel beam which is supplied. (£5·50) (Marshall Ward)

'Marx' Copter squad machine gun. Authentically detailed gun has a replica of continuous belt ammunition feed, mechanical trigger action pull and realistic 'chopper' sound. Forward hand-hold flips down to form tripod and scope sight provided. (£3·50) (Marshall Ward)

Powermite Toy Workshop. Comprises battery powered Jig Saw with extra blade. Drill, Bits, Square, Hammer, Screwdriver, Bench Vice, Wrench, Blue prints, Styrofoam material and Instructions. (£6·40) (Quality Post)

Action Man Deep Sea Diver Outfit. Now you can make your action man dive or surface, with this fabulous outfit which contains so much: a white fabric suit, a diving helmet, boots, belt, gloves, hammer, buoy, compass, knife, scabbard, rope, and an oxygen pump and hose. Also enclosed is an instruction leaflet. (£2·85) (Quality Post)

The worlds conjured up by these toys are very different, and emphasise the very different presents and futures of males and females in Britain. Overall, I think the toy market in Britain is very similar to that in the United States as reported by Goodman *et al.* (1974). They conclude that girls' toys are simple, solitary and passive, boys' toys are more varied, more expensive, and are complex, social and active.

Apart from toys and games, children's lives will be influenced by the mass media and by books in school if not at home. These influences are discussed in several recent studies, such as Weitzman *et al.* (1977), Sharpe (1976), Braman (1977) and Koerber (1977). All conclude that the view of the world offered to children is unreal, and heavily biased towards exaggerated gender-stereotyping. Women are frequently omitted from stories altogether, and where they do appear they are presented as frightened, passive, domestic bores. Carmel Koerber's (1977) work on television will serve as an example of a recent feminist analysis of such material. She presents an analysis of the TV programmes for 7–13 June 1975 – or rather the BBC programmes and those for the two London ITV companies (an interesting example of unconscious regional chauvinism accentuated by classifying Welsh as a 'special interest' programme). Koerber found the children's TV on all channels, including pre-school and teenage programmes, made up 27 hours 40 minutes of time, 14 hours 10 minutes on BBC 1, 2 hours and 5 minutes on

BBC 2 and 11 hours and 30 minutes on ITV. Koerber analysed the content of the programmes and offered the following comments (p. 135):

> Pre-school programmes like BBC's *Playschool* are fairly innocuous, focusing as they do on things around us – trees, animals, shells. There's painting and singing and a man and a woman share the presentation fairly equally . . .

However,

> By and large the boys are simply the more interesting characters – the ones who have the adventures, the ones who succeed. Even the pets belong to the boys, with the exception of ponies . . .

Koerber points out that in the June week children could see *Yao, African Prince, Devlin* (a motor cycle stuntman in the United States), *Kim & Co.* (boy author) and *The Boy from Sula* all from BBC, all featuring young heroes, and nothing centring on a girl. I examined the programmes for the week beginning 8 April 1978 and found *Lorna Doone* showing, although she was heavily outnumbered by *Fish* (a male detective), *Tarzan, Captain Nemo, Batman, The Canal Children, Snacker* and *Doombolt Chase* (all with heroes).

Detailed analysis of the *content* of all these programmes is a job for a professional, and a time-consuming task at that. However, many of the series for older children centre on boys or adult men, while the programmes for young children are no better. Jane Bergman (in Stacey, 1974, p. 110) makes the following point about the highly praised American series *Sesame Street* from which many of the more progressive programmes have drawn an inspiration:

> In the puppet universe, when a female appeared – which was seldom – she was almost invariably a strident mother, a hapless, hopelessly vague mother, or a simpering, querulous little girl with pigtails and a squeaky voice.

Feminists are concerned about the gender-stereotyping in children's books, comics and in the mass media.

SCHOOLDAYS

This final section of the chapter on childhood before adolescence concentrates on life in school. I have written about the part played by the school in gender role socialisation (Delamont, 1980) and this section is therefore brief. I argue there that most educational classes for young children are reinforcing even more rigid gender-stereotypes than the wider society in which they are embedded. Data from classroom observation are necessary to substantiate this, and more data need to be collected. However, we can summarise here what is known about little girls in school.

The large-scale studies of national samples have shown that girls have consistently produced superior academic attainment in the primary school in all subjects except mathematics (Douglas, 1964· Davie *et al.* 1972). There is also evidence that girls get rated more highly for good behaviour and personality by teachers. A study in London by Ingleby and Cooper (1974) demonstrates this female superiority. They collected teacher ratings on 180 children in the London area in primary schools. There were West Indian, Asian, Anglo-Saxon and other kinds of children in the sample, and they found that girls received more favourable ratings than boys on all the rating scales used except for sociability. Girls were seen as superior in character, brightness, work, home background and language skills. Over the course of the school year the gap between boys and girls narrowed on all the scales *except* work. There were substantially worse ratings for all the non-white children all through the year which did not improve, but the gender gap was equally pronounced within each non-white group. That is, West Indian girls were rated better than West Indian boys, Cypriot girls better than Cypriot boys.

Of course teacher ratings of children are only important if they relate to behaviour or are communicated to the children. There is considerable evidence that teachers' expectations for children do relate to their interactions with them (Brophy and Good, 1974). Certainly there is evidence that boys get far more disciplinary contacts with teachers than girls do (Jackson and Lahaderne, 1967), because they get reprimanded much more often. More detailed work on this needs to be done in the United Kingdom, but what we have suggests that boys get more teacher attention, but much of what they get is negative – 'telling off'. Over and above this the classroom is deeply divided by gender as an organising principle. Children are listed in two groups, lined up in two groups, seated in two groups, play games separately, and even enter the school by different entrances. Lobban (1975) has reported on observation of two London schools where children led almost separate lives by gender because of all these organisational differences. We need more data on inter-action processes to see how far this segregation and separation is common throughout nursery, infant and primary schools.

In so far as nursery classrooms mirror the basic patterns of later classrooms, the study by Joffe of a parent-run nursery school in San Francisco (Stacey, 1974) shows sex differentiation operating from an early age. Joffe observed this nursery in 1970 and 1971, and found that although it was racially mixed and concerned about stereotyping races and sexes, in fact different behaviours were reinforced in boys and girls. Often the particular teacher behaviours observed seem trivial, but Joffe suggests they are only the surface manifestations of a much deeper process. Thus although the two teachers tried to encourage boys and girls to take part in 'cross-sex' activities, for example by getting boys to cook, and had unsegregated lavatories, Joffe found consistent differences in teacher behaviour. First, she found that girls' clothes and appearance were far more frequently complimented than boys' *and* that girls got more compliments when wearing dresses. Then, also significant, boys were much more likely to be admired for fighting – so that teachers would make comments like 'he really can take care of himself like a man'.

Clem Adelman (1979) has recently studied classes in East Anglia in classes for pre-school children of 3 to 5 years. Although Adelman's work was not intended to focus on gender differences, the fieldnotes he took show both gender differences in behaviour and the kinds of interpretations we put on them. Adelman had a camera mounted in a robot-like structure he called Charlie. When he first took Charlie into a class the 'children were struck silent'. Then 'Sharon . . . went to Mrs S. and cuddled up to her in some sort of fright maybe, whilst at the same time a young new girl who was drinking milk with the nursery nurse began to cry'. Quite soon though, children came forward to inspect Charlie, and then 'there were ten or twelve children, the majority of them boys, painting very vigorously the surfaces of Charlie'. Here we see two stereotyped kinds of behaviour: the little girls show fear and cry, the boys come boldly forward to try a new activity. These seem to be typical of studies of young children, and two questions arise. First, are small girls really more fearful of novelty, or is there a difference in adult interpretation of the behaviour? Secondly, could schools encourage children to behave in less stereotyped ways, and if they could, should they?

Some of the teachers Adelman observed certainly believed that even at 4 boys and girls should not be treated the same, and there are examples in the data of the same kinds of behaviour noted by Joffe. Thus in fieldnotes from 14 January 1975 the teacher is reported as saying:

'Look pretty, don't shout.'
'You are just so beautiful.'
'Wendy, what a lovely name.'
'Oh, don't you look beautiful. Oh, my favourite lady.'

and

'You look absolutely smashing. Oh, isn't it pretty.'

All these comments were made to girls, dressing up and holding a pretend tea party in the Wendy House. During the same long extract, which covers five pages of typescript, no boy is complimented on appearance at all. Throughout Adelman's extracts, which are taken from a reception class, a nursery class and a nursery school, this pattern recurs. Girls are frequently complimented on their clothes and appearance, boys are frequently ticked off. Fieldwork data collected in an open-plan primary school in Scotland by David Hamilton (1977) and by French and McClure (1979) show similar patterns.

Certainly the fieldwork I conducted watching 9-year-olds in two middle schools in England in 1977 is peppered with examples of stereotyping and differentiation imposed by both teachers and pupils upon the children. The children held very rigid stereotypes of what boys and girls could and should do, and these were reinforced by all kinds of organisational arrangements and everyday interactions. Towards the end of the fieldwork, for example, in one classroom the pupils had to complete a worksheet which asked them to measure various features of the room such as the window sills, the height of the doors, and so on. Throughout one morning the teacher encouraged the class to hurry and complete this work, and her incentive was a race between boys and girls. Beating the other gender was intended to be, and seemed to be, a successful motivator. Thus throughout the morning I recorded interactions such as:

Miss Tweed announces, 'I'm still waiting for most of the boys to do that measuring' . . . (Later). Yvette has finished measuring work sheet. Miss Tweed says 'Another girl finished' . . . Later when Tammy and Ştephanie are up Miss Tweed says 'Only seven girls to go'. Someone asks how many boys and the answer is lots . . . Later when Kenny is up for marking Miss Tweed says 'Only five girls to go now' . . . 'How many boys?' . . . 'Nearly all of them'.

This was in a progressive school called Beaconsfield, but (the more traditional) Adderly Hill was equally characterised by gender-typing. For example, in a cookery lesson the home economics teacher said:

Boys – is it boys who are making so much noise or is it a group of girls? . . . Be careful boys that you get your tables all nice and straight.

Playing one gender off against the other is a common strategy with the 9-year-olds in the two middle schools. Together with the separation of the genders for organisational purposes, the children themselves hold very clear stereotypes of male and female behaviour, and keep themselves and their work distinct. The work they complete also shows quite clear gender differences in interests where free choice is offered. Fieldnote extracts show these self-segregating features of school life in the two middle schools, and how teachers often reinforce them further. For example, at Beaconsfield the children had written essays on 'my favourite place' which I read. Many of the boys had imagined favourite places such as the jungle/submarines/pirate ships – and lots had to do with fighting. No girl had invented a location. Most had chosen real places, zoos, stately homes, fairgrounds, and so on.

At Adderly Hill in a PE lesson in the gym the children were told to get into threes, but the numbers of boys and girls were wrong. I wrote:

> The PE teacher puts Terence with Coral and Laurette to make a three. The other boys regard this as a great joke and giggle . . . This trio never actually do the exercises.

The children obviously kept themselves apart voluntarily, and were unwilling to work in mixed-gender groups. This is illustrated by the previous example, but is also substantiated in systematic observation data across over sixty classrooms in England by the ORACLE project team (Galton, 1979). When boys and girls are expected to co-operate they do not, and this is hardly surprising when their differences, and even opposition, are constantly stressed to them. Thus a teacher who says 'This is one for the girls' when offering reading books, and one who says 'That's one for the boys really, I suppose' when asking for a sentence using the three words 'soldier', 'army' and 'tank', can hardly be surprised if the children do not share and co-operate when occasionally asked to.

Certainly all the other features of life in the nursery, infant and primary schools do nothing to break down any gender stereotypes the children may have. The toys, pictures, games, books and equipment surrounding the children are segregated and highly gender-differentiated as I have discussed elsewhere (Delamont, 1980). One example, the reading schemes in common use, will suffice here.

Reading Schemes

We have an excellent British study of gender roles in reading schemes done by Glenys Lobban (1974, 1975). Lobban took six reading schemes in common use in infant and primary schools in

Britain: two from before 1960, two from the 1960s and two more recent schemes. Between them these six schemes have been used to teach, or fail to teach, most British children to read. The two recent series Lobban analysed are *Nippers* and *Breakthrough to Literacy*, the two from the 1960s are the Ladybird Books featuring Peter and Jane, and *Ready to Read*, while the two pre-1960 schemes are *Happy Venture* and *Janet and John*. Lobban coded the content of 225 stories from these series, 179 of which had human characters as opposed to animals only. Her analysis focused on the human characters.

Lobban found that there were very clearly segregated sex roles for adults and children. In all the series, the 'feminine' behaviours were domestic, passive, expressive and centred indoors, while 'masculine' behaviour was instrumental, active and outdoors. Lobban coded the adult roles presented, the new skills learnt, the leadership roles assumed in mixed activities, the activities shown, and the toys and pets owned by the children. The severely limited world inhabited by the people in reading schemes came through clearly. Boys and men have more of everything than females: there are far more masculine activities, toys and pets, adult roles, new skills and leadership activities. Lobban's 179 stories contained 71 heroes and only 35 heroines, and most of those heroines were starring in traditional female roles, such as learning to care for a new baby. Seventy-three stories had a hero and heroine, but Lobban says the boy was nearly always dominant.

Anne Coote (1976) made a similar point commenting about Ladybird's *Key Words Reading Scheme*:

> Poor Jane, what a weed she is, tagging along behind her brother . . . She wears a white dress and never gets dirty. You can see her in the back of the picture, sitting quietly with her hands folded in her lap. 'Peter is in the water with his new boat in his hand.'

Coote wrote as Ladybird were updating the series and eight of the thirty-six volumes had been revised. (Lobban used the earlier edition.) Coote asked – comparing the schemes,

> how emancipated has Jane become? She wears jeans, has longer hair and looks a lot happier. Her Mummy wears trousers and her Daddy is sometimes caught washing up.

However, as Coote points out, some things do not change. The modernised version of Vol. 1 has the children buying toys. Jane still buys a doll (now black) while Peter buys a mechanical toy (passive/active again). Later in the book Jane is still watching Peter kicking a ball, and when it gets stuck in a tree, although she now climbs it with Peter, she does not actually get high enough to rescue the ball.

The Northern Women's Groups Education Study Group (Wandor, 1972) had earlier raised similar doubts about the Ladybird scheme, complaining about not only its sexism, but also the static 'middle-class world' portrayed (p. 146):

> it is always summer – except when it is Christmas . . . Peter and Jane . . . are nearly always free to play with their huge selection of expensive toys in a garden where rolling lawns and deep herbaceous borders are surrounded by a mellow brick wall . . . The house is detached . . . inside . . . it is all very comfortable . . .

As Lobban showed in her more scholarly analysis, this is not strictly accurate, because Jane does *not* have a huge selection of expensive toys, Peter does. The adult roles are rigidly segregated so that father works and does outdoor maintenance, and teaches the children interesting skills like photography. Mother stays home doing housework, and only teaches domestic skills.

The northern collective also looked at the *Through the Rainbow* series, where photographs of real people are used as illustrations occasionally. Here they found one book where Father and John go up in an aeroplane while Janet stays earthbound with Mother, a picture they find 'particularly outrageous – would any family . . . give such a treat to only *one* of the two children?'.

Lobban also points out that boys are shown spending time watching adult men, not relatives, performing their occupational roles and tasks. Girls do not. They see only mothers. Given that mothers are never seen to have jobs except in the *Nippers* series, girls are not shown *any* adult occupational roles.

This leads naturally into a consideration of other texts available in infant and primary schools, elementary textbooks. Here we are dependent on American analyses (see Delamont, 1980) whose conclusions are summarised by Nilsen (1975, p. 208):

> It is ironic that in recent years, little girls lost out in two different ways. Boys are the dominant figures in the non-fiction section of the library because they are thought to be *more* able than girls in such fields as maths, science, and statesmanship. Then they are the dominant figures in the beginning-to-read books for just the opposite reason. They are thought to be *less* able than girls in the field of language arts.

Thus schoolbooks show little girls as more restricted and living in a more gender-segregated world than the real world they inhabit outside school. School life lags behind the outside world in the area of gender roles.

Chapter 4

Adolescence

> Although adolescence has held social scientists spellbound, it has also seemed to make them lose their heads. (Mungham and Pearson, 1976)

Sometime around the age of 11 to 13 the girl child becomes an adolescent. Three things are important in this change, the physical onset of puberty, the transfer from middle or primary school to upper or secondary school, and the acquisition of the label 'teenager'. While the physical symptom of menstruation is not marked in modern Britain by official public ceremony, unlike many other cultures, it is an important event, but the *social* aspects of adolescence are of equal significance. The social construction of adolescence is much wider than the physical changes, but the importance of the bodily changes – the blood, the spots, the 'need' for a bra, the sweat and the hair – cannot be underestimated, and is discussed later in the chapter.

Adolescent girls have been neglected by researchers and by social theorists, as this chapter will show. There is, however, one paper by Rachel Powell and John Clarke (1975) which, although tantalisingly brief, offers an important theme which can be used to organise the research that is available. Powell and Clarke argue that the 'problem' of adolescent girls can be formulated as 'how to manage the "dangerous passage" of young girls, from parental care – out from one family – and into a maternal role – back into a new family'. This approach allows the researcher to examine girls' relations to the major social institutions, when these relations may differ from those of boys. Powell and Clarke argue that the traditional way to examine girls' participation in subcultures is to treat them as *marginal*. By this they mean that authors explain society, and subcultures within it, 'in terms of what men do, and *then* the activity of girls can be explained through a further, more subtle subdivision of categories . . .'. In other words 'women's participation is perceived as peripheral to the major tensions, conflicts and negotiations that compose a specific class situation'. They suggest that this model is totally inadequate, and go on to discuss other possible ways of fitting adolescent girls into the social system, ending by presenting a model of their own. Put at its simplest, Powell and Clarke are arguing that adolescent boys and girls pass through major institutions on different tracks. In this chapter the different paths through home, school and leisure are plotted for adolescent girls and boys, after a brief discussion of *physical* adolescence, because this is important to teenage girls.

PUBERTY

Marje Proops (1977, 60–1) has described vividly how many adolescent girls are thrown into confusion and misery by the physiological changes:

> If a girl hasn't started menstruating by the time she is thirteen, she begins to worry about her sexual development . . . If her breasts are slow in growing, she is afraid she will be passed by . . . Weight is also a serious obsession . . . Common to both sexes is acne, which causes the deepest embarrassment.

Later she elaborates on the last point, telling how girls with acne 'won't go out, won't even, in extreme cases, go to school and roam the streets playing truant rather than face . . . the classroom' (p. 164). Thus adolescent girls write wanting help to become taller or shorter, fatter or thinner, and to change their hair colour from brown to blonde and vice versa, away from red to anything, and so on. Then come problems of sexuality or lack of it, the girls who fear lesbianism or promiscuity with boys, those believing the myths that masturbation will produce hairy palms or sterility, and those who write because 'As soon as a boy starts to kiss or touch me I just go rigid' (p. 61).

The data from the National Child Development Study sample at 16 provide the most recent comprehensive information on physical change in girls (Fogelman, 1976). Table 4·1 shows the age at which the girls in the sample had started their periods. The medical examination of the sample showed that 63 per cent of the 16-year-olds had fully developed breasts, 37 per cent intermediate development and 0·2 per cent undeveloped breasts. The growth of pubic and axillary hair is shown in Table 4·2. These data show that between 11 and 16 the vast majority of girl children attain adult bodies. With these physiological changes come problems, most noticeably painful menstruation or dysmenorrhoea. Fogelman (1976) shows that 36 per cent of the girls in the NCDS sample suffered

Table 4·1   *Age of First Reported Menstruation*

Age	%
9	0·2
10	2·0
11	13·0
12	24·0
13	34·0
14	20·0
15	5·0
Not yet	2·0

Table 4·2   *Pubic and Axillary Hair Percentage*

	Pubic Hair	Axillary Hair
Adult	60·0	49·0
Absent	3·0	2·0
Sparse	6·0	18·0
Intermediate	34·0	31·0

badly enough for their parents to report it to researchers, while 1·3 per cent of girls had suffered enough to lose more than one week's schooling in the year. Interestingly only 3 per cent of the cohort had been to their GP with the pain, suggesting a resignation among the girls and/or their mothers. Certainly these data, collected from about 12,000 16-year-olds, suggest that the physiological changes are unpleasant for many girls.

The *social* significance of menstruation is not great in Britain except among certain Islamic groups. This was not always the case. Just before the First World War, Naomi Mitchison's first period resulted in her being removed from the boys' prep school she had been attending, and her confinement at home with an inferior governess. Her freedom, both physical and intellectual, was strictly limited until she was married (Mitchison, 1975). While such a dramatic change seems alien it is very similar to the experiences of Muslim girls in Britain today. Patricia Jeffery (1976) studied Christian and Muslim Pakistani families in Lahore and Bristol, and presents data on the adolescent girl which reveals experiences similar to Mitchison's sixty years earlier. Jeffery points out (pp. 61–2) that:

One reason why the women do not generally know English is that English is introduced only in the higher grades . . . and many of the women were taken away from school before they had started learning English . . . Ruxsana left school at twelve and Akhtar at fourteen.

In Bristol the parents of adolescent girls, or those approaching adolescence, face considerable problems. Jeffery says (p. 104):

> Most want their daughters to be well-educated. However, they are worried about co-education . . . they fear that the girls will be corrupted by mixing with boys . . . Rashid intends to circumvent this problem by returning to Pakistan with his two daughters; Ruxsana commented . . . 'we shall go back with the girls . . . We couldn't let the girls go through college here – we want them to train as doctors in Lahore.'

Such dislike of co-education is directly related to the maintenance of proper Muslim standards, especially relating to *izzet* (honour) and *purdah* (the maintenance of social distance between women and men). Ideally *purdah* involves segregation between the sexes before or at puberty, among other practices, and thus the onset of menstruation brings the values of British education into direct conflict with the Islamic ones. Verity Saifullah Khan (1977, p. 85) in her study of Pakistani families in Bradford and Mirpuri found a similar pattern of parental reaction to British education and says that some see the answer to be a single-sex or a Muslim school in Bradford. Thus we can imagine that the onset of puberty for a Muslim girl may produce a dramatic change in her social life, of a kind uncommon or unimaginable in the majority culture.

The physiological changes, and the anomalous position of the teenage girl with her adult body and child's status, mean that female adolescents are frequently seen as being in moral danger. However, generalised anxiety has not led to any systematic body of research, and girls are neglected compared with boys by social scientists. Not that the research on boys has necessarily been well carried out, but it does, at least, exist. Data on adolescent girls are sparse, as the following sections on home, school and leisure will show.

THE ADOLESCENT GIRL AT HOME

Although the popular stereotype of the adolescent is one of rebellion and rejection of adult standards, in fact a whole series of studies has shown that in most spheres of life the adolescent stays close to home, both physically and in his or her attitudes. Most adolescents live at home and share values with their parents on important issues: marriage, work, class, politics, religion and morals. Clashes with parents occur over 'trivial' issues, such as dress and music, not over core values. This is, of course, closely related to the class position shared by adolescent and adult alike. This attachment to home by shared values is common to boys and girls, whereas there is a sex difference in the degree of physical attachment. From an early age, 7, or even 4 (Newson and Newson, 1978), boys are allowed – or take – more physical freedom. Boys escape, or are sent, to play in the street, in the park, on the dump, on the bomb site, while girls are kept closer to home. By adolescence boys are certainly more likely to be 'out', girls more likely to be 'at home', whether helping with domestic work or retreating into their private world.

McRobbie and Garber (1975) point out that many of the activities of the postwar 'teenage' culture could be appropriated by girls into the home, into what they call 'the culture of the bedroom'. This culture, discussed later, consists of 'experimenting with make-up, listening to records, reading the mags, sizing up the boyfriends, chatting, jiving' and depended on access to some space within the home, such as a bedroom. The physical circumstances of the home are of crucial importance for the adolescent girl (especially, of course, for those of Muslim families, where *purdah* is maintained). The National Child Development Study provides some data on the home circumstances of adolescents, which shows, compared with those on the children at 7 and 11, greater material prosperity of the homes. Fogelman (1976) says that 90 per cent of the sample (of 11,500 16-year-olds) lived in houses or bungalows, while 9 per cent were in flats or maisonettes. Coming to the crucial point for McRobbie and Garber's arguments, 61 per cent of the sample had their own bedroom, and 92 per cent had their own bed. Only 0·5 per cent were sharing their bed with two or more other people. This suggests that at least half the teenage girls would have a private space in which to engage in the culture described by McRobbie and Garber.

Home, then, is the place where adolescent girls derive many of their core values *and* where some of them, at least, also engage in their 'youth culture'. It can be the scene of bitter disagreements and of close family harmony, but there is no evidence in any of the research of the supposed generation gap. The Eppels (1966) in their study of 250 young people, half girls, between 15 and 18, attending day release classes, found a large degree of family harmony among the girls. For example, 52 per cent of the girls said they had no desire to be anyone but themselves, and as the Eppels say (1966, p. 126) 'the vast majority of contented subjects, particularly the girls, attribute their attitude to a very happy family life . . .'. Typical quotations are:

I like being myself . . . I have brothers and sisters, a mother and

father who are all very good to me. We have plenty to eat, a
clean bed to sleep in.

I like being myself . . . I have 2 brothers and 3 sisters. We live
in a three bedroom house, and we have a good laugh . . . We
all share what we have and I have a very good mother.

I don't want to be like anyone else, . . . I'm happy at home with
my family . . . (p. 127)

Again, when the sample completed the sentence

I'd give up a lot for . . .

56 of the 103 girls mentioned personal relationships. Twenty-five of
these specifically mentioned parents or siblings, in comments such
as 'my parents' happiness', 'to know my family was happy', 'our
home to be just right to live in, so my mother could stop work and
my father leave Fords' (Eppels, 1966, p. 109). Then the sentence,
'My greatest wish . . .' produced 60 of 120 girls who wished for
happy personal relationships, especially in their families. Typical
quotes are 'is that I can show my parents how much I appreciate
what they have done for me' or 'to see my home with every latest
mod. con. then my mother wouldn't have so much hard work' (pp.
113–14). Boys were much less likely to express such sentiments, being
more likely to wish for nights with Brigitte Bardot, or sports cars.
     Ten years later, a team of researchers interviewed forty-three
adolescent girls in the Swansea area (Ward, n.d.) mostly between
14 and 16. Swansea was a useful area in which to look at the family
lives of adolescent girls, because of earlier work done there by
Rosser and Harris (1965) and Barker (1972) which is discussed later
in the book. Ward and his collaborators found little evidence of
major disagreements or a generation gap, although minor arguments
('Housework, smoking, boys and coming in late were regularly
mentioned as sources', p. 30) were common. However, as Ward
points out, the endless disagreements over 'trivia' are only tolerable
'with someone to whom one was bound by personal constraint . . .
or who were in some way intimates' (p. 32). Yet Ward thinks
intimacy is probably not the right word, for the girls talked of
'getting on' with parents, which he says is a way of describing a
middle ground relationship where continuous interaction takes
place, but neither love nor hate are intense. Ward argues that
parents are 'a territory' for the girls, rather than a sphere in which
personal relationships can be practised. Parents were not used to
share activities, or as confidants either in intimate matters or on
theoretical issues such as religion. In short, daughter–family rela-

tions are not 'worked at' but 'worked from' (p. 37). For example, 'None bar the most extremely . . . afflicted of these girls had any ideas of even wanting to move out into flats or lodgiings . . .' (p. 33), a finding which parallels Barker's (1972) study of the value attached to 'keeping close' by young adults in Swansea. If the ordinary working- or middle-class girl is likely to get on reasonably well with her family, and shares their values, this is equally so for the Muslim and Sikh girls studies by Jeffery (1976), Khan (1976, 1977) and Sharpe (1976). The areas of conflict mentioned by Ward – 'almost inevitably going out, coming in late, clothes and make-up, boys and housework' (p. 32) – are all to do with the idea of 'youth' culture, with specifically teenage behaviour and mores. It is to these the chapter now turns.

ADOLESCENT LEISURE

In their introduction to *Working Class Youth Culture* Mungham and Pearson (1976, p. 1) point out that adolescents are portrayed either as 'rebellious, ill-fitting members of a well-ordered world or glorified as potential rebels . . . who will overturn a world which is sick, lifeless and dull'. Attempting to bring some order to the confused debate, Mungham and Pearson emphasise the sloppiness of most writing about young people, which talks loosely of 'generation gaps' and 'problems'. They prefer to see 'youth culture' not as a unitary phenomenon but as something differentiated by class, occupation, education, ethnic identity and sex. However, their own collection of conference papers, and the volume from Hall and Jefferson (1975) which appeared at the same time, both perpetuate one of the worst flaws in the literature on adolescence: its total neglect of gender divisions. Mungham and Pearson claim (1976, p. 4) that they could not find anyone to write about the lives of working-class adolescent girls; while Hall and Jefferson include one theoretical note and a short article which draws on data collected in a youth club (McRobbie and Garber, 1975).

The social scientist who wishes to keep her head when assimilating the vast literature on youth or adolescence is faced with three main problems. First, most of the research has been focused on deviant or delinquent youth; secondly, nearly all of it has neglected class and region to concentrate on age alone; and thirdly, there are no data on 'normal' adolescent girls collected in a scholarly, unbiased way. In other words, gender differences have not been considered when adolescence is discussed. Irene Jones (1974) analysed the research literature on adolescence in Britain and the United States, making a particularly detailed study of twenty five original, empirical research reports published since 1945. Although the literature on the subject of youth is large, it is noticeable that there were few empirical studies of non-delinquent adolescents for Jones to examine. She found that only one of the twenty-five was based on a sample of girls only, ten (40 per cent) were based on boys only and fourteen (56 per cent) on mixed samples. Twenty of the twenty-five studies (80 per cent) were conducted by a man or men, two (8 per cent) by mixed research teams and three (12 per cent) by women. Within the fourteen studies which included both sexes in the sample, they were rarely equally represented, even in numbers. Often very small proportions of the sample (e.g. 20 per cent) were girls.

Jones suggests that research on adolescents is negligent about girls for three reasons: traditional attitudes about women being socially insignificant (especially in studies of careers and higher education), the male predominance within the research community (most researchers, particularly senior ones, are men) and, finally, the low delinquency rates among adolescent girls. Similar points are made by McRobbie and Garber (1975) and by others who have recently surveyed the field. More seriously, the methods used in nearly all the studies are biased by the conscious or unconscious preconceptions of their devisers. This is clear from Jones's (1974) detailed scrutiny of Murdock and Phelps's (1973) work on adolescent life-styles.

One particular aspect of the research struck Jones forcibly because of its implicit assumptions. The researchers offered a sample of 322 girls and 299 boys a series of teenage role models with which to identify. Some of these role models were common to both sexes, but some were only offered to either the boys or the girls. Jones argues that by offering certain roles only to one sex and not the other Murdock and Phelps were *creating* polarised results, and forcing the two sexes into different, stereotyped roles, rather than undertaking a truly scientific study without preconceptions. The roles offered to both sexes were 'good pupil', 'rebel', 'ritualist', 'good bloke'/'good friend' and 'pop fan'. Boys were also offered 'street peer', 'sports fan', 'boyfriend' and 'natural leader'; while girls were given 'homemaker', 'tomboy', 'girlfriend', and 'fashion follower'. While the girlfriend/boyfriend pair were matched, the other roles offered only to one sex or the other reinforce very crude stereotyping. The role of natural leader was omitted from the girls' list altogether so no data are available on what proportion of girls saw themselves as leaders. Equally stereotyped is the offer of roles as homemaker and fashion follower to girls, while denying them the option of street peer or sports *fan* (the tomboy is a participant in sports), yet not offering boys any home-centred role (model-builder, carpenter, etc.), or any interest in fashion and clothes. Effectively, therefore, Murdock and Phelps pre-ordained that girls would come out home-centred and sheep-like, boys street-centred and aggressive.

Jones goes on to highlight some further biases in the research. She contrasts the male sports fan with the tomboy. The boy is good at sport and goes to matches and watches TV sport. The tomboy likes swimming and gym, but 'doesn't like dressing up and would rather wear her old jeans all the time'. Thus the tomboy has to be scruffy as well as athletic, as if sport and attractiveness were opposed. Not only is there no sports fan – no role of soccer fanatic or cricket scorer – there is a dowdiness attached to participation. The boy's image is all positive – no suggestion that he is unattractive, unfashionable or dirty as well as athletic. In contrast, the boy is forced out of the home. No role offers itself to cover the adolescent described by Jones who spends 'a great deal of time repairing bicycles and go-carts, making model aircraft and ships, and eventually tinkering with motor cars' (p. 70). Nor, despite Murdock and Phelps's own finding that 73 per cent of boys liked buying clothes, is there a 'fashion follower' role for boys.

Following on from this, Jones argues that Murdock and Phelps are guilty of accepting the boys' definitions of situations rather than the girls', treating boys' evidence as data but describing girls' evidence as 'claims'. This was particularly apparent when the issue of mixed or single-sex peer groups was raised. The majority of the boys (72 per cent) preferred all-male groups. The girls were more evenly divided, with 52 per cent preferring an all-girl group and 48 per cent a mixed group. Murdock and Phelps call these 'hangers on', and thus, Jones says, ignore social reality. While boys may *prefer* all-male groups, *in fact* many girls go round in groups with boys. To treat the male statement as fact and the girls' statements as 'claims' suggests a pre-definition on the grounds of expectations which is not shifted to take account of the findings. Since Jones wrote, a similar point, supported by evidence from adolescent girls, has been made by Lesley Smith (1978). She found teenage girls who were active, integrated members of adolescent gangs. Although their involvement lasted on average only two and a half years to the boys' four years, it was as intense while it lasted and did not depend on attachment to one particular boyfriend. Lesley Smith's findings directly contradict nearly everything previously written about delinquent teenage girls, and show that research on all types of female adolescent is urgently needed to see if the common assumptions there are also unfounded.

Bearing in mind the probable biases in the literature, we can piece together a picture of what adolescent girls actually do in their spare time. Two things are shown clearly by the literature: a gender difference in preferred leisure activities which could be a reflection of biased research instruments, and a widening gap between those, mainly working class in origin, who are eager to leave school at the minimum age; and the minority, mainly middle class in origin, who intend to take 'A' levels or continue with their education beyond the compulsory leaving age, and train for 'careers'. These are examined in turn.

Sex Differences in Leisure
The first 'finding' which seems to turn up in many studies is that girls choose not to go out as often, or are not allowed out as frequently, as boys. Thus among 14–18 year olds in Bury, Lancashire, Smith found that 85 out of 137 boys were out five or more nights a week, but only 61 of 132 girls were (Smith, 1978, p. 173). Similar findings from 14-year-olds were reported by Quine and Quine (1966). However, not only is there this quantitative difference between boys and girls of the same age, there is also a qualitative difference. Girls are expected to do more housework and child care in their homes than boys are. McRobbie (1978) reported between twelve and fourteen hours of domestic work per week among girls between 14 and 16 using a Birmingham youth club. More data on this aspect of adolescent girls' lives is necessary, because McRobbie's findings run counter to those of Barker (1972) who found little domestic work being done by daughters. The report of the National Child Development Study on 16-year-olds (Fogelman, 1976) has not provided break-downs by sex. However, the information offered is based on a large sample (over 12,000). A large number of the sample spent their 'leisure' working. Half the NCDS cohort had a job in term-time, although the number of hours worked varied widely. Commonly, an average 16-year-old worked from three to nine hours every week, and earned between £1 and £3 (at 1974 wage levels). However, one-twentieth of the whole sample worked for more than fifteen hours a week, and earned £6 per week or more. Given the debate which has gone on since the 1950s about adolescent affluence, these figures can be usefully compared with those for pocket money received, to gain an idea about money available to adolescents. Only 7 per cent of the sample said they had no pocket money, 40 per cent had less than £1 per week, while 15 per cent had over £2. However, without data on sex differences (if any), holiday jobs and the overlap between pocket money and earnings (if any) we cannot make any statements about disposable incomes among adolescent girls. It is probable that boys' jobs pay better than girls' jobs, but sex differences in pocket money are completely unknown. The activities and objects bought with the money are also under-researched, although some data are available on popular activities.

The NCDS asked about leisure activities and Table 4·3 shows their respondent's answers, while their satisfaction with local amenities is shown in Table 4·4. The NCDS data have not been broken down by sex, and so the possible sex differences in leisure

Table 4·3 *Leisure Activities of 16-year-olds in the NCDS Sample (N 11,070) (%)*

	Often	Sometimes	Never/hardly ever	Like but no chance
Leisure reading	27	46	24	3
Sports and outdoor games	38	35	24	3
Swimming	21	44	27	8
Indoor games and sports	25	32	32	10
Watching TV	65	29	5	1
Parties in friends' houses	19	48	26	7
Dancing (discos/dancehalls)	39	31	24	5
Voluntary work	7	30	46	16

Table 4·4 *Adolescents' Satisfaction with Neighbourhood Facilities (%)*

	Satisfied	Uncertain	Dissatisfied	Not bothered
Playing fields/pitches	44	13	26	18
Places for young people to meet clubs/coffee bars/ dance halls	20	11	56	13

Source: Fogelman, 1976, p. 39.

are not known, nor are class or regional variations. In addition, the researchers offered a restricted list of eight activities, rather than allowing the pupils to mention anything they did. Unfortunately, we have very little recent data on adolescents' leisure activities on anything like the same scale, and so have to create the picture of class and sex differences from older studies and small-scale research reports, such as Scottish Council for Research in Education (SCRE, 1970), Murdock and Phelps (1973), McRobbie and Garber (1975), McRobbie (1978) and Ward (n.d.). What all these show is a clear pattern of sex differences. For example, Quine and Quine's (1966) 14-year-olds in Southampton were at a school with an attached youth club; 58 per cent of the boys used this club frequently, but 60 per cent of the girls never used it. Instead the girls went to dances at the local community centre and to commercial clubs in the town centre, which the 14-year-old boys never visited. The Quines said 'girls do attend certain types of clubs more often than boys of the same age: but the clubs which they tend to prefer are those whose main activity is dancing. While we were doing the survey it became apparent that the children had a definite grading of clubs in terms of desirability. The most popular were dancing clubs in the centre of the city where a live group would play pop music, second were non-school youth clubs, run by churches, labour clubs or community centres, and finally at the bottom of the list, came the school youth club'. Quine and Quine point out that the 14-year-old girls regarded the boys of their age as 'kids', and went to places to meet older men. Overall, girls went out less, but always went to a definite place, while boys went out more just to hang around.

A similar gender difference was reported by SCRE (1970) from a sample of 15-year-olds in ninety-seven Scottish schools. They concluded (p. 118) that:

In general, the girls in the group took more part in leisure activities than did the boys. The exception was games, where 74 per cent of the boys were involved compared with 57 per cent of the girls . . . Games and sports, reading, hobbies and dancing enjoyed the greatest support. The more cultural pursuits, such as the theatre and music, were not popular . . . [except with those] still at school or in non-manual occupations . . . Although reading was the second most popular leisure pursuit in the group as a whole, it is much more a pursuit of those still at school or in full time education (47 per cent), than of those in employment (21 per cent) . . . Dancing . . . was associated with employment rather than with continuing education and was much more popular with the girls . . . than with the boys.

Here we can see not only the sex differences but also the widening gap between the school leavers and the stayers.

The SCRE study gave a breakdown of different types of youth organisation attended by their sample. They found (p. 119) that church and non-church youth clubs were the most used (226 and 221 members). Next came the Scout and Guide movement (193) and the Boys' and Girls' Brigades (136). Less popular choices were athletic clubs (57), pre-service organisations (47) and political clubs (11). Membership in all these respectable, worthy youth organisations was more common among those still at school, or in non-manual work. Youth clubs were more popular with girls than boys, while the pre-service and political groups were almost exclusively attended by boys. Here a sex difference and the split between 'leavers' and 'stayers' both show vividly.

The study reported by Ward (n.d.) of forty-three girls in Swansea and the surrounding area in 1972–3 contained girls still at school and at work, from class backgrounds very similar to those researched by McRobbie (1978) in Birmingham. Of course the sampling frame is crucial in studying adolescents, and by basing herself in a youth club McRobbie obviously got an atypical group of teenage girls. Ward gives no indication of how the sample was drawn, although it does include some girls who never go out, or engage in unusual activies. Overall, however, the two studies show a similar picture.

Both sets of girls led highly circumscribed lives. McRobbie's sample 'rarely left the estate. They bought their clothes from the local shopping centre or more often from catalogues ('clubs'). Apart from visiting an older sister . . . their days and evenings were spent moving between school, youth club and home with monotonous regularity.' This is contrasted with their middle-class school peers, and their own brothers, who travelled much farther afield. Ward similarly found that lack of transport confined the girls to places in walking distance, or on bus routes. Yet Ward's sample went to more places than McRobbie's, they went out a great deal and when they did stay home it was either to do a 'feminine' task as hair washing or dressmaking, or under some constraint babysitting, homework, housework. Otherwise 'staying in', defined in opposition to 'going out', is an acknowledgement of nowhere to go, or being in a bad mood. Ward found that half the sample were out every night of the week, and nearly all were out three or four nights. Nearly every night involved a social activity: youth clubs, discos, meeting friends or a boyfriend. Visits to friends' houses, or to relatives, were rare. Again in the Swansea study the difference between school leavers and school stayers was clear, in that girls doing 'A' levels stayed in to do homework. McRobbie had no 'stayers' in her sample.

Two aspects of the lives of teenage girls also turn up in all the studies, the importance of the best friend, and the issue of femininity and attracting boys. I want to turn to the 'culture of femininity' and 'bedroom culture' as McRobbie calls them, and to the relationship with boys. She too suggests that the best friend is a crucial relationship, absorbing emotional energy and useful for pursuing boys. McRobbie and Garber (1975) suggest that the elements of the 'bedroom culture' involve talking, make-up, listening to the right music, reading magazines and dancing. Of these, dancing, the music and the magazines have been analysed to some extent, although very rarely in terms of the meaning they have for adolescent girls. The magazines have probably received more attention than any other aspect of the teenage culture, from Alderson (1968) through to Sharpe (1976). Sharpe (p. 119), writing when *Jackie* sold a million copies a week, argued that a diet of romantic magazines produced an apolitical, apathetic teenager, and summarised the forces which create the dominant culture of femininity as follows:

By the time a girl reaches adolescence, her mind has usually been subjected to an endless stream of ideas and images incorporating sexist values. She has struggled through reading primers and children's books, watched endless hours of television, has absorbed thousands of comics, keeps *Jackie* in her school desk or borrows it from a friend, she browses through her mother's *Woman*, listens to the radio, and . . . follows her current music idols . . . no connection between their lives at school and their growing sense of womanhood is ever portrayed.

Murdock and Phelps (1973) have discussed how different subgroups of adolescents look to different sectors of pop music, a point re-iterated by Murdock and McCron (1976). The relationship between the music and the centrality of dancing in the lives of the adolescent girls has not been properly explored, however. Dancing seems to fulfil for girls what football does for boys, allowing physical exercise and displays of skills – with the difference that dancing can take place in the home, and certainly never takes place on the street. Overall, however, we lack any detailed knowledge of how 'femininity' is acted out – just as we lack information on the relationships with boys.

Teenage sex, and especially the 'illegal' sex of the under-16s considered in this chapter, has created considerable public concern, but facts about it are very scarce. The large study conducted by Schofield (1965) found very few girls under 16 who were not virgins, and suggested that a few 'promiscuous' girls were 'serving' the higher proportion of sexually experienced boys, while the overwhelming majority of girls stayed 'good' or 'nice'. Certainly the double standard described by Schofield as *fact* is firmly in the heads of most adolescent girls studied more recently. McRobbie's sample describes explicitly how girls who 'give in' become labelled on the estate and lose girlfriends as boys treat them as easy, and a similar dilemma was found by Deidre Wilson (1978) in a sample of 13- to 15-year-olds in a northern city. Wilson's sample might have sex with a steady boyfriend and remain a 'nice' girl, but once a girl was labelled 'an easy lay' she lost girlfriends and her reputation. The pressures on the working-class girl are certainly towards saving oneself for, if not marriage, at least the engagement ring. How many actually yield to the pressures from boys, and how many to the social pressures of keeping one's reputation, is always likely to be unknown. The only clear data one has refer to are the casualties – the girls 'put away' for promiscuity, and the pregnancies that come to the notice of the official statisticians.

Certainly the total number of 'casualties' of pre-16 sex is not numerous. In 1975 1,512 babies were born to girls under 16. What is not known is the ration of non-virgins to these conceptions, and this probably never can be known accurately. The best data available are probably those collected by Christine Farrell (1978) who carried out interviews with 1,556 adolescents (16- to 19-year-olds) in 1975. She found that 12 per cent of the girls reported illegal sexual experience before they were 16. Farrell found no significant class differences between girls who had had sexual intercourse and those who had not. However, in 1977 *Honey* published a survey of unmarried girls aged 18 to 26 which included questions about their sex lives. Unmarried girls of 18-plus are not representative of the population of women of that age-range, but one in three of the sample said they were virgins, and of the two-thirds who were not, only 22 per cent had had intercourse under 16. The girls who had stayed on at school to do 'A' levels were more likely to have kept their virginity longer, and so were girls in the north. In other words, the most likely people to have had sex at an 'early' age were working-class girls with no 'O' levels in the south of England.

Sexual experience is discussed in more depth in the next chapter, on the young adult woman, and here I want to emphasise the blanket of uncertainty which shrouds most interactions with the opposite sex, an uncertainty which is beautifully encapsulated by the following letters to problem pages:

> This may sound silly, but I want to know whether I should keep my eyes open or closed when I kiss my boy friend. Most of the time my boy friend has his eyes closed and I don't know what to do myself. (reprinted in *This England*, 1965, from *Daily Mirror*)

> ... I think there must be something wrong with me. As soon as a boy starts to kiss or touch me I just go rigid. I can't respond and all I want to do is run away. I am fifteen and most of my friends sleep with their boy friends. (Proops, 1977, p. 61)

If the girls themselves are frequently uncertain about what to do, they are likely to be under scrutiny. Adults will watch them closely for signs of 'trouble'. Harrison (1975) reports the following conversation from Stevenage:

> Andrea, aged eleven ... wants to be a drum majorette when she grows up. Her best friend, Mandy, aged 13 ... doesn't often go out with boys. 'I feel embarrassed cause my mum takes the mickey. If we build houses in the playground here, they won't let us go in them with the boys. They think we're up to something but we're not really.'

Learning to manage one's own sexuality in the context of adult scrutiny and suspicion, a double standard of morality and a good deal of hypocrisy is obviously hard for the adolescent girl. However we lack data on how girls deal with these pressures. The only thing upon which all the recent commentators agree is that the pursuit of boys, the best friend and the 'culture of femininity' distract girls from the irrelevance of school, to which this chapter now turns.

THE ADOLESCENT GIRL AT SCHOOL

The school lives of adolescent girls are chronically under-researched, a surprising fact when one considers that the change from high achievement in primary school to poor performance in secondary school is one of the most vivid examples of educational wastage in Britain. Yet as King (1971) and Shaw (1976) have pointed out, this failure of adolescent girls to achieve their potential has hardly been *noticed*, much less studied, by anyone. Inequalities in terms of class and sex can be found in studies of access to education and of educational achievement in both Britain and the United States. The inequalities of class are a matter for political and popular concern and are the subject of governmental programmes. (The American and British governments both funded compensatory education programmes in the 1960s aimed at lower-working-class and ethnic groups traditionally failing in school.) Inequalities of sex have not been the subject either of popular concern or governmental intervention of a compensatory nature. The sex gap in educational access and success is ignored not only by politicians and the public, but also by social scientists. A search through the educational research literature reveals few studies of girls or women and of those which do exist few have an adequate analysis of class differences. Ronald King (1971) is about the only sociologist to have pointed this out, and his ideas are discussed further in Delamont (1980).

The school experiences of pupils have been researched quite extensively in the last decade, but nearly all the researchers have studied boys, as Jenny Shaw (1976) has pointed out. In this section a few facts about the kinds of schools teenage girls attend are presented first, followed by some discussion of how they experience schooling.

The first and most noticeable fact about adolescent school experience is that most of it is received in state schools (93 per cent), and a great deal of it in comprehensive schools (59 per cent) (Fogelman, 1976). Only a small proportion of pupils are in independent schools (3·7 per cent), direct grant schools (2·3 per cent) or grant-aided schools in Scotland; 10 per cent are in grammar and senior secondary schools, and 21 per cent in secondary modern or junior secondary schools. Nearly all these pupils were at day schools, with only $3\frac{1}{2}$ per cent at boarding schools full or part time. In other words, nearly all were living at home with their families. Most of the NCDS sample were at co-educational schools (74 per cent), and only 13 per cent of the 16-year-old girls were at single-sex schools (Fogelman, 1976). Thus the majority of the 16-year-olds in Britain in 1974 were at mixed comprehensive day schools, a type of school about which we have absolutely no information of any sociological merit relating to girls and their school lives. The NCDS sample data give us some information about the size and organisation of the comprehensive schools attended, and the teaching groups within them. Thus we can see that the majority of teenagers are in schools with fewer than 1,000 pupils (62 per cent); while 38 per cent were at schools with between 1,000 and 2,000 pupils.

Most of the adolescent girls in Britain were attending schools in the 1970s which arranged the pupils in streams or sets for their academic subjects, and only 17 per cent were taught in mixed-ability groups. We know that streaming causes all sorts of polarising effects on boys in single-sex schools (Hargreaves, 1967; Lacey, 1970) and in mixed schools (Banks and Finlayson, 1974), so that those put in top streams improve their academic performance and adopt the school's values while those in lower streams do less homework, lose academic ground and adopt anti-school values and behaviours. We do not know if similar patterns occur for girls, because the equivalent research was not done in the old grammar and secondary schools, and is not being done in the comprehensive schools. Lambert (1977) did some research in a girls' grammar school which was not streamed. The friendship groups here were extremely complex, but did not show the same pattern of polarisation as found among boys. Mandy Llewellyn's unpublished material on a girls' grammar and secondary modern school does reveal polarising effects of streaming, although her analysis would suggest that the pattern in girls' school lives is not identical to that found in the classic studies of males. Certainly we need more research on girls' school lives in streamed and unstreamed classes, although it is clear from the NCDS sample that mixed-ability teaching which might mitigate against polarised pupil cultures is very rare in the key subjects. Only 9 per cent were in mixed-ability groups for mathematics, and only 21 per cent in mixed ability groups for English.

Many of the pupils in the NCDS were attending schools which were badly equipped and under-staffed. The heads of the schools were asked to rate the adequacy of their facilities in seven areas, and the results of these inquiries are shown in Table 4·5. The table shows clearly that a great many pupils are in poorly equipped schools, where truly comprehensive education cannot take place. Only one-third of schools were rated by their heads as having adequate facilities in all these areas. The meaning of these inadequacies for female pupils is not clear, but it is likely that shortfalls in several of the facilities shown in Table 4·5 would particularly affect girls. Pupils taking commercial subjects and home economics will be mainly female, and shortages there will affect

Table 4·5 *Inadequacies in British Schools*

	Percentage of Schools
Sports facilities	34
Commercial subjects	25
Science laboratories	23
Library	21
Wood/metalwork	20
Domestic science/home economics	15
Audio-visual facilities	15

them. It may also be the case, though, that it is boys who suffer from inadequate facilities in 'female' subjects because they are closed to boys. We do not know. However, inadequate sports, science and library facilities certainly handicap girls' educational progress. Not only are two-thirds of secondary schools poorly equipped in some respects, many of them have oversized classes in basic subjects. Thirty per cent of 16-year-olds were in classes of more than thirty pupils for English or mathematics, while only a small percentage were in classes of under twenty for English (12 per cent) and mathematics (15 per cent). These large classes may be responsible for the 1·6 per cent of the NCDS sample whose teachers said they could not read well enough for everyday life, and the 2·6 per cent whose mathematics was not up to doing basic calculations.

Of course we cannot know how far the inadequacies of secondary school contribute to the disenchantment with schooling experienced by so many adolescent girls. Many people have suggested the problem is more in the atmosphere of the schools, and especially their insistence on rules and uniform. Two-thirds of the NCDS sample were in schools which had uniforms which were partially compulsory or voluntary, and 30 per cent had compulsory uniform throughout the school. Only 4 per cent of the sample attended schools where no uniform existed. The existence of a uniform is probably not, in itself, enough to drive girls away from school, but the wider system of institutional control over pupils of which it is a part may be sufficient. Certainly it seems likely that girls will resent an institution like the girls' secondary modern in London described by Eileen Moody (1968) where an atmosphere of 'overwhelming pettiness' prevailed:

There was the teacher in the habit of stopping girls with short skirts and unravelling them herself, at the waist – in public. There was the ban on jewellery because, as one teacher explained, it looked 'cheap'. Maybe it was: cheaper than hers. There was the continual nagging about uniform. And the preoccupation with make-up.

In the absence of any research into the problem it is perhaps not surprising that there are *no* satisfactory explanations of the terrible waste of educational potential among working-class girls, and the relative underachievement of all women. The facts are stark. A majority of the pupils in the National Child Development Study intended to leave at 16 (62 per cent) and 67 per cent of these had no wish for further full- or part-time education. The girls among these leavers probably would not have any further education facilities available, as Eileen Byrne (1978) shows only too clearly. Of those pupils planning to stay on at school till 17 or 18 or later (30 per cent) there were relatively few (12 per cent) intending to enter universities, polytechnics or central institutions (in Scotland), although there was a sizeable proportion (21 per cent) for other kinds of training. These teenagers reported that they wanted to leave school to earn a wage and be independent, because they did not feel good enough to stay and that they did not like school (Fogelman, 1976). These overall figures mask considerable sex and racial differences among adolescents. Girls, in study after study, are more favourable towards schools, yet they still leave without fulfilling their academic potential.

Linda Dove (1976) studied 545 adolescents of 15 and 16 in three London comprehensives, attended by Cypriots, West Indians, Asians and whites. In all groups girls were more favourable towards school than boys of the same group, although Cypriots and Asians of both sexes were more favourable than West Indians and whites. Asian girls were the keenest on staying on to do 'A' levels of any group; white boys were the keenest to leave and get apprenticeships. The educational attitudes of Cypriot and Asian women are discussed further in the next chapter. Sue Sharpe (1976) provides some data on Asian and West Indian girls, again in London. She found the West Indian girls nearly all had very strict parents with whom they were often at odds, due to different values. Education was one sphere of conflict, for Sharpe argues that the West Indian girls were deeply ambivalent about the school system. They wanted qualifications for jobs, but did not like school. Some experienced severe racial discrimination. The Asians in Sharpe's sample were mainly from India and East Africa, and so differ from the Pakistanis studied by Khan (1976), Jeffery (1976) and the Ballards (1977). Sharpe found the Asian parents and girls were very ambitious, and the girls could use education as a way of postponing marriages arranged by parents.

Sharpe's white London girls mostly saw no point in staying at school, but wanted to get out to work. There is no clear explanation for this, although Sharpe suggests the American research on 'fear of success' in women (Horner, 1971) which has been found in American high schools (Baruch, 1974), the sexist nature of the curriculum, and the overwhelming pressure from media, society and even the school, towards marriage not careers. These need to be mentioned in turn, although there is no British research on any of them. In the original 'fear of success' experiment, college students were asked to complete a 'story', in which a girl (if they were women) and a boy (if male) had come top of the medical school class. The women college students wrote stories in which academic success for the woman was *negatively* perceived. Friends and fiances were lost, misery and isolation resulted for the successful woman. Baruch attempted a similar experiment with 11- and 16-year-old girls in American schools. The stimulus sentence was 'Anne has won first prize in the science fair for her exhibit on car engines'. The 11-year-old girls were not overwhelmingly hostile to female success; 29 per cent showed this fear, 52 per cent did not, while 19 per cent described Anne coping with the problems of success. However, boys of the same age were overwhelmingly unafraid of male success (75 per cent). Baruch shows that many girls offered stories in which Anne *shared* her success to avoid its negative consequences ('Her friends Mary Anne and Beth also helped') although none of the boys did this. Female confidence among 11-year-olds had faded among the 16-year-olds. Under 40 per cent of the older girls showed no fear of success, and classic Horner-type stories appeared:

She is standing in front of her exhibit, smiling and feeling proud, yet she also feels sort of funny because she is a girl, and girls don't usually think about car engines . . . all the boys are laughing at her because they don't think she is feminine.

In another story 'Paul is a poor loser and said he will never sit with Anne again, because she is too smart for him'. These fears of male rejection of the clever woman are reflected in another story reported by Baruch from a stimulus of two women who have won a Nobel Prize. They use the prize money to go on a cruise to meet men! The belief that men dislike clever women, and are unable to love and cherish women who beat them at anything, is deeply ingrained in both British and American culture. This was shown nearly thirty years ago by Mirra Komorovsky (1946) who reported how college girls 'played dumb' to boys, lowering marks, misspelling words and generally acting like passive idiots. In the 1970s a replication on male students' attitudes (Komorovsky, 1973) showed such strategies were still necessary: many men *were* frightened of clever women. In Britain, Galloway's (1973) research in Scotland showed similar perceptions by women: men would be scared off if they were intellectuals. Sharpe and others think this is an important element in discouraging girls from educational achievement.

Sexism in the curriculum has been much more widely studied in the United States (Stacey, 1974; Maccia *et al.*, 1975). Although British textbooks and curricula are probably just as sexist as American ones, there is no evidence on this. Studies of 'O' level history texts, geography books, maths questions, and so forth need to be carried out. There is more evidence that many schools do not offer girls proper science, or woodwork, metalwork and technical drawing, but we have little evidence that girls want these subjects. Sharpe (1976, p. 149) quotes girls who had wanted such subjects: 'We did a lot of cookery and needlework at school. No technical drawing, no science subjects except biology ... ' and 'I wanted to do art, so I couldn't do technical drawing.'

Both the curriculum and the fear of academic success probably pale into insignificance beside pressure into work and marriage from parents, media and even teachers. Yet we have no *causal* research on these pressures, and until we have the failure of girls will not be explicable. All we can say is that the majority of adolescent girls, especially in the working class, do not dislike school as much as their male contemporaries (e.g. Willis, 1977) but still reject anything it can offer them at the earliest opportunity.

Chapter 5

Young Adults

I've been going steady with my boyfriend for two years and we both intend getting engaged – we're both 19. He says he'll never marry a girl who's not a virgin and so to be sure that I am one he wants to have intercourse with me before we become engaged. (Problem Page, *Woman's Own*, 1965)

I'm 19, and have grown fond of an 18year-old girl. We've been going steady for four months, and she's just confessed that, when she was 15, she tried to make love with a boy. Although they didn't succeed, knowing this has spoilt everything. I despise her now ... Will I ever recover my love for her? (Problem Page, *Woman's Own*, 3 June 1978)

Although the dominant cultures of Britain do not allow for any particular ceremony to mark the girl becoming a woman, apart from marriage, there is a clear sense in which the age of 16 marks a division between adolescence and young adulthood. Sixteen is the legal age for consent to sexual relations, the age at which marriage can take place and the school leaving age, as well as the time when smoking and drinking become legal. This chapter examines the lives of young women in Britain between 16 and 21. The chapter is chiefly divided into two distinct sections: the first deals with the lives of girls who leave school at the first moment they can; the second with the minority who choose to stay on at school or attend further education, and continue on to higher education.

Staying on at school after 16 may seem a small difference between one woman and another. However, the decision to stay or leave has far-reaching consequences: it is likely to affect their age of marriage, earning power and their relationships with men. The actual age of marriage is definitely related to completing fulltime education, for early marriage is associated with one partner being out at work. *Social Trends, 1977* shows that three-quarters of women and over half the men aged 16 in 1975 will be married by the age of 25. In 1975 the most popular age of marriage for women was 19, and the average age 22. For men, the most popular age was 22 and the average 25. After dropping steadily for twenty years up till 1970, the age at which first marriage takes place for women has actually risen slightly and is now back near 21.

The distinction is clearly there between the earlier-than-average marriage of the working-class early leaver, and the later-than-average marriage of the middle-class 'stayer-on'. As with marriage, so too with sexual relations. In June and July 1977 the magazine *Honey* published a survey done on 290 unmarried women between 18 and 26 which studied their sexual activities and attitudes. This survey showed clear differences between the regions of Britain, between the classes and, noticeably, by education. Women who had stayed on at school to do 'A' levels had significantly different patterns of sexual behaviour, and attitudes. Such women were less likely to be sexually experienced than early leavers: of the 29 per cent who were not virgins at 17, 59 per cent had left school without taking 'O' levels. Sex before the age of 16 was most common among southern English girls of working-class origin who left school without 'O' levels.

Once the women who stay on at school or college to do 'A' levels have experienced sexual relations they were more likely to use contraceptives (97 per cent) than those who were early leavers. In the sphere of attitudes, the 'stayers' were more likely to say they would consider having an abortion if necessary, and to say they would consider a relationship with a man of a different colour, race or religion. They were also more likely to stress the importance of fidelity, not only when 'going steady' and in marriage, but also when a couple lived together. The *Honey* staff comment: 'Perhaps this is because they, more than other groups, feel they may live in that way for a time.'

The 'stayers' were not totally different from the leavers, of course. For example, they were just as likely to want to marry eventually although at a later age (25–7 rather than 22–4). Of course, by sampling only single women, the survey was biased in that many working-class girls are married by 20 and so the older women are unlikely to be 'typical'. However, the differences between 'stayers' and 'leavers' is clear enough, and supports earlier work of a more scholarly kind such as Kalsall *et al.* (1972). The vast majority of young women, those who do not do 'A' levels and/or enter higher education, are considered first, and then the minority who opt for voluntary education.

LEAVING SCHOOL AND ENTERING LIFE

The girl who leaves school at 16 with or without any qualifications faces three main problems: finding work, getting along with her family and managing her relationships with men. These three aspects of her life are considered in reverse order, starting with sex, courtship and marriage, and then coming back to family life and work. This is because, for the vast majority of young women, managing the transition to adulthood is predicated on her relationships with men. These relationships are, as the quotes at the chapter opening show, heavily imbued with a 'double-bind' or 'Catch-22' which enslaves nearly all young women. The letters, over a decade apart, show that the double standard is still prevalent in Britain. Virginity and inexperience are still valued by young men, and where a young woman's sex life is considered, she is still damned if she does, and damned if she doesn't.

Sex, courtship and marriage are interrelated, and the majority of young women must try to negotiate themselves into marriage by using their sexuality – either by pregnancy, or virginity, or some intermediate position between the two. As Mungham (1976) has argued, there is no social or economic role for the semi-skilled or unskilled working-class woman, who must marry. She is denied apprenticeships into high-paying skilled work, has left school and cannot enter professions or semi-professions, and so must be supported. In addition, there is no housing, and no social life, for the spinster in the working class or the lower-middle class today.

Thus, there is a harsh realism in modern Britain which dictates that the woman who leaves school at 16 is unlikely to be able to support herself, and must find herself a male partner. Unfortunately we know almost nothing about courtship and dating in Britain although there is a vast literature on the topic in the United States which accompanies school and college courses on how to set about it. Young women are likely to marry someone of a similar or slightly higher educational level, who has lived near them, and is of the same race and religion. But how the 'choice' is made, or even whether choice comes into the process of courtship, is unknown. To talk of 'choosing' a husband may be a middle-class notion, quite inappropriate to the non-autonomous working-class women. Then, there is one group who may be said to be 'forced' into matrimony, the 'victims' of 'shotgun weddings'.

Many such young women 'catch' a man by pregnancy. In 1976 nearly one-third of the marriages contracted by young women under 20 involved pregnant brides, about 20,000 women. Forty thousand other women under 20 in 1975 had an illegitimate child or an abortion legally – while others may have miscarried or had illegal terminations. Talking of 'catching' a man by pregnancy suggests plotting by women which, in the absence of any data, is not really justified. However, it seems reasonable to treat the sexuality of young women as one of their few bargaining counters in the attainment of adulthood. The issue of virginity is important in many ethnic mintority groups in ways which are only slightly different from its importance in majority culture.

Farrell (1978), whose research on the sexual attitudes and experience of 1,556 young adults (aged 16 to 19) was mentioned in the previous chapter, found that 42 per cent of her female sample were sexually experienced. These were all single people, and the married young women of the same age would obviously include many others who were sexually experienced in their teens. Farrell says (1978, p. 23) that one girl in eight has lost her virginity before she is 16. *Honey* (June and July 1977) reported that one-third of the 290 single women surveyed were virgins (25 per cent of those between 21 and 23, 36 per cent of those between 18 and 20). Virgins were rarest among southern middle-class women of over 20 who were living and working away from home. The two-thirds of the sample who were not virgins had mostly 'lost' their virginity before they reached 20 (90 per cent).

'The 'decision' to 'give in' to some young man or other is likely to be a difficult one for a young woman to make, as we can see from the letters on the problem pages, both those at the chapter head and these similar ones:

I'm 17 and expecting my fiance's baby. We're planning to marry this year but he has said that if I were pregnant before our wedding day he'd never forgive me. I wouldn't like to hurt him by telling him I'm pregnant. (*Woman's Own*, 1965).

I have heard that it is harmful to have sex when not fully physically developed. When I was fourteen I had intercourse twice but no more since then. Has this caused me any harm? ... Do I have to wait until I'm twenty-one before I can have sex again ... I'm very worried in case, having done what is meant for the developed, my body has responded by ceasing to mature normally. (*Cosmopolitan*, April 1978)

If these pathetic letters from young adults are one source of information about the double standard young women face, another excellent one is Paul Willis's ethnographic survey of boys in the English midlands, *Learning to Labour*. Willis describes how the lads he studied held deeply rooted sexist attitudes, and says (1977, p. 44):

Although they are its object, frank and explicit sexuality is actually denied women ... she is a sex object, a commodity, she is actually diminished by sex; she is literally worthless; she has been romantically and materially consumed ... On the other hand ... there is a fear that once a girl gets sexually experienced ... she will be completely promiscuous ... The 'girlfriend' is a very different category from an 'easy lay'. She represents the human value that is squandered by promiscuity. She is the loyal domestic partner.

Willis quotes one of his informants on this topic: 'After you've been with one like ... well they're scrubbers afterwards, they'll go with anyone. I think that once they've had it, they want it all the time.' The adolescent and young adult women studied in another area of the midlands by Mandy Llewellyn were confounded by similar attitudes from the men in their neighbourhood. If they stay virgins they may be labelled 'frigid' or 'lesbian', if they do not they may slip from 'nice girl' to 'scrubber'. In some ways young women in various subcultures where the norms are clearer have an easier life, because the rules are or were absolute.

Pamela Constantinides (1977) says of the Greek Cypriots she studied in London and Cyprus that there have been changes in the pattern of courtship in London which have given more autonomy to young people, although virginity is still a central value. The traditional Cypriot marriage was arranged, via an intermediary, and a betrothal was formalised by a priest in church. Breaking off a betrothal was as serious as a divorce, and brought dishonour to the young people. Constantinides says:

> Girls are expected to be virgins at the betrothal, though after that it is conceded, though not necessarily approved, that sexual relations may take place ... This is what makes a broken engagement so dishonouring for the girl, and substantially reduces her further marriage chances.

The dishonour to the young woman comes from the assumption that her fiance has discovered she was not a virgin. This traditional pattern was breaking down among the Greek Cypriots in London, where Constantinides found more young people being allowed some choice of partner, and the engagement being used as a period in which the couple got to know each other. Associated with this has been a decline in the religious betrothal in favour of an announcement and a party. She comments: 'This of course makes them easier to break, and, of necessity, less shame and dishonour comes to be attached to the broken engagement.' Indeed engagements were being used 'simply as a means to go out freely with a member of the opposite sex'. Constantinides argues that because of the insistence on virginity Greek Cypriot girls are kept to very restricted lives, and the engagement is the only way to gain British freedom.

If the Greek Cypriot girl is restricted in her freedom to make decisions, the Turkish Cypriot in London is even more confined, as Sarah Ladbury (1977) shows. *Spare Rib* (No. 39, 1975) carried extracts from interviews with three such girls, all very unhappy about their lack of autonomy. All were doing 'A' levels, although this decision was viewed with suspicion by their families.

> Since I never had a father my uncle acted like one. When he heard that I was staying on at school for the sixth form his first question wasn't 'Are you staying for a better job and grades?', it was 'Is there a boy or teacher you love, is that why you're staying on at school?'. One of my real reasons was that if I left I probably would have got married.

All three of these girls were under pressure to enter arranged marriages, and all were using sixth form work to prolong their freedom. Thus what may constrain some British girls by keeping them defined as 'schoolchildren' even at voting age is actually a precious state of liberty for others. Just as this is the case for the Muslim Turkish Cypriots, it is also for young women in the various Asian communities of Britain.

Thus the Ballards' (1977) study of Punjabi Sikhs in Yorkshire showed that virginity was crucial for young women, and arranged marriages were still favoured. They comment that 'because their chastity is of such great importance to the family honour, girls tend to get into greater difficulties with their parents than do boys'. The educational achievements of Sikh adolescents and young adults can serve to exacerbate these generational conflicts for, the Ballards say, parents with no education and a peasant background may lack confidence in arranging matches for highly educated, urban children. Thus an educated daughter may have more say in her marriage because her parents cannot be so confident of their superior judgement. Certainly they found that young people were able to veto marriages they particularly disliked.

The conflict of the Asian young women and their parents is accentuated because, as Verity Khan (1977) says, her Mirpuri Pakistanis in Bradford 'are unprepared for their children's adolescent period. In the village there is a sudden transition from the status of daughter and girl, to that of wife and woman.' The prolonged adolescence and young adulthood in Britain must be very confusing and disturbing to such parents. Patricia Jeffery (1976), in her study of Muslim and Christian Pakistanis in Bristol and Lahore, found similar confusion among parents about young women and marriage. In the Muslim community, Jeffery says (p. 34):

> During the upbringing of a daughter, her parents must take great care that nothing occurs which might cause their proposal of marriage to be rejected. Any hint of romantic attachment on her

part would probably result in such a rejection, and would also reflect badly on her younger sisters and make their marriages more difficult to arrange.

The 'honour' of the local caste group and the kindred is linked to finding appropriate marriage partners for the young people, and there is a preference for marrying first or second cousins, whose status is known. Arranged matches are usual, and highly valued. Sometimes the young woman is allowed a chaperoned meeting or meetings with the chosen man, sometimes she sees a photograph, but some women never see the man before the ceremony. The amount of freedom young women have varies, so Jeffery says some may have no choice at all while 'others may be asked to select a spouse from several possibilities, while some have in effect only the power of veto' (1976, p. 30). The parental involvement is crucial for the maintenance of honour. Jeffery comments (loc. cit.):

'Love marriages' are rare and generally bring disrepute to the families involved. While films hinge on romantic attachments, parental opposition and the fear of ostracism, the segregation of the sexes from puberty onwards and the very restricted and clandestine contexts in which young men and women can meet, all hinder love-matches.

While such segregation of young people, and the lack of opportunity for them to meet, may seem strange and un-British, a lack of opportunity for 'courtship' was not unknown in traditional British society. The area of north Montgomeryshire studied by Rees in the 1939–49 period was equally characterised by a segregation of the genders, and a lack of opportunities for courtship as we are now accustomed to it. Rees (1950, p. 85) says:

One seldom sees unmarried couples going for walks together; indeed custom offers few opportunities for couples to meet out-of-doors . . . Courtship is a private matter which has no public expression. Young couples usually behave nonchalantly towards each other in public and seldom acknowledge their friendship at social gatherings. At the end of such gatherings the young girls will set out for home in groups, followed at some distance by the young men, and they will not usually divide into couples until they are well out of public view.

Rees points out that it was not respectable for the unmarried girls to go out except for a definite purpose (chapel, shopping, etc.), although the men could come and go without inquiry. Courting took place in the girl's home at night – the man threw something up to her window, and if she was interested she came down and gave him tea and even a meal in the kitchen. The illegitimacy rates in the area were so high that Rees argues that sexual relations during courtship were common, although he has no accurate evidence on the point. Courting in bed, with a bolster between the young people, or a sewn-up nightdress, was in disrepute or decline when Rees did his study. However it was extremely difficult for Rees to collect any firm data on courtship because (p. 85)

[it] is a secret to be concealed from both parents and neighbours as long as possible. The parents will usually have heard of the courtship from third persons long before it is disclosed to them by the young people themselves.

Similar courtship patterns were found in the rural areas studied by other researchers in the late 1940s and the 1950s, but by the time Frankenberg came to study his Welsh border village he found a more public form of courtship 'very different from courtship in Llanfighangel . . . but not very different from the pattern of working-class youths in towns all over Britain' (1966, p. 93). Unrelated unmarried young people seen together were assumed to be courting, lost touch with the same sex peer group, and were expected to announce an engagement and plan a wedding.

While Frankenberg claims that the pattern found in his border village was the usual one found among working-class people in Britain, there is little or no evidence on the point. Even if courtship is no longer hidden from parents, peers and the community, it is still a private relationship which is rarely available for study. We have very little information on how young women meet men, how relationships develop and how decisions are made about engagements and marriage. Diana Barker's (1972) study of marrying couples in Swansea is an isolated piece of research, and there are no Scottish or English equivalents. The leisure activities of adolescent girls have been discussed in the previous chapter, but the data on the leisure activities of young workers are sparse. The popular idea is that the majority of initial contacts with eventual partners are made at dances or while dancing, or failing that via pubs, parties, mutual friends or at work. Dancing preoccupies the leisure-time of many adolescent and young adult women (Ward, n.d.; McRobbie, 1978) but we know nothing about dancing and dancing places as experienced by women.

Mungham (1976) has written an account of one kind of dance hall, the large and highly respectable commercial *palais* run by multinational companies. There are no equivalent pieces on the dances held for young people of the upper-middle and upper classes by charities, individuals, or golf, hunt and yacht clubs. Nor do we have recent information on village hall 'hops', discos, community centres and other working-class dancing milieux. For accounts of meeting and dating in such environments we are thrown back on to novels (nearly all written by men) and journalism. Mungham says that 'few male youths dance well, even fewer seem to enjoy it and the majority settle uncomfortably for shuffling around the floor with a girl when the group is playing its slower numbers'. Mungham goes on to describe the well-known male strategy of propping up the bar until nearly the end of the evening, and only asking women to dance in the closing stages of the dance. This saves money (no drinks to buy), and avoids dancing. Mungham says that this is unpopular with young women who feel that they are being treated as a last resort. However, the account of the night out at the Mecca ballroom leaves out two aspects of dancing: those men who do enjoy it, and the way it is *experienced* by women. For young women dancing is not only a way of meeting men. It can be both an area of life where young women can obtain and display skill and expertise, and a way of taking exercise, producing the kind of exhilarating exhaustion men gain from football. No male writer, social scientist or novelist has ever captured the sheer physical and mental pleasure which can be gained from executing complicated dance movements, rehearsed in privacy, in a large and glamorous arena. Completing a difficult dance movement is just like serving an ace, making a fine late cut, or dribbling round the opposing full back. Seeing young women's dancing only as a form of courtship is severely limiting to the young women, for whom dancing is also a sport, a skill and even an aesthetic expression, and must be understood as such.

One crucial class difference in the use of dancing as a forum for meeting possible partners which has been left relatively unstudied concerns the variety in gender roles appropriate at the dance. In the working class, it is common for young women to dance together, and for pairs of men to approach couples of women already on the floor and 'split them up' for the duration of the number. Working-class young people 'hunt' in pairs, and women do not need to be talked to. This pattern is not acceptable in the middle class and above, where women have to wait to be asked, and people are more likely to *come* in couples or mixed parties, rather than single-sex pairs or groups. These differences in gender roles are a public reflection of the separate roles for the two genders in full adulthood.

Other places to meet probably include work, pubs and friends. Chamberlain (1975) found one 19-year-old who met her future husband via amateur radio activities; but even here dancing was involved (p. 81):

I met Kevin on the radio. I used to talk to him and then he came over for a Dinner and Dance for the Amateurs, and I met him, finally, there ... At the moment, Kevin has digs over the road, which is convenient. We can say goodnight on the radio. And he can use the shed out at the back, for the radio.

This is an unusual meeting and courtship for a young woman in East Anglia. The other young women Chamberlain quotes offer accounts of boredom, enlivened only by premarital sex. One 20-year-old said (p. 82):

I was seventeen when I got married, but I was pregnant then. I wish I had waited ... I suppose I got pregnant the first time because there weren't nothing to do in the village.

A 25-year-old said: 'Although I'd never actually slept with my husband, we used to drive to some woods and make love there.' While another 20-year-old recalled (p. 86):

We used to make love, before we was married, in front of the fire at his parents ... And then when I learnt to drive, we did it in the back of me Dad's car ... I got pregnant on purpose, so's we could get married. My husband's parents didn't like me at all. So if I was pregnant, we'd have to get married. No question.

This last account raises an interesting issue about pre-marital pregnancies, which, on accounts like this and those reported in Sally Macintyre's (1976a) work, may well be planned and wanted, if only to force parental acquiescence to marriage. This will be discussed further in the chapter on parenthood, but it needs to be remembered that some, many or all of the pregnant brides mentioned above may be deliberately pregnant. For the more conventional, or lucky, or undersexed, courtship proceeds towards a formal engagement.

THE ENGAGEMENT

The engagement ring is the first step on the road towards a great deal of expense which will be incurred before the *rite de passage* is completed, turning girl into wife. The magazine *Wedding Day* printed a questionnaire for its readers to complete about the costs of marrying in 1977. There were replies from 351 couples, whose digested answers were published in the magazine's June/July 1978 issue. The average cost of an engagement ring had been £73, the minimum £10 and the maximum reported £205. It is surprising that the respondents were prepared to talk about the prices, because three of the four engaged couples (a Jewish couple in their twenties, an aristocratic young farmer and a show business divorcee) interviewed in the *Observer* (12 February 1978) were reluctant to talk about such a private matter. Only the trainee chef and waitress from Birmingham aged 19 and 17 were prepared to admit to a £31 eternity ring. The young woman regarded this as a substitute for 'a cluster of diamonds or at least a solitaire which would have set us back about £80', a staggering sum when their earnings were £27 and £21 a week. This couple were engaged – or 'eternalised' as the young woman called it – while saving for a home. The aristocratic farmer and his upper-class bride were engaged for three months and said it was 'a good time to find out what each other is really like'. Saving was clearly not an issue, as the man was 'geared up for marriage', having bought a 400-year-old farmhouse and 70-acre farm in Wales and owning 'lots of furniture and paintings'. The Jewish couple were waiting a year before marriage due to a family death, but in any case, they regarded an engagement as a natural part of practising Jewishness. The young woman said: 'Engagements are particularly important for the older generation who feel it gives more permanency to a relationship.' This couple had four engagement parties.

Probably more 'typical' are three women interviewed in *Brides* magazine (Summer 1978). One 22-year-old in Potters Bar, married in May 1978, said:

For the first year of our engagement we really enjoyed life. We went out for meals in exciting places like the Post Office Tower and the Playboy Club; we had a holiday in Minorca. Then, during the year leading up to our wedding we began saving and went to the opposite extreme.

This pair had to raise £3,000 for a house deposit. Bonita put her whole salary into the building society:

I carried saving to ridiculous lengths. If we went out for a drink I would just have a fruit juice. I was paying my mother £5 a week, but as Terry stayed with us at weekends, she really had to provide for the two of us.

A similar tale is reported by an 18-year-old bride, who with her 20-year-old husband had saved £850 in eighteen months. This couple had also borrowed £100 from her father and, in addition:

I did pay my mum £3 a week when I first started earning, but during the last two months before the wedding things were so tight my parents told me to keep it.

It seems clear from these interviews that the engagement period (unless one is a rich woman) is characterised by saving: by going without clothes, holidays and treats to save money. In part this is because the wedding and the setting up of the home are both expensive, as the next section will show. However, there is another feature of these accounts which parallels the more academic work on courtship and marriage, Diana Barker's (1972) study of Swansea. Barker has argued that two of the central features of the lives of the young adults in Swansea were 'spoiling' and 'keeping close'. That is, parental, and especially maternal, indulgence of the young adult, plus a life centred on home and family. This latter point – the keeping close – is dealt with in the section after marriage: here I want only to discuss 'spoiling', which comes clearly through the two interviews in *Brides*. Barker found that her sample had, once they began work, negotiated with their mothers a sum for their keep. This was usually far below what it would have cost them commercially. As Barker says, this leaves the young people ignorant of the cost of living which can come as a shock to them on marriage, and quotes several examples of young women facing economic reality:

Mothers 'help' by taking little board money from apprentices, from those on the dole, and from engaged couples who are saving up to get household goods or a deposit on a house.

In a second sense, too, Barker found that the young women were 'spoiled'. They did very little around the house, and only when they 'enjoyed' or 'felt like' it. The young men, of course, did less.

Indeed many of the young people were *waited* on by their mothers; their food was put on the table in front of them, their slippers were put by the fire, their dirty washing was removed and replaced automatically.

This lack of domestic practice by the young women is at odds with the heavy domestic loads mentioned by Angela McRobbie (1978). The interviews in *Brides* support the Barker finding of spoiling. The 18-year-old said 'I suppose I was a bit lazy at home. My mother did all the washing and I am finding it hard without a washing machine'. The 22-year-old reported:

I was rather spoilt at home. I only occasionally had to do a bit of washing and ironing. I knew I would have to pull my socks up once I was married.

This woman misses 'being able to put her feet up when she gets in from work'. Inexperience of domestic labour presumably explains the list of domestic catastrophes *Wedding Day* (Summer 1978) describes, with young brides cooking spaghetti bolognese in one pan, roasting chicken with the plastic bag of giblets inside and mistaking apple pie for steak and kidney.

If the engagement is a time for saving and self-denial financially, it is also a time when sex relations can probably take place without too much censure in many British subcultures. There may even be disquiet if a sexual relationship is not established at this stage, as a letter to *Brides* (Summer 1978) makes clear:

We've been engaged for six months and have fixed the wedding day... My problem is that my fiance has never attempted to have sex with me, very rarely kisses me – and then it's only a brotherly peck – and shows more animation to his men friends than to me. When I try to talk about this he just says that sex is something to do, not to discuss, and that it can all wait until we're married.

This young woman fears that her husband is gay. Such a concern, with its underlying implication that either sexual relations, or some attempt at them, is normal in the engagement period, is relatively new. Fifteen years ago the problem pages dealt more with the guilt of those who felt unable to wait.

There is little data on the length of engagements, but whether long or short the next stage is to move on to planning a wedding. This event, the only public status passage, or *rite de passage*, for women in all cultures in Britain, moves a woman firmly into adulthood, whether she is 16 or 25. It also involves a great deal of expense, forward planning and emotional turmoil.

MARRIAGE

If one follows the advice offered by *Brides*, getting married is a complex and long-term business. Once you are engaged, *Brides* suggests you put the announcement in the press, and then, before you can choose a date, the young couple must decide where they want to marry and make sure the register office, synagogue or church is free. The same is true of places for receptions. Once a date has been fixed, (and *Brides* thinks three months is the minimum it takes to arrange a wedding) a range of other plans have to be made. *Brides* offers a checklist which reads like a battle plan. The happy couple and their parents are advised to see the registrar or religious official, arrange the reception, fix a guest list, order cars, book a photographer, organise cake, print invitations, pick bridesmaids, best man and ushers, choose wedding clothes, book a dressmaker, choose attendants' clothes, see about family planning, order flowers, order wedding ring, pick music, print service sheets, make up present list, buy honeymoon clothes, choose attendants' presents, buy wedding cake boxes, and so on. There is not an equal division of labour here between the young man and woman. One item for the bride says: 'Check that your fiance has got himself organised for the wedding – the ring; his clothes; the honeymoon.' In other words, the man is reduced to a task which the woman has to deal with before the wedding, like the cake and the photographer. The *Sunday Times* (3 July 1977) had one example of a minor role for the groom in a wedding reputedly of an ordinary working-class girl. Her husband 'was under simple orders: hire a chocolate-coloured morning suit from Moss Bros, give the bridesmaids presents, and don't get drunk at the stag party'. A truly marginal role in the ceremony.

Apart from the organisation involved in staging such a complicated ritual, there are staggering costs involved. *Wedding Day* printed a questionnaire on wedding costs in 1977 which was returned by 351 couples, and the results were printed in the issue for June/July 1978. Table 5·1 shows the minimum, average and maximum sums reported by these respondents under the headings provided. These headings are in themselves very revealing about wedding customs, in that, for example, no question is asked about honeymoon clothes for the groom. No one seems to think a man needs special night clothes for his honeymoon, or even new swimming trunks! Also missing from the *Wedding Day* questionnaire were items on the costs of licence, church, choir, rabbi, and so on, although these can be very expensive. The *Sunday Times* (3 July 1977) told its readers that marriage at the fashionable church of St Margaret's, Westminster, would cost £93 without the choir, who are thirteen strong and cost £4.20 each. Even without the costs of the civil or religious ceremony, the *Wedding Day* readers reported tremendous costs. Table 5·1 shows clearly that the 'cheapest' wedding would have cost £87, the 'average' £977 and the most expensive £3,807. This, of course, ignores all other costs of establishing a new 'family' with home, furniture, and so on.

It is impossible to tell how far these costs reported to *Wedding Day* are 'typical'. They certainly reflect the kinds of advertising and editorial matter in *Brides* and *Wedding Day*. The costs of the bride's outfits are a good example of this. Table 5·1 shows that the maximum reported for a bride's clothing was £1,000, the minimum £25 and the average £110. I examined all the bride's outfits shown, with prices, in editorials and advertisements in the summer 1978 issues of the two magazines, and calculated the average cost of the dress alone. In *Wedding Day* the average price of the dresses shown in the editorial pages was £143, in *Brides* it was £130, while the

average price of the dresses advertised was £51. The dress, of
course, is not the whole story: headdresses are shown at £10–£20,
veils at £15 upwards, and then there are the rings, shoes, and so on.
Both magazines show 'dream' dresses at £500 and above: *Brides*
features a design inspired by the film *Star Wars* at £670.

Table 5·1   *Reported Costs of a Wedding Day*

	Minimum	Average	Maximum
Bride's clothing for wedding day	25	110	1,000
Bride's trousseau	nil	48	300
Groom's clothes	nil	44	100
Bridesmaids' dresses	nil	35	150
Car Hire	nil	26	87
Photography	nil	45	100
Flowers	nil	27	60
Stationery	nil	24	130
Ring	12	36	60
Reception:			
Premises	10	28	70
Catering	40	215	650
Liquor	nil	108	500
Cake	nil	32	50
Honeymoon	nil	199	550
	£87	£977	£3,807

Source: Wedding Day, June/July 1978.

Of course, the totals recorded on Table 5·1 are unrealistic, because couples are unlikely to have spent the minimum or maximum
on every item. The *Sunday Times* (3 July 1977) featured the costs
of four weddings, at £16.79, £250, £500 and £1,500. These have to
be seen as modest, for three years earlier they had printed a similar
article in which they talked of 'lavish' £5,000 weddings and costed
five couples' expenditure at sums between £153 and £1,016. Leaving
aside the £16.49 wedding which was an emergency dash to a registry
office to cope with an expiring work permit, the cheapest 'proper'
weddings were working-class couples marrying in church with forty
to seventy guests. In 1974 a Catholic gas fitter married for £153,
while a similar wedding, paid for by a retired messenger and a
bakery worker, cost £500 in 1977. The only people who do not seem
to be swept along on this tide of romantic weddings are the readers
of the *Observer*. A selection of correspondents (13 February 1977)

had rebelled against formal clothing and religious ceremonies. One woman said she wore 'a long plain green dress having made up the five yards of fabric which I'd bought from a jumble sale for a shilling'. This is, however, unusual. In 1977 half the weddings in the country took place in churches, or other religious buildings, and the lush advertising in *Brides* and *Wedding Day* suggest that most young women yearn for their big day.

The popularity of the ceremony and the institution itself among young women is undiminished. The strains of the new marriage are not, however, usually anticipated or easy to handle. But where the realisation of sexuality was once the most feared aspect of marriage, *Brides* (Summer 1978) suggests that 'the first real break from home and family' on marriage is likely to be one of the most serious problems for the young bride. One interview, with a 22-year-old, describes how, after the wedding when moving from Yorkshire to Cheshire, she cried all the time, and 'every time we sat down for a meal I used to burst out crying because there were only the two of us'. This woman had a twin sister and three other siblings, and though a nurse, 'had never been away from Scarborough before, except once for a fortnight's holiday'. Six months later she still longed to move back near her mother and sisters. This attachment to the parental home, although quite at odds with myths about youth in Britain, is in fact a common finding of research, and leads us from marriage back into a discussion of the familial relations of the young adult woman.

The Importance of Mum

If *Brides* thinks leaving home is a strain for the new bride worth writing about, it is a strain experienced by most young women at marriage. Barker (1972) found that 90 per cent of the young women in her sample were living at home at the time of their first marriage, and so were 86 per cent of the men. Despite these high proportions, 30 per cent of the women and 40 per cent of the men had had *some* experience of living away from home while training or working, but, as Barker stresses, this was seen by everyone concerned as a temporary and enforced absence rather than a leaving. Young people saw absence as a temporary expedient necessary to learn skills or earn money, not as a pleasure. The parents, according to Barker, attached strong positive values to keeping children 'close' before and after marriage. This was transformed into a strong pressure on young people to stay at home, especially the young women. Barker (1972) suggests that women have a brief flowering period of about five years between school and marriage when they can enjoy themselves, but that much of this time is occupied by serious courtship and preparation for marriage. Young women are, however, kept close to home because commercial entertainment is too expensive and parents want them at home. This contrasts with Ward's (n.d.) findings that his sample were all out a great deal, and it is hard to know which is more accurate. However, what is clear is that women's wages will not allow very much freedom from home, either to live away or to go out a great deal. The work which the majority of school leavers enter is poorly paid, has no prospects, and offers little incentive to leave home to the young women.

THE YOUNG WOMAN AT WORK

Women's paid employment is discussed in some detail in Chapter 6, so this section only mentions those aspects of the labour market which affect the girl who leaves school at 16 or 18 and goes straight to work. The most important fact which faces the school leaver is that access to the highly paid, highly organised skilled manual trades, which are entered mainly via apprenticeships, is almost entirely closed to her. Openings for girls are either into respectable 'white blouse' work, as secretaries or clerks, or into semi-skilled and unskilled work in trades where pay is low and union organisation is weak. Whatever sphere of work they enter, opportunities for day release and other kinds of further education are poorer (Byrne, 1978), and chances for promotion slight. Mackie and Pattullo (1977, p. 97) show how in 1974 only 15,500 women school leavers got apprenticeships, while 118,000 men did; while 96,000 women got clerical jobs only 19,000 men did, and so forth. Those women who did get apprenticeships nearly all entered hairdressing, a field where wages are very low, promotion possibilities limited, and equal pay is non-existent. Women school leavers in shop work, and in the clothing, textiles and footwear industries, are immediately caught in a vicious circle. These employers are unlikely to send anyone on day release courses, so women are doubly deprived of possibilities for further development – not only are they, as women, unlikely to be included in training schemes or promotion plans, they are also in industries where educational opportunities are scarcer anyway. Young women are caught because no one believes that they are going to take their work seriously, managers least of all as Audrey Hunt's survey (1975) showed, and because they themselves have lost any ambitions they might have had by the time they leave school – or have lost the courage to mention their aspirations or strive for them. The cleverer girls opt for 'people' occupations such as nursery nursing, and flock to secretarial and clerical jobs where they expect – apparently – to meet interesting people and earn reasonable money without getting dirty, while the rest go to factories, shops and the dole queues. As recent work on the work experiences of secretaries, clerks, shop assistants and young girls in factories is non-existent, it is hard to discuss what work means to these people. The only recent data are based on mothers who had left work to rear children (Hobson, 1978; Oakley, 1974*a* and *b*) and their accounts are coloured by nostalgia, not so much for the work as for the companionship.

Hobson (1978) quotes one woman who had been in a factory, in Woolworth's, in a second factory and at Butlin's, a second who had worked in Lewis's department store and two factories, and a third who had worked in two kinds of shop and an office. Hobson argues that the satisfaction or otherwise of young women in wage labour is due to the personal friendship with other workers as much as anything intrinsic to the task. Thus Anne is quoted saying that she liked the jobs she had except:

> the dirty one, as I said, the one where they made wire. It was rather, you know, boring, more boring than a lot of factory jobs because it was too noisy to talk.

While Ann Oakley found that overall it was the housewives who had left the more glamorous jobs who most disliked their domestic role, many of her sample also expressed nostalgia for quite menial jobs. Thus one woman had been a chambermaid and says (1974*a*, p. 76) that she:

> enjoyed it very much. It wasn't the work, it was the company – the environment. And I had a lot of time to myself – there was always somebody there and we had a television set and rest room there, and there was always about twenty or thirty girls in it.

It is noticeable that the company, and sometimes the intrinsic interest of the job or the responsibility of it, are mentioned by these women, not their own money. Most working-class women will never have earned enough to enable them to live autonomously in any comfort, and will have been subsidised by their homes. Why the majority of young women are content to 'choose' jobs on the basis of company, and do not want training or promotion, is a complex question, which would be illuminated by studies of young working women which we do not yet have. Given the overwhelming social and parental approval for secretarial work for young women it is perhaps surprising that any women go on to higher education and train for anything else! The motivation and attitudes of the minority are the subject of the final section of this chapter, to see how far apart from their contemporaries they really are.

THE STUDENT PRINCESS?

Men outnumber women in nearly all sectors of higher education, except teacher training. This is made clear in Table 5·2, which is adapted from *Social Trends, 1977* (p. 76) and shows data for 1974/5.

Table 5·2 *Destinations of School Leavers 1974/5 by Gender*

	Teacher training	Degree courses at Universities	Polytechnics	Other Institutions	Other further education
Young women	11,900	14,200	2,000	300	57,300
Young men	2,900	24,700	4,100	300	31,700

Source: *Social Trends, 1977*, p. 76

All these figures are dwarfed by the numbers who went straight out to work, which 338,100 young women and 353,700 young men did. However, the table shows that women outnumbered men in teacher training colleges and on low-status further education courses, while men are predominant on degree courses. Since 1974 there has been a dramatic change in higher education provision, which has affected women particularly. The government has decided that teachers should no longer be trained in specialist colleges, isolated from other students; and that the falling birth rate means that there is slackening demand for primary teachers now, and for secondary ones later. This means that women's higher education opportunities have been drastically curtailed. The *Times Higher Education Supplement* (19 August 1977) commented:

> The drastic reduction in places at the colleges of education which have traditionally provided education as well as training for both young and mature women is a setback to the slow progress which women have been making in the world of higher education ... Three times more women than men entered teacher education last year, more than half of them with one A level. Many must now turn elsewhere for higher education.

The *THES* went on to argue that alternative arenas for women's higher education should be found.

The reorganisation of higher education has already been recognised by the compilers of government statistics, in that no figures are now given for colleges of education in England and Wales. Table 5·3 shows the breakdown of higher education institutions by gender, with the reclassification clearly evident. This table shows that the number of women in all sectors of higher education grew between 1965 and 1975, although the percentage of women did not change dramatically, for the numbers of men in higher education also rose in that decade (from 191,400 to 301,300). The proportion of women rose from roughly a quarter to about 30 per cent, over a period when the proportion of working-class students stayed stubbornly near a quarter. Indeed, it can be argued that women

Table 5·3 *Women in Higher Education* (thousands)

Full-time students:		1965/6	1972/3	1973/4	1974/5	1975/6
Universities		46.1	76.3	80.4	85.3	90.6
Colleges of education		61·0	89·7	91·5	85·3	10·6
Advanced courses elsewhere		11·8	29·9	33·4	37·4	113·0
	Total	11·89	195·9	205·3	208·0	213·9

Note: The 1975/6 figure for colleges of education refers to Scotland and Northern Ireland, as colleges in England and Wales have been included in the other categories.

students, mainly from middle-class homes, had increased their foothold in the universities at the expense of an increase in the proportion of students from working-class homes. Thus as women rose from being six to every ten men in 1965/6 to seven to every ten in 1975/6, working-class students stayed still. This has been documented most carefully for Scotland by Hutchison and McPherson (1976). They show how 'as increasing proportions of women joined a more sluggishly expanding body of men in applying for scarce university places, prevailing admissions standards were raised'. Students from middle-class homes were better qualified to meet those rising standards. Hutchison and McPherson point out there are two aspects of this 'displacement' of working-class males by women, one real, the other less so. The real displacement took place because working-class males were more likely than middle-class ones to be in non-science, non-vocational areas, like arts and social science, and these were the areas to which the better-qualified women also applied. The 'false' displacement was due to the uneven expansion of university places in the arts and social sciences, which *de facto* increased the proportion of women, because they tend not to study science, applied science or the vocational degree subjects.

This subject imbalance at university is paralleled in other spheres of higher education, and reflects the subject choice at 'O' and 'A' level. Forty-three per cent of male sixth-formers take science 'A' levels, while only 18 per cent of females do. Where girls do any science it is mainly biology, so that girls are only 28 per cent of physics candidates at 'O' level, and 18 per cent at 'A' level. In universities there is only a small gender imbalance in 'pure' sciences, where there is one woman for every three men, but in engineering and technology there are twenty men for every woman. Women were also badly under-represented in medical schools, because they all operated quotas on women, until the passing of the Sex Discrimination Act 1975. Some of the medical schools kept the proportion of women as low as 10 per cent, while the majority allowed between a quarter and a third. Either by design or lack of applicants, women are a small proportion of students in all spheres of higher education but teacher training.

Such bare facts tell us nothing about student lives, opinions and attitudes, and unfortunately we have little or no research on contemporary student lives. The data we have on students, postgraduate students and graduates in society are all badly out of date. Kelsall and his collaborators (1972) offer material on the graduates of 1960, for example, but recent data are needed to cover student life in different institutions in the late 1970s. For the purposes of this chapter, however, the data from Kelsall's survey are combined with a more recent project of Margo Galloway's (1973) to show that those women who do choose to go on into higher education are very similar to those who do not in many of their attitudes.

Kelsall and his collaborators, Anne Poole and Annette Kuhn, surveyed, in 1966, adults who had graduated in 1960, before the vast expansion of higher education. The basic facts about the women in their sample were, for a feminist, miserable. The majority of graduates were married, had small children and were doing no paid or academic work six years after graduation, while those who were working for money were mainly in teaching, and were suffering worse pay and promotion prospects than their male contemporaries. Successful career women with equal pay and responsibilities were rare, and the full-time housewives said they were happier than the working women did. Anne Poole argued that these women, who had come from middle-class homes in the main, were contented, conservative, middle-class women six years after graduation and not a force for change. Judging by the findings of Galloway (1973), the graduates of the 1970s are set to follow a similar pattern. Galloway's data were drawn from detailed interviews with women at Edinburgh University and Moray House College of Education in the early 1970s and, although unrepresentative of English or Welsh students, they are rich and illuminating.

Margo Galloway was interested in the women's careers to date, and their expectations about their future. The overwhelming finding was that these students held conventional ideas about the role of women, the division of labour in marriage and their own futures, such that their lives were likely to follow those of Kelsall's sample. There was evidence collected throughout the second half of the century that American women were scared of being seen as clever by men in case it jeopardised their social success. Galloway's sample felt strongly that while men did not mind women being clever and successful, they did dislike women who were 'intellectual'. Thus women said things like 'It's very foreboding [sic] and 'I don't want to be very intellectual because I don't want to be very anything' (1973, p. 84) and 'men don't like you to be too emancipated'. All but one of the sample said they wanted to marry, most thought marriage and motherhood were their main aims in life, and most wanted a husband who was superior to them in age, intellect, earning power and judgement. Typical comments were 'Marriage would mean more to me than any career' (p. 87) and 'I think the male should be dominant in any family' (p. 92). One young woman produced, in one answer, the 'typical' worldview of the majority of Galloway's sample. She had expressed a desire to go to Turkey for visits and collect folk material but added (p. 103):

I'd like something small but nothing big. I wouldn't like to be famous or anything like that.

INTERVIEWER: You wouldn't like to go down in history as the woman who unearthed all the important Turkish folk tales?

GIRL: I'd rather be the wife of the man that did it.

This was an extreme case, but not that extreme. The women saw the housework as their duty and did not think men should do very much around the home. A typical woman said: 'I don't mind a man helping with just the dishes but nothing else. I can't stand to see a man running round the house with an apron on' (p. 96). Washing clothes and bed making were seen as particularly unmanly tasks, although Galloway did not ask about nappy changing, which seems to be the actual task at which men baulk, as the later chapters of this book show. There were certainly going to be nappies in these women's lives for the majority were sure that children completed a marriage, wanted two or more, and planned to stay home for seven to ten years with them. These women based their conventional views of the future on a belief that gender differences are grounded in biological facts, so that they believed women made better mothers for reasons such as 'I think women are born more patient' (p. 109).

Galloway was especially interested in why women who were technically qualified for university had chosen to attend Moray House College to train for teaching. She had expected them to hold less 'emancipated' views of women's role, and believe university was less feminine than primary teaching. However, this turned out not to be the case. While the majority of the university students had come to university as 'the next step', expected of them by their homes and schools, the college students had usually thought about what higher education they wanted. Those women who were objectively qualified for university but did not go fell into two groups. Some were committed to teaching and chose college as the best available professional training, while the others were convinced that they were not intellectually capable of university work. Both groups had stood firm against all pressures on them to go to university. With the shortage of teacher training places in the future, the higher education of the second group in particular is in jeopardy. None of the girls reported either her school or parents trying to stop her going on to higher education; indeed the college girls reported pressure to aim higher than they themselves wished to go. The university sample were more likely to have better-educated mothers, and mothers who wanted them to have a higher education and qualify for a good job. Overall, though, the picture of parents telling young women to do something that will make them happy comes clearly through. The sample did not feél pushed into low-status courses, but left to make their own choices (of course, women whose parents are totally hostile to higher education will not have appeared in this research). It is, however, important to note that these women were following arts courses in the university and training for primary teaching, so they had not broken the conventions of female behaviour. The women medical students at Edinburgh in the early 1970s, in contrast, told Paul Atkinson (1976) that they experienced opposition to their plans for becoming doctors from schools, who told them to be nurses, or read pure sciences, because entry to medical school was so hard. Thus opposition may arise if women have high occupation aspirations, which Galloway's sample did not have.

Overall, therefore, Galloway's sample revealed themselves as conventional young women, with attitudes much like those of their less educationally successful contemporaries. The most important factor in determining whether women students intended to have careers at all, or be permanent housewives, was the mother. Those whose mothers had worked intended to work, while those whose mothers had never worked did not intend to do so themselves once they were mothers. Not only was the mother the crucial role model, she was also a central person in the women's lives. Most of Galloway's sample were close to their families, had no serious disagreements with them, and were dependent on them. One girl said 'I don't like being left in the house when she is out' (p. 142). Thus these students were like their non-student contemporaries, and quite unlike the image of the rebellious student. In the absence of any data showing the contrary, we can argue that the woman who opts for student life is only different from her contemporaries in that her age of marriage is deferred. In attitudes, opinions and relations with her family she is similar, and even in her eventual work she is unlikely to enter male fields of work or earn large sums of money. The main difference is that she has a longer period of not being an adult – although adulthood is an uneasy state for women, as the second half of this book shows.

Part Two

Adulthood

Introduction

The largest part of this book concerns the adult lives of British women, and various aspects of women's adult lives are presented in the remaining six chapters. However, calling women 'adults' raises certain important problems, because there are many senses in which British women are *never* accorded the same adult status as men. This is expressed neatly by the cry of 'women and children first', which classifies women with non-adults, but can be traced into more serious legal and social disabilities which are only now being gradually whittled away. The most vivid denial of adult status to women was their lack of a vote before 1919 and 1928, when women were classified with children and convicts as non-persons. While women are now allowed to vote, the same classification exists, if not so often in law, in the hearts and minds of most people. A famous experiment demonstrated this belief very neatly. A researcher asked psychotherapists to rate the qualities of the ideal healthy man, woman and child. They rated the healthy adult woman very like the healthy child, and quite unlike the adult male (Broverman *et al.*, 1972).

For the purpose of this volume I am taking a social definition of adulthood which is based on a combination of three factors: reaching 21, marrying and/or having a first legitimate child and graduating from higher education. While women of all classes and ethnic groups reach 21 (the average age of marriage for women), the social features – marriage, motherhood and graduation – are distributed very differently across groups in Britain. Working-class girls rarely graduate from university, for example, and marriage ages are very different in different subgroups. However, what follows in the remaining chapters is material on *adult* women – that is those over 21, those who are married, those who are mothers and those who have graduated into occupations. In other words, women who are no longer legal minors, who are no longer in the dependent status 'student', who have attained the 'adult' label Mrs. These definitions of social adulthood may seem rather vague. However, as there are no generally recognised initiation rites into adulthood in Britain, as there are in many other societies, some rather nebulous definition has to be made. I am arguing, therefore, that a woman has legitimate claims to adult status if she has achieved one or more of the factors listed, and that this adult status should be accorded in other spheres of life. These other spheres, work, community, health and illness, politics, religion, parenthood, class and power, are the subjects of the remaining chapters.

In fact, as these chapters show, neither sociologists nor the wider society have accorded women adult status in these spheres with any consistency, but have tended to treat them as essentially childlike. This treatment by sociologists and by the wider society has its roots in a central paradox of adult women: on one hand they are less deeply involved in many spheres of life than men and more deeply involved in their family life. *Yet* on the other hand a concentration on seeing women solely or primarily in terms of their family lives and their dependence on men has led social scientists to neglect or misrepresent the roles women play in society as a whole. Social scientists treat men differently. They are seen as occupying multiple roles in different spheres of the society – so men are shown as worshippers, voters, workers, Scout leaders, shop stewards and so on, and treated as independent autonomous adults in each sphere. This is so even when men deviate from the norms of the society. Male criminals, terrorists, drug users, and so forth are treated as rational, autonomous adults, who have reasons for engaging in deviant or anti-social activities. Women deviants are seen as *dependent* deviants, led into error by weaknesses, especially by men or by hormones and other 'biological' factors. Thus a male housebreaker is seen as robbing for gain, a woman thief is mentally unbalanced, or her chemistry is disturbed, or her husband made her do it.

In the following chapters, numerous incidents and perspectives on the literature of this kind will be demonstrated. No more needs to be said about the sexism of the research literature, but the sequencing and ordering of the material on adult women in the next four chapters needs some explanation. Most noticeable is the absence of a chapter on 'marriage and the family'. There seems little point in trying to change the stereotyped view of women current in sociology for several chapters and then reinstating it by a chapter on marriage and the family. Instead, I have arranged the material round the non-marriage themes of work, community, class and power first, turning to parenthood, old age and widowhood in the last chapter. By treating women's lives as if they were not centred on marriage, a novel perspective emerges.

Chapter 6

Work, Deviance and Leisure

> I do my bedroom out every day – sweep it and dust the furniture
> – and I do something else every day, like I dust the tops of the
> cupboards or I give the wardrobe a polish. Every second day I
> wash out this room – because it's only lino. And every fortnight
> I wash the curtains – the net ones and the heavy ones too . . .
> Friday night and Saturday night are my busy nights. Friday night
> I wash the carpets – I start about 10 p.m. and finish about
> midnight. (Jill Duffy, quoted in Oakley, 1974)

Raymond Williams (1976, p. 282) has argued that the notion of
work has become specialised over the last century or so, so that it
refers primarily to paid employment, as opposed to other types of
labour or effort. Williams says that this specialisation 'is the result
of the development of capitalist productive relations'. He goes on
to claim that:

> To be in work or out of work was to be in a definite relationship
> with some other who had control of the means of productive
> effort. Work then partly shifted from the productive effort itself
> to the predominant social relationship. It is only in this sense
> that a woman running a house and bringing up children can be
> said to be not working.

Here Williams has raised the central flaws in the literature on
work: it focuses on paid employment rather than 'voluntary'
labour. Thus it neglects women because so much of their labour
is of the 'voluntary' kind, and because their wage-labour is seen as
secondary to their voluntary activities they are treated as marginal
to the labour force. A recent volume by Anthony (1977), *The
Ideology of Work*, shows this bias. The only index reference to
women leads the reader to a comment on managers' wives. The
fundamental ambivalence about working women which charac-
terises public opinion and industrial sociology was revealed in a
study by Ann McKay and colleagues in 1970 (McKay, Wilding and

George, 1972). A sample of adults interviewed in Nottingham, consisting of over 350 people in three areas of the city, were asked about their views on single-parent families and work versus child care. Respondents were asked to say whether a single-parent father should go out to work or stay at home with the children· and then whether a single-parent mother should do the same. Overwhelmingly, the sample chose different work/child care patterns as appropriate for the two genders. Fathers were thought to need paid work for their mental health and self-respect, and often it was felt that a man who stayed home with children was sponging on the welfare state or scrounging. Nor were fathers thought to be good at looking after young children or running homes. In complete contrast, single-parent mothers were considered suitable to rear their children, and it was thought that they should not work full time. Where any paid employment was considered, part-time jobs were seen as a good idea. The woman single parent who could manage to work part time was thought to benefit from 'meeting people' or 'getting out of the house'; no mentions were made of career-building. Most noticeably, the authors remark: 'No one felt that she should go out to work because it is her place in society or that she should not sponge on the state.'

In other words, the overwhelming majority of this sample thought that men belonged at work, not at home, and women belonged at home, not at work, even when the adult concerned was equally responsible for the sole care of pre-school children. It is this strong belief, held unconsciously by social scientists, that I want to challenge in this chapter. It is argued in what follows that throughout social science, while the man who is not engaged in paid work is either ill or deviant or a victim of harsh economic circumstances, the reverse is true for women. Women who *are* in paid employment have been judged by social science as somehow peculiar. Further than this, the very notion of 'health' as applied to men – where it means they are fit for paid employment – cannot be safely applied to women because many healthy aspects of womanhood are in fact characterised in women as sicknesses preventing employment. Thus this chapter examines the work done by women in modern Britain, and the ways in which social scientists have discussed it, and then looks at the ways in which illness and deviance keep women from work, or drive them out from home into work.

A WOMAN'S WORK

There are three distinct kinds of work which women do in modern Britain, which need to be kept separate in any analysis of female work. These are *housework* – which is nearly always done unpaid for love, *voluntary work* – which is, by definition unpaid or poorly paid and done for love or charity, and *paid employment* – which is done for money but, when badly paid, for love as well. Information about all three kinds of women's work is limited, and social scientists have been particularly slow to study housework and voluntary work. In this chapter the emphasis is placed on paid employment and housework, and the discussion of voluntary work has been postponed until Chapter 8.

HOUSEWORK

Housework has recently been the subject of an acrimonious debate in the women's movement because one group of feminists is campaigning for Wages for Housework (James, 975; Dalla Costa and James, 1972). In addition, the growth of the women's movement and of women's studies has produced a series of academic investigations of housework and housewives by Ann Oakley (1974*a* and *b*), Jean Gardiner (1976), Leonore Davidoff (1976) and Dorothy Hobson (1978) which follow on from the American work of Helen Lopata (1971) and Hannah Gavron (1966). Housework is also the one thing that almost all women have in common, whether they are old or young, married or single, rich or poor, childless or childfree, and whether or not they have paid employment full or part time outside the home. Even the richest women, with houses full of servants, have the responsibility for seeing that the domestic work gets done properly. Even between couples who wish to break down the traditional division of labour (e.g. Rapoport and Rapoport, 1976), the responsibility for housework stays with the woman, and in communes, too, women appear to bear the weight of home maintenance (Abrams and McCulloch, 1976; Rigby, 1974). Even women in full-time paid employment are unlikely to be able to shelve not only the responsibility for the housework but, more seriously, the actual labour involved. Most men, and most children, are serviced by wives and mothers, so that they emerge into the world fed, clothed and pampered by someone else. Women workers leave home fed, clothed and pampered only by themselves. The physical and mental servicing of wage earners and school pupils in the home is seen as essential to the proper functioning of a complex capitalist industrial society both by structural-functionalists such as Talcott-Parsons (1948) and by Marxists such as Jean Gardiner (1976). The Marxists have popularised the term 'reproduction of labour power' to cover the bearing and rearing of children, and the mental and physical refurbishing of employees and pupils. A discussion of the domestic role of women couched in terms of the reproduction of labour power certainly sounds much more impressive than one which talks of housework, and the term also serves to locate the labour done by women firmly in the economic system of the country, rather than leaving it as a private thing between one woman and her 'nearest and dearest', a 'labour of love'. Thinking in these terms has also given rise to a women's movement song in which a housewife sings that she is her family's 'maintenance engineer'.

Any discussion of women's domestic work has, like all the other topics raised in this book, to be seen in class terms. While there are similarities between the household duties of all women of all classes, there are also considerable variations in the working conditions and the attitudes of women in different social classes. In part these stem from the time of the industrial revolution at the beginning of the nineteenth century, and they are related to women's participating in the labour market.

Since the industrial revolution two quite distinct trends in women's paid and domestic employment based on class lines have been apparent. While the working-class struggle was aimed at raising male wages to remove the necessity of woman and child labour, upper-middle-class women were campaigning for the right to enter gainful employment. The industrial revolution had forced women into mines and factories where they were shamefully exploited. As the nineteenth century progressed skilled manual workers gradually gained wages which allowed their women to stay at home, as the women of the middle- and upper-middle class had done all century. A decent male wage which supports a wife is still a powerful working-class ideal, and domestic life is still an obtainable dream for many working-class women, who are forced to earn to live. In contrast, ladies in the nineteenth century were forced to be idle, and to stay at home as ornamental objects, visible symbols of the financial prestige of the man who maintained them. The early feminists campaigned for education, training and work because this idle existence was stultifying and, for spinsters, widows and other unsupported ladies, dangerous. If they had no man to support them, ladies could easily slip down the social scale into terrible poverty. In the first phase, feminists campaigned for careers for celibate women mainly on financial grounds. (See Delamont, 1978, for a more detailed discussion of this relation between celibacy and careers.) However, it is possible to see the movement among middle-class wives and mothers since the Second World War as a further development of the early protests against the stifling boredom of an entirely domestic existence. Certainly there has been as vigorous a controversy over the 'right' of middle-class women to independent careers even when they are mothers as any of the parallel debates in the nineteenth centry.

The quality press regularly carries acrimonious exchanges about whether middle- and upper-middle-class women should concentrate on domestic duties, or should be able to pursue independent careers.

Such debates are normally sparked off by an article or feature on a woman who either finds the domestic existence intolerable and asks for help, or who has gone out to work and complains about her tax position or the lack of state help for working mothers generally. Such women are then showered with advice, and often abuse, by other correspondents who are nearly always women. The publication of Hannah Gavron's (1966) *The Captive Wife* sparked off just such a debate (see, for example, the *Observer* 8 and 15 May 1966); and much more recently, when the *Sunday Times Magazine* (7 May 1978) featured a captive wife who survived on Valium a comparable debate ensued there.

The types of argument offered have varied very little over the past fifteen years. Women who complain about the job of house-wife do receive some sympathetic support from others who dislike the job as much, but more typically, other women tell them to count their blessings, either because they are middle class with nice homes, or because the role is 'really' wonderful. Thus correspon-dents write:

What would I and a thousand others give for a beautiful old house in a remote area, with leisure time to devote to garden, family and so on. Count your blessings. (The *Observer*, 27 March 1977)

and

The complaining young wives who write to you don't know when they are lucky. My young children have grown up and gone away, and I am free to do as I please; but I would give anything to be 'captive' again. (The *Observer*, 17 May 1966)

Such comments obviously cut little ice with the despairing women who write to problem pages, the quality press, and those inter-viewed across the United States in the early 1960s by Betty Friedan (1963). She was probably the first modern commentator to put her finger on the malaise associated with full-time housework when she called it 'the problem with no name'. Yet to outsiders it is not clear what it is about the job of the housewife which is so contro-versial. Research on the lives and work of housewives is not ample, and is biased towards full-time housewives *and mothers* in the midlands or the London area. Ann Oakley (1974*a* and *b*) sampled forty mothers between 20 and 30 in London, nearly all of whom were at home full time. Dorothy Hobson (1978) used young mothers at a clinic who did not have jobs as the basis of her Birmingham area sample. We can use these data, however, to throw some light on the conditions of work. Oakley in particular examines house-work within the framework of the sociology of work, breaking down the role into a set of tasks and looking at the ways in which middle- and working-class women relate to each task rather than the role as a whole. In other words Oakley treats housework as work.

Oakley found that, while there were class differences between middle- and working-class women, the discontented housewife was by no means a middle-class phenomenon. While both classes of women got little pleasure from housework as work, the working-class had far more invested in the role, and searched for satisfaction in it. The overall reaction to the tasks involved in housework was negative, however, even by women who claimed to be 'satisfied' as housewives. Thus Oakley found the 70 per cent of her sample came out of the interview as 'dissatisfied' overall. One of the commonest complaints made by all the women is loneliness. Oakley points out that workers tend to value social relationships as an important part of the job, and thus it is likely that the lack of social interaction would be associated with dissatisfaction with housework. In contrast, autonomy is the most valued aspect of the work, because women can control their pace of work which most could not do in their paid employment. Housework shared characteristics with assembly-line factory work, in that most women found it monotonous, fragmented and excessively paced. The monotony was especially disliked, whereas the fragmentation was seen as an essential part of house-work and was not minded so much. Overall, however, housewives experienced higher levels of monotony, fragmentation and excessive pace than factory workers.

The fragmentation of housework was related to different valu-ations of the various tasks involved. The task least liked by the sample was ironing, followed by washing up, cleaning, washing and shopping, whilst cooking was the most popular. Overall, the house-work tasks were the worst aspects of the role of housewife for this sample, although the role of housewife was also disliked because it has such low social status. The low status was experienced especially by women who had had high-status jobs before becoming full-time housewives. Thus the women who had held posts like fashion model, manicurist at Claridge's and computer programmer had suffered an acute loss of status, and resented the role of housewife more than the rest of the sample. Overall, the more a woman had enjoyed her previous work, the less satisfied she was with full-time housework, whatever the status of that previous work.

Oakley's sample was found to have a very long working week. The average woman in her sample worked for 77 hours per week, while the lowest number of hours worked was 48 (by a woman with a full-time job) and the highest 105 (by the woman quoted at the head of the chapter). In addition to the sheer length of the working week, Oakley also found that many of the women set themselves routines and standards of work to which they were then forced to adhere. The women were their own task mistresses, and many of them were extremely severe on themselves. Oakley offers three explanations for this high specification of tasks. She argues that this is one way of gaining rewards for household tasks, for women can gain satisfaction if they reached the standards. Then, self-imposed standards are a way of emphasising the housewife's autonomy, and a way of breaking down the fragmentation and imposing unity. While the self-imposed rules provide certain satisfactions for women, however, Oakley also argues that the rules become objectified and seen as external, and can actually destroy the autonomy, by enslaving the woman to what were, originally, her own standards.

Oakley draws a distinction between the sample's attitudes to the tasks of home maintenance and their overall satisfaction with the role of housewife. While most of her sample did not like housework, they did like being housewives. Thus in Oakley's study it is possible to distinguish between the woman who enjoys housework but does not like being a housewife, and the woman who enjoys being a housewife but dislikes housework. Oakley found that her working-class women were more likely to fit the second pattern (liking the role, but not the work) whereas the middle class were more likely to follow the first pattern. Interestingly, Oakley's study also shows that there may be considerable conflict between child-rearing and housework, for time spent on one is not available for the other.

Oakley's sample thus found housework a low-status, monotonous, fragmentary activity which involved them in long hours of work at an excessive pace usually in isolation. Hobson's (1978) sample can be seen to express similar sentiments towards their tasks, although her women seem to be even more isolated than Oakley's. Findings of this kind do not convey the actual differences in the nature and amount of housework done, of course, and for that one has to quote women themselves. Oakley quotes extensively from the interview with Catherine Prince, a middle-class woman who dislikes housework, and Jill Duffy, a working-class woman who loves it. Catherine Prince gets up at 8.30 with the baby, while her husband gets himself up and gets his own breakfast. She feeds the baby, reads the paper, does some washing, reads a book, goes shopping, has lunch, reads a book, plays with the baby, puts it to bed, then cleans the house if necessary, does the adult supper and then knits or does dressmaking. She says 'I've got very low standards! You see I think housework is a waste of time, I don't do it, or I do a minimum' (Oakley, 1974a, p. 103). In contrast, Jill Duffy, who loves housework, does all her washing by hand ('I don't believe in washing machines') and in one day goes shopping, does out the bedroom, vacuums several times, feeds her 3-year-old to avoid her making a mess, washes and changes the children's clothes once. She claims her standards have dropped for the older child used to be changed twice a day. When her husband changes she washes his clothes immediately. Her cleaning standards, detailed at the chapter head, involved washing her curtains every two weeks, and her carpets every week (at night because her husband plays drums in a group and is not at home then). She only sits down when he is home 'and he's not in much' (1974a, p. 109). These two women, and the four whose interviews are reported at length in her follow-up study (Oakley, 1974b), are probably 'typical' of the housewife in the south-east of England, if not in Britain as a whole.

Their lives are a far cry from that portrayed in the latest book on how to run a home, Shirley Conran's (1975) *Superwoman*. Conran argues that housework is horrible, the home should be only 'as clean as you can get away with' (p. 4) and then goes on to plead for the elimination of most of the tasks on which Oakley's sample spent time. Thus Conran argues against ironing things that do not go on public show, and even suggests that each member of the family should do his or her own washing up. However, she actually belies her own advice by filling fifty pages with hints on doing all the chores, and another twenty on shopping and cooking. In contrast, the parallel book for men, William Rushton's *Superpig* (1976), manages to deal with domestic work in under thirty pages, and passes on to mixing cocktails and chatting up women. Even Shirley Conran is a victim of the mythology about domestic work which enslaves so many of Oakley's sample. Only the positive orientation to the role of housewife keeps many of these women going through the range of tasks, and, in many cases the relatively unattractive alternatives of poorly paid manual work. Paid employment for women in Britain is not an attractive prospect and suffers from many of the same defects as housework. Except for a privileged minority, paid employment is of low status, produces low pay and offers little intrinsic interest, as the next section will show.

PAID EMPLOYMENT

Just as there have been different class orientations towards women becoming full-time housewives, with the working class often holding as an ideal what the middle class is struggling against, so too middle- and working-class women have traditionally occupied very different spheres in the labour market. While both middle- and working-class women may meet in secretarial and clerical work, in general the two groups are firmly segregated in the occupation sphere. This will become clear when some detail on women's role in the workforce is set out below, after some basic points about paid employment and women have been made. Four points in particular have to be borne in mind when considering women's employment:

(1) There are a large number of women in paid employment and most of them are married.

(2) Sexual inequalities in work conditions and pay accentuate class inequalities, so that women in higher-status occupations have greater equality with men than those in manual work.

(3) Industrial sociology and the sociology of work and occupations have neglected women and offer very little insight into their lives.

(4) Many women in paid employment do not go 'out' to work, but undertake 'outwork' or 'homework', something rare for male workers.

These four points need to be examined in turn to complete a picture of women's employment. *Social Trends*, 1977 shows that Britain had a labour force in 1976 of over 25 millions, of whom over 1 million were registered as unemployed. This labour force was made up of 15·9 million men and 10·0 million women in 1976, of whom 6·7 million were married. The government's predictions of the size of the labour force in 1981 were for 10·6 million women (7·1 million married) and 16·2 million men. The most significant change in the composition of the labour force since the Second World War has been the increased work participation of married women, and especially of mothers of school-age children. In 1961 less than a quarter of married women with two or more dependent children were in full- or part-time work. By 1971, this had risen to 35 per cent, and the prediction was that it would reach 50 per cent in 1977. This increased work involvement has not been uniform across the regions of Britain for, as Paul Wilding (1977) shows, in 1961 only 28 per cent of Welsh women were in work as opposed to 37·5 per cent of *British* women, while by 1971 the Welsh figure had reached 37·5 per cent, but the British figure had got to 42·7 per cent. Wilding comments: 'No Welsh county – not even South Glamorgan which embraces Cardiff – has a rate of female economic activity which even approaches the average of Britain' (1977, p. 5). In general, where there are low rates of female employment there is a poorer region, but this does not mean that women's pay is actually equal to men's or anywhere near it, despite the Equal Pay Act, which came into force in 1975.

Sex Inequality at Work
Westergaard and Resler argue (1975, p. 101) that

sex inequality in pay . . . reinforces class inequality: it strikes hardest at the lowest levels of the occupation hierarchy.

They do not offer any data on pay inequalities between men and women in occupations in social class I – higher managerial and professional workers such as doctors – probably because there are so few women in these occupations that pay differentials between the genders cannot be safely calculated. However, they offer startling figures on gender inequalities in the three main categories of occupation below social class I: semi-professional, routine white-collar and manual workers. In social class II (teachers, social workers, nurses and parallel occupations of a 'semi-professional' kind) women earn about one-fifth less than men in similar jobs; in social class IIIA (routine clerical work) women earn about one-third less than men in similar jobs, while in manual work (classes IIIB, IV and V) women earn only about half what men earn. Thus Westergaard and Resler are arguing that there is a stepped inequality in earnings as one moves down the social scale, as Table 6.1 shows.

Table 6.1   *Sex Differences in Pay* (£s)

	Men		Women	
	1971	*1976*	*1971*	*1976*
Non-manual workers				
mean	39·1	81·6	19·8	48·8
Manual workers				
mean	29·4	65·1	16·3	39·4

Source: Adapted from *Social Trends, 1977*, p. 102. Table 6·12.

The explanation of these continuing inequalities is partly located in the kinds of work women do (for example, women are rarely apprenticed to the highly skilled, high-paid manual occupations) and partly in the length of service and seniority attained. In teaching, for example, few women get into the better-paid promoted posts (Byrne, 1978; Delamont, 1980). Yet the gender inequalities in work are not restricted to pay, because women also suffer worse conditions. As Westergaard and Resler (1975, p. 88) point out, both welfare benefits and fringe benefits provided by employers are not distributed equally across classes and genders. Fringe benefits include such things as company cars, school fees and cheap mortgages, and welfare benefits include sick pay, life insurance and superannuation. In 1970 only about 65 per cent of male manual workers were covered in occupational sick pay schemes, but over 90 per cent of male non-manual workers. Pension schemes showed a similar pattern, for men. The authors comment: 'Coverage on both scores, and especially in respect of pensions, was poorer for women in full-time employment' (1975, p. 88) and then continue: 'The exclusion of women from sick pay and pension schemes provided by employers is far more marked in the lower . . . reaches of the occupation hierarchy'. Westergaard and Resler show in a table (p. 89, Table 12) that in 1971, among non-manual workers, 75 per cent of men employed by private firms were in an occupational pension scheme, but only 36 per cent of women; whereas in the public sector the figures were 94 per cent and 60 per cent. In manual work, 45 per cent of men in the private sector and 68 per cent in the public were in such schemes, whereas the figures for women were a shameful 19 per cent and 25 per cent.

The majority of women are employed in sectors of the economy where men are rare, and vice versa. Thus women in the semi-professions are concentrated in teaching, nursing and social work where women predominate, while women manual workers are concentrated in service industries and in food, textiles and footwear. Thus *Social Trends, 1977* shows that there were 6 million women working in service industries compared with 3 million women in manufacturing industries. The 1971 census showed very clearly that women are concentrated in female ghettos, so that 96·6 per cent of those employed in hand and machine sewing were women, 91·2 per cent of those in nursing, 96·4 per cent of canteen assistants, 98·6 per cent of typists and 96·6 per cent of maids. These sectors are traditionally low paid. In addition, where women are employed in the same sector as men the wages are not equal. Thus a survey of NALGO members conducted in 1974 showed that of employees in the public sector far more women were below the TUC low-pay target of £30 per week. This is shown in Table 6·2.

Table 6·2 *Percentages of NALGO Members Earning Less than £30 per Week in 1974*

Service	Men	Women
Local government	8·0	33.0
Health	4·5	36·5
Gas	5·0	32.0
Electricity	12·5	48·5
Water	10·5	42·5
Universities	0·0	33·0
New towns	5·0	36·5

Source: Adapted from CIS (n.d.).

Ross Davies (1975, p. 17) points out that:

Among manual workers, only one woman in eight, as opposed to nearly one man in three, works in the seven industries where men's average earnings are highest (vehicles, paper, printing and publishing, coal and petroleum, shipbuilding and marine engineering, bricks, pottery and glass, metal manufacture and transport and communications). Yet more than a half of all women employed, compared with a quarter of all men, are in the lowest-paying industries: textiles, clothing and footwear, distributive trades, professional and scientific services, public administration, miscellaneous services, agriculture, forestry and fishing.

Of these low-paying occupations, women are concentrated in the first five rather than the last three. The most noticeable differences about the two lists are the power and influence of the trade unions and the difficulties about entry. The male, high-paying occupations demand skills, usually only available via a traditional apprenticeship, and are served by old-established, powerful trade unions who operate a closed shop which effectively cuts out women. Women cannot get apprenticeships in occupations such as printing, boiler-making and steel working. The elite trade unions have kept their occupations closed to women as effectively as they have kept their members' wages relatively high compared with other manual workers.

A parallel situation exists in non-manual work. Here the majority of women are employed in the semi-professions which are classified as social class II and which carry relatively low pay and relatively low status compared with the top jobs. Thus women are nurses, schoolteachers and social workers, while men predominate in medicine, university teaching and the law. Mackie and Pattullo (1977) offer figures for 1974 concerning women's participation in the elite jobs of social class I which tell a depressing story.

In the university sector, although women form a third of the undergraduate students, and a quarter of the postgraduates, they make up only 12 per cent of the teaching staff at lecturer level, 6 per cent of the senior lecturers and about 2 per cent of the professors. None of the top administrative posts – registrar and bursar, principal or vice-chancellor – is held by a woman. In medicine, about 27 per cent of qualified personnel are women, but only 12 per cent of the hospital consultants who wield the real power in the profession. Women are particularly scarce in the high-prestige specialities such as surgery, particularly brain and heart surgery. In law, women are about 4 per cent of practising solicitors, and the number of barristers, county court and high court judges is tiny. In architecture about 4 per cent of the members of the professional body, RIBA, are women. The figure for vets and dentists are similar to those for law and architecture, and women are not yet allowed to enter the clergy on the same terms as men in most denominations. Yet the professions offer more chance to women than business, commerce and industry. Only 1 per cent of the members of the Institute of Directors were women in 1974, and successful women in fields like merchant banking, stockbroking and insurance are almost non-existent. This dismal picture of unequal employment in top jobs and manual ones might be alleviated by the position of women in the semi-professions. Yet detailed studies show that even in those occupations which are fully integrated by gender, such as teaching, men are better paid, largely because they have cornered most of the promoted posts (Byrne, 1978; Delamont, 1980). This is also the case for nursing (Austin, 1977*a* and *b*) and social work.

The two books which examine the inequalities of women at work (Davies, 1975; Mackie and Pattullo, 1977) are both by journalists, and much of the other evidence is presented in pamphlets (Lloyd, n.d.; CIS, n.d.). The only academic text is Chiplin and Sloane, 1976, which is largely incomprehensible to the non-economist. None of these texts offers any good explanations of the inequalities in conditions, pay and promotion, so one might wish to turn to sociological work on industry or occupations for illumination. This is a course of action doomed to produce more heat than light, however. Recently Richard Brown (1976) for the United Kingdom and Pamela Roby (1975) and Rosabeth Moss Kanter (1975) for the United States have reviewed the literature on the sociology of work, occupations and industry. All three commentators show a neglect of working women in the literature.

Bias in the literature
Richard Brown's (1976) critique of industrial sociology starts from the premise that the authors have either ignored gender differences altogether and thus treated women as identical to men, or they have focused on the 'problem' working women cause for either their employers or their families. Brown's examination of texts in industrial sociology shows that few have bothered to discuss gender stratification in the labour market, while most authors have either ignored women workers except as a 'problem' or left them out of account altogether. Brown then suggests several reasons why the literature has developed in this sexist way, and examines some of the stereotypes about women workers which are perpetrated in those books which do discuss the female part of the workforce. Women are, typically, seen as more compliant than men, more subservient to management, more indifferent or hostile to trade unions and less in favour of strikes. Brown shows that many of these stereotypes have not been based on a dispassionate consideration of the relative

importance of gender differences and the conditions of various sectors of the labour market. Thus, for example, unionisation rates are known to be lower in small firms and plants; far more women work in small units, so women's low rates of unionisation may be an outcome of their work situation as much as of their gender. No texts in industrial sociology raise this point.

The major texts in industrial sociology never discuss how the lower rates of unionisation among women workers may be related to the nature of trade unions in the Unted States and the United Kingdom. Such books do not discuss how male workers, and male-dominated trade unions, have deliberately kept women out of many occupations and sectors of the workforce and thus away from the better-paid and highly unionised jobs. Thus, the way in which women were allowed into such occupations during the two world wars but forced out of them when peace was declared by an unholy alliance of government and male unions is only discussed in books on women at work, not in books on industrial sociology and the sociology of work. Brown, quite rightly, points out that because social scientists have not faced the sexism of male workers they have misrepresented several of the points they make about women workers. Women workers may correctly and rationally perceive that trade unions are hostile to them and their interests and this is as likely to 'explain' their anti-union attitudes as any natural conservatism or deference to management.

Brown also raises the interesting point that most of the central studies in the sociology of industry have been carried out in industries in which very few women are employed, although usually the researchers claim to have been attracted to those industries for other reasons, such as a high degree of social and technical change, or a high strike record, or unusual working conditions. Thus the classic studies have been carried out on shipbuilders, car workers, seafarers, navvies, steelworkers, printers, lorry drivers, dockers, deep sea fishermen, and coal miners. Newby's (1977a) recent work on male farm workers is a recent contribution to this tradition. The classic studies in industrial sociology are, therefore, of hard, dirty, highly paid, masculine work of a particularly 'exciting' kind. It is almost as if the sedentary male social scientists were compensating for their own 'pansy' occupations by studying occupations undertaken by 'real men'. These occupations are also the arenas in which heroic struggles of men against wicked employers and a harsh environment can be lovingly and loathingly portrayed by left-wing social scientists. It is hard to imagine creating such an aura around the unromantic industries in which women workers are confined. Can you imagine a book called *Shoes Are Our Life* or *The Shirtmakers* or *Above Us the Laundry Baskets*? Studies of the textile, clothing, food, tobacco and boot and shoe industries and the vast service industries of shop work, laundry work and catering are few and far between, very out of date and distressingly unscholarly.

Pamela Roby (1975) has recently pointed out that whereas in the United States the period 1900–25 saw a considerable amount of research on women in working-class jobs, the next fifty years saw almost nothing. Thus in eighty years the *American Journal of Sociology* has published only seven articles on blue-collar women, and all seven were before 1910! Of course, this neglect of working-class women's jobs could be a blank spot in a thorough coverage of other women's work, but it is, in fact, just one manifestation of a general neglect of *both* women's jobs and women in predominantly male occupations at all levels of the work hierarchy. Women workers have lost out on academic attention in all spheres of work. If a job is a female ghetto, like secretarial work or night cleaning, it is neglected because it is an unimportant job too trivial to study. If there are a handful of women in a predominantly male occupation, such as medicine, then researchers tend to leave the women out of the study because they complicate the research.

Indeed in Britain women in routine white-collar jobs and in the high-status professions have been as badly neglected by researchers as working-class women workers. In the high-status professions the history of women's struggle for entry and the present position and life-styles of female members are both of interest, and both are badly under-documented. There are several biographies of early women doctors and accounts of women's entry to medicine (see Manton, 1965, and Moberly Bell, 1953) although far more research needs to be done on the topic. However, medicine is unusual. There are no scholarly studies of women entering law, engineering, architecture, dentistry, veterinary medicine or the armed services; few biographies of the pioneers; and to my knowledge none of these deficiences is being remedied. There is a history of women civil servants (Martindale, 1938), but this occupation is unusual precisely because it has been documented.

Work on the current position of women in top jobs is equally scarce. Apart from one piece of research on management, the civil service and the BBC (Fogarty *et al.*, 1971) there is nothing recently published on women in medicine, law, dentistry, veterinary medicine, architecture, the armed services, accounting, the senior police, universities or engineering except for a few scattered articles. Neither is there any British book to parallel Cynthia Epstein's (1970) key text on women in professional occupations, *Woman's Place*. This is especially disappointing, for Epstein's book has several faults. The sociology of the professions has fallen into two main parts: studies of the internal dynamics of occupations such as socialisation into the work, interaction with clients and with peers, and so on, and studies of the position of 'professions' in the class structure.

Epstein's book is clearly in the first tradition, emphasising the internal dynamics of the professions and how these serve to keep women marginal and subordinate. It does not begin to address the important questions raised by Johnson (1972) and Atkinson *et al.* (1977) about professional power, autonomy and knowledge. A scholarly work which draws together Epstein's insights on professional processes, the data on women in professions in Britain, and the recent theoretical insights is urgently needed. At the moment we do not even know how far Epstein's arguments about the invisible barrier to women in the professions are true in Britain.

Epstein has suggested that women are likely to be relatively unsuccessful because many aspects of everyday routine among men are closed to them or difficult for them. Thus men traditionally progress in professional occupations via sponsorship or patronage from a senior male. Epstein argues that senior men are unlikely to sponsor a young woman, but such sponsorship is the only way a woman can get on. Then much male business is done in informal settings, which *de facto* exclude women, such as golf courses, male lunch clubs, bars, and so on. Perhaps most serious is the issue of visibility and status inconsistency. By these, Epstein means that not only is the woman professional always visible because she is a minority in her occupation, but also that, because for most people 'woman' and 'lawyer', 'woman' and 'doctor', 'woman' and 'accountant' are not congruent statuses, whenever a woman professional appears she causes others to be disconcerted. Women in professional occupations are thus always noticeable, and their presence causes discomfort to others, which has to be constantly allayed if any work is to be done. While Epstein documents these phenomena for women lawyers in the United States, and shows how they are worse in contexts where lawyers must work in teams, it is not known how far they apply in Britain. Kanter (1975) discusses other American research on how professional women learn to survive in these conditions, but again we do not know how far these findings can be applied to Britain.

Sponsorship and patronage in professions in Britain are probably as important as in the United States, and certainly the medical students in Edinburgh studied by Atkinson (1976) were well aware of this. Studies of successful women in academic life in Britain also show clear evidence of sponsorship being necessary – so that the relatively large number of women in crystallography can be attributed to J. D. Bernal being willing to encourage women scientists. The difficulties experienced by women when excluded from informal settings is very well documented in science with the case of Rosalind Franklin and DNA. Franklin's role in the discovery of DNA was denigrated by James Watson in his best-seller *The Double Helix*. Watson called her ugly, feminine, secretive and unco-operative.

Years later it transpires that she was not only far more central to the discovery than Watson admitted, but was also excluded from most of the informal discussions which took place during the research at King's College, London. Ann Sayre (1975) has pointed out that at King's in the 1950s the staff common room and dining room were for men only, so that Franklin was excluded from all the social intercourse between the other scientists. While the men ate and talked in comfort, she was forced to go elsewhere for her meals and conversation. Watson never mentioned this fact – probably never noticed it – although it no doubt accounts for her 'unfriendly' attitude. Given that Watson claimed to have discovered the double helix while drawing on a table napkin, it is clear that crucial scientific discourse went on over meals and drinks, so it is little wonder that Rosalind Franklin appeared less 'chummy' than her male co-researcher at King's. (Interestingly, Watson also says that Rosalind Franklin was unattractive and wore glasses, although in fact she did not, but he was clearly not interested in the truth about her on any level.)

The issues of visibility and status inconsistency are in urgent need of research in Britain. The kinds of occurrences reported by Kanter (1975) such as the man having lunch with a woman manager being reported to his wife as having been seen with a lover, and the assumption that any woman answering a telephone *must* be a secretary not a doctor or lawyer, are no doubt common here, too. Certainly women academics report that hotels, travel agencies and the like always assume that reservations are being made for a male superior. ('I'd like to reserve a room for the night of the 10th please.' 'Name, please.' 'Dr Delamont.' 'Does he want a bathroom?') Data on these questions would be easy to collect and would be very illuminating.

If we are seriously short of data on women in 'bottom' jobs and 'top' jobs, it would be natural to assume that the semi-professions where women predominate would offer a literature on working women. Yet studies of women in social work (Walton, 1975), teaching (Partington, 1976) and nursing (Austin, 1977a) are few in number, and have not been very clear about analysing the *relative* importance of features of the occupations and the fact that most employees are women. Overall, both industrial sociology and the sociology of work and occupations have neglected working women in all spheres of work. Perhaps the most startling omission is the total neglect of one major type of female work, although it fits in with all the stereotypes of women's main interest lying in their families, the omission being homework or outwork.

Homework and Outwork

Although homeworkers were the subject of inquiry in the nineteenth century, relatively little attention has been paid to them recently. Emily Hope and others (1976) undertook a small study in north London in 1972, and there have also been studies done in the midlands by trades councils and by the Low Pay Unit (Mackie and Pattullo, 1977). Serious academic workers have neglected homework as have the major trade unions, and it has been left to radical pressure groups of various kinds to study the conditions, rates of pay and attitudes to work of homeworkers.

Homework has three major characteristics: it is largely done by women, it is desperately poorly paid and it is highly insecure. Homeworkers are common in the garment industry, but other tasks done at home include knitting and crochet, lace making, assembling Christmas crackers, fishing tackle, hair rollers, ball point pens, painting model figures, or packing contraceptives. They are nearly all classed as self-employed, and the wages they receive are derisory. Polly Pattullo, writing in the *Observer Magazine* (11 July 1976) quoted a woman painting model footballers who got paid £1·60 a week for 500 models. Rates of 10p and 15p an hour are common for homeworkers, who rarely realise how little they are being paid. The trades in which homeworkers are common are often seasonal, and all homeworkers fear losing the work, either because the employer takes it from them for some reason or because the local authority stops them using their homes for work. All the accounts of homeworkers show that attempts to organise workers or raise wages, even to the lowly minima laid down by wages councils, result in loss of work.

Hope *et al.* (1976) quote one homeworker, Jean, who machines pillow ticks. She has four dependent children and a husband in a low-paid job in a shoe factory. Her work history is given as follows:

> At first she could only make twelve ticks in an hour. When she is working at speed she can make a pillow tick in $2\frac{1}{2}$ minutes. She is paid 2p for each tick ... she machines for $1\frac{1}{2}$ hours and is paid 72p ... She earns roughly between 36p and 54p an hour if only the machining time is taken into account.

> After the ticks have been machined they have to be turned inside out, the corners poked out, then packed and labelled with Jean's name in case of any complaint. This work is always done by John in the evenings and takes a considerable amount of time.
> ... Jean earns between £9 and £10 a week
> ... does between $19\frac{1}{2}$ and 28 hours machining
> ... This does not take into account John's contribution ... nor her overheads ...

In their survey Hope *et al.* interviewed twenty-one women and found that nearly all had dependent children. None was a single parent, and the authors suggest this is because homework is too badly paid for those without a partner also earning. Most of the homeworkers held traditional views about their role as house-keepers and mothers, had no skills and did homework purely for the money which was needed for necessities. Hope *et al.* says: 'The homeworker is a casual labourer exploited on the basis of her ascribed role as a woman/wife.'

This is the view from the commentators. It should be pointed out that Pamela Constantinides (1977) presents rather a different argument from her study of Greek Cypriot women in London. While most studies of homework have revealed that many of the women involved are 'immigrants' and argued that they are forced into homework by language difficulties or husbands who will not let them go out to work, Constantinides' sample saw things rather differently. She suggests that 80 per cent of Greek Cypriot women in London do some kind of work in the garment industry and says that outwork is the norm for those with pre-school children. She goes on:

in most... households the ubiquitous sewing machine will be found in a convenient corner... The sewing is done on piecework rates for Cyrpiot dressmaking manufacturers who deliver the fabric... Though the piece-rates are rather low, women can earn large sums each week by working long hours... these women consider it their right and duty to further the financial welfare of their family and they resent attempts, official or otherwise, to persuade them they are being exploited. They equally resent attempts by some local councils to put a stop to outworking... where the council investigation is prompted by complaints of neighbours about noisy machines, women tend to feel that they have been victims of the prejudice or envy of their non-Cypriot neighbours.

It is in this climate that Hope and her colleagues learnt: 'The Greek women in our area thought our project was aimed at taking work from them to give it to English women.' Such is the insecurity of homework, and the importance of it to its workers.

In many ways, however, homework is typical of women's work. Most homework is put out by industries which typically employ women, and the workers are unskilled, poorly paid, poorly organ-ised, have low job security and have been ignored by researchers. The women who do homework also conform to the prevailing social norms, in that they are doing 'feminine' jobs, subordinating them to their husbands and children, and are staying at home. It is no accident that ethnic groups with very strict segregation of gender roles provide many of the women homeworkers, for the traditional female role is well suited to sweated labour.

If the conventional woman is one who stays married and stays at home, the conventional man goes out to work. Women who work seriously are either bad or mad – that is, deviant or sick – while men who do not work are bad or mad – that is, deviant or sick. In the rest of this chapter the ways in which ideas about conformity and deviance and health and illness are differentially applied to the two sexes are examined.

DEVIANCE AND WOMEN

Deviance is the opposite of conformity. Thus anyone who differs in ideas or behaviour from the opinions or actions of the majority in his or her society is a deviant. However, all societies have some rules, laws or norms which are not taken very seriously, so that those deviations do not matter much, and others which are taken seriously, and breaches of which matter immensely. Thus in modern Britain the law contains prohibitions on offences of a serious and a minor kind. Breaking the speed limit and dropping litter are not taken very seriously, while killing policemen and sexually attacking children are. Similarly, refusing to wear a wedding ring is a minor breach of custom for a woman, while admitting to being a lesbian (gay) is a major breach, although neither are illegal. The litter dropper, the child molester, the ringless wife and the gay woman are all deviants, but the scope and seriousness of their deviation differs. Not only are there different degrees of deviation in terms of seriousness in Britain, but as the country is not one culture, but a combination of many subcultures, what is regarded as deviant in one subculture may be normal in another, and vice versa. Thus Gypsy and Muslim women must not show their legs, while many head teachers forbid girl pupils to cover them up with trousers or long skirts; in Christian churches men must uncover their heads, in orthodox Jewish synagogues they must cover them. Because of the multiracial, pluralist nature of modern Britain, many apparently deviant groups turn out to be conforming to the norms and values of some other subgroup. Studying the norms and values of different subgroups in society is one of the main tasks of sociology, as it is important to understand the perspective of the deviant, and the processes by which 'moral panics' are created about deviant acts.

Deviance, particularly the more spectacular and sexual forms of deviance, is a major source of public entertainment. Crime, perversion and the breaking of social rules form the subject of 'news' in the mass media, and of much fictional entertainment in literature, films, TV and radio. There are large numbers of people who want to see or read about murders, robberies, adulteries and drug taking, and about less criminal forms of deviance such as 'welfare state scrounging'. Sociologists are no exception to this. Ever since Durkheim became interested in suicide, sociologists have been keen to study criminals and other kinds of deviant in society. In particular, sociologists have been enthusiastic about studying groups of flamboyant and exciting deviants, both criminals and those inside the law, such as drug users, adolescent street gangs like teddy boys, and jazz musicians. Nearly all these studies have been done on males, so that prostitutes are the only category of deviant women to have received consistent scholarly attention. It is necessary to see why this is so, before examining what kinds of behaviour are considered deviant in women.

There are two excellent overviews of the research on deviance, criminology and women by Marcia Millman (1975) and Carol Smart (1976). Both show how in the United States and Britain sociologists have studied the male criminal and the male deviant, and women criminals and deviants have been neglected. Both discuss the possible explanations for this neglect, and rehearse the theories which have been put forward about women's deviance and criminality, so there is no need to go into detail here. It is, however, important to explore the relationship between deviance and crime among British women, because while many women are deviant, apparently few of them are criminally deviant.

One of the reasons that criminologists have neglected women is that British women *apparently* commit very few crimes, and those that they do commit are minor and non-violent. It is important to stress the 'apparently', because most of what we know about crime is based on prosecutions and convictions, and it is *possible* that women commit large numbers of crimes for which they are not prosecuted or convicted. (One man, Otto Pollak, 1961, actually argues this very forcibly, believing that women are so good at concealing crimes and evading justice that they are the mistresses of crime.) However, if the figures for prosecutions and convictions relate to the numbers and proportions of offenders in the population, there are clear differences between the genders in the number and type of criminal activity. Thus in 1976 in England and Wales 350,000 men were convicted of indictable offences and only 65,000 women (*Social Trends, 1977*, p. 204). Not only did women, apparently, commit fewer crimes, but theirs were nearly all non-violent offences involving theft, while men were convicted in large numbers for violent attacks on others (35,000), for serious burglary (65,000) and for criminal damage (38,000).

It is possible to explain some of the apparent gender differences in criminal activity as being due to the law and the legal processes in Britain. Some laws treat the sexes differently, so that, for example, female homosexuality is legal, while male homosexuality is illegal in Scotland and only legal in a restricted form in England and Wales. Thus there are men indicted for an offence which does not have a female equivalent. In contrast, only women are prosecuted for aborting themselves, for infanticide and for prostitution. (Since male prostitutes are lumped with other kinds of homosexual contact in public, being a heterosexual male prostitute is not an offence.) Most laws do apply to men and women equally in theory, but there is speculation, that needs research evidence, that the processes of law may differentiate between the genders. Thus women may be indicted in their crimes, or cautioned not prosecuted, or acquitted not convicted, more often than men 'guilty' of the same offences. Social norms may have an important effect on the treatment of women offenders, so that, for example, a woman caught with stolen goods may claim she was under threat from her husband, while no man could expect to claim he was under a similar threat from his wife. Thus, the whole question of whether women are more conformist than men, and actually less criminal, cannot be answered. We can only say that women are less likely to be prosecuted or convicted for serious or violent crimes than men, and that female crime is apparently trivial, non-violent and centred on petty theft.

Women criminals such as the shoplifter are not glamorous, and have not attracted attention from sociologists of deviance. However, as Millman (1975) has pointed out, criminologists and sociologists of deviance have also failed to study the criminals who have women *victims*, especially rapists and wife batterers, the men who use criminal women, such as pimps and the prostitutes' customers, and those who have to put up with male deviants and criminals, their victims and their wives. Women have thus been doubly invisible in the sociology of crime and deviance, neglected as practitioners and victims.

Because women criminals are such a tiny minority of British women this chapter does not go into detail about them, except to point out that most female crime is related to women's housewife and mother roles. Although as many men as women are convicted of shoplifting, it is seen as a female crime, because so many criminal women are shoplifters. However, Smart (1976) points out that women are caught stealing food and clothing, usually of low value, while men are caught with expensive goods and not food. Women criminals are thus women shoppers who have not paid, rather than deviants from the female role of provider.

Deviance and crime are not, as we have seen, synonymous. Women are deviant in many non-criminal ways, and in this chapter I want to examine these, because they concern far more women than crime does. In particular, I want to discuss how women regarded as deviant in modern Britain frequently have their behaviour 'explained away' by the mass media and by social scientists as being due to badly adjusted sexuality or mental or physical illness. Thus deviant women are rarely credited with responsibility for their own actions, but are seen as 'carried away' or 'not responsible'. In contrast, I shall argue, the victims of crimes against women, especially rape, *are* regularly held to be responsible for their plight. There are nine categories of deviant and victim women whose conduct is related to their sexuality or their health that I want to mention briefly: the political terrorist, the shoplifter, the baby snatcher, the prostitute and the lesbian are the deviants; the rape victim, the battered wife, the divorcee and the unmarried mother are the victims. Despite the apparently disparate nature of these e.amples, there are underlying similarities in their social categorisation, and social scientists have failed to collect data or to challenge the categories, or subject them to critical scrutiny.

Women engaged in violent political action are not new, but in recent years the involvement of women with the Angry Brigade and the IRA in Britain, with the Baader-Meinhof group in Germany, and the cases of Angela Davis and Patty Hearst in the United States have led to widespread mass media attention. Media coverage of these women does not credit them with genuine political beliefs and commitment, although male terrorists are so credited. Female participation in violent political activity is 'explained away' by love. The woman terrorist became sexually involved with a male activist, and was not 'responsible' for her subsequent actions. Thus Angela Davis became a terrorist because of her love for George Jackson, Bridget Dugdale because she had an affair with a leading IRA man. This 'explanation' is doubly insulting to women because it reduces their commitment from political to personal, and defines them as conventional women who are at the mercy of biological urges towards monogamy and blind devotion. Academic study of women's political beliefs has neglected their seriousness and commitment, as Chapter 8 shows, and extremist women are equally trivialised.

The woman caught stealing from Sainsbury's may seem to be very different from the woman hijacking a plane. Yet explanations of women's shoplifting locate this behaviour in her home and family life (her children have left her), her physical health (the menopause) or her mental state (depression). These explanations, proposed by popular and academic writers, take away women's autonomy, her responsibility for herself, and locate her crime in her feeble womanly nature or her relationships with husband and children. The lack of a husband and family allied to a strong maternal instinct is also used to 'explain away' the crime of the woman who steals a baby. Such a woman is also denied responsibility for her 'crime', because she is obviously 'sick', she did not 'really' want a baby, but was swept away by her biological drives. No criminologists have studied women who have stolen babies as if they were rational, and when a judge gave one such woman a heavy prison sentence – which suggested she was responsible for her actions – there was a public outcry which led to her release on the grounds she was sick. No male kidnapper would be treated in this way, because he would not be credited with a paternal instinct.

Prostitutes are one group of deviant women who have received scholarly attention. However, as the reviews of the literature in Smart (1976) and Smart and Smart (1978) show, most of the research and comment has been biased by current preconceptions about prostitutes, rather than truly scholarly. Thus prostitutes have been described as women who have failed to mature into proper adult women (i.e. 'sick' women), as lesbians (i.e. 'ill') and the victims of broken homes (i.e. not responsible). None of the commentators has treated women who sell their bodies as rationally economic women, although virgins who preserve their maidenhood for marriage are seen as behaving 'normally', 'responsibly' and with maturity. A study of prostitution which does not take the existing pattern of male dominance for granted is urgently needed. However, in this book the important point I want to make concerns the widespread use of the term 'prostitute' or one of its many synonyms to insult *any* woman who has 'annoyed any man. The history of the English language shows that nearly all the insulting words used about women began with, or acquired, the meaning of prostitute (Thorne and Henley, 1975). Any woman who steps out of line in modern Britain, even if the offence is not sexual, is liable to be given the label of prostitute or one of its synonyms, and also risks being called a witch and a lesbian. Thus Una Kroll, whose only social deviation is to want to be ordained an Anglican vicar, is regularly called all three. Given that one characteristic of witches was their 'unnatural' sexual practices, we can see that all three categories of insult are actually accusations of unnatural sexual activity – that is, sex with many men, with women or with animals and devils. While sociologists have no belief in witchcraft in modern Britain, their writings on lesbian women and prostitutes show as little rationality as the insults flung at Una Kroll. Both prostitutes and lesbians have been 'explained' by reference to psychoanalytic ideas and not studied sociologically at all. Because neither group of women devote their sexuality to one man in wedlock and or bear children for one man, both are condemned. No serious scholarly studies have been made of the lives and attitudes of either group.

The first five categories of deviant women are actively engaged in anti-social or disapproved practices. In the consideration of the last four categories of deviant women I want to show how women who are 'victims' are actually judged by society and sociologists to be as guilty as women who deviate actively. Thus the victims of rape, marital violence, divorce and extramarital pregnancy are all blamed for their predicament, and the blame is laid at the feet of their sexuality. Sexual activity is only legitimate for women inside marriage, and all extramarital activity not only disgraces the woman but is almost certainly her fault. If the woman has not brought the calamity upon herself by uncontrolled sexuality, or denial of legitimate sexuality, she is certainly ill or mad.

Rape is the classic case of a crime where the victim is nearly always blamed. Only very young girls and very old women are not blamed for arousing the uncontrollable male lust. The onus is on women victims to convince the male world that she has been violated. A woman cannot claim to have been raped by her husband, and it is hard to prove an accusation about any other man. If she knows the man, then she is accused of leading him on; if she does not, then she probably provoked him by wearing flamboyant clothes, or going out after dark, or ventured into a lonely place alone. If she has any sexual experience outside marriage, then the 'rape' is seen as unimportant, for she is already spoilt or second hand, and one more experience is not serious. Commentators (e.g. Brownmiller, 1975; Toner, 1977) suggest that the stigma and blame attached to the victim prevent many women from reporting rapes to any authority. It is estimated that, for whatever reason, two-thirds of all rapes are not reported to the police. The legal processes once a rape is reported do not encourage women to make complaints, for many of the more distressing aspects do not count (oral sex, objects such as milk bottles forced into the vagina), and the sympathy of police, court and press are with the man unless he is exceptionally violent. The only sociologist to have studied rape scientifically is an American, Amir (1971), who found that none of the popular stereotypes of victim or rapist was found in the majority of cases; but no equivalent research has been done in Britain and here the myths are unchallenged. (See Smart and Smart, 1978.)

Even if the rapist's victim is not blamed for her assault, there is another woman who can be blamed for the rape – the wife or girlfriend of the rapist who denied him 'legitimate' sex. Thus women can be seen as guilty if they express their sexuality and if they lack sexual feelings or deny and repress them. Women can be blamed for lack of sexual control and for controlling it too tightly. Thus the next victim to be considered, the battered wife. Male social scientists have not produced any serious work on violence in marriage which does not blame the woman victim. Gayford (1975) actually argues that women invite the violence by flirting with other men, or denying their husbands sex, or talking too much. Rebecca and Russell Dobash (1977) have argued that over half the violent crimes in Scotland consist of men assaulting their wives, yet this is not seen as a serious crime. Only Women's Aid have consistently argued that the women are genuine victims and the men are criminals (Hanmer, 1976).

The same kind of stereotyping about too-free or too-controlled sexuality is also applied by society to the last two groups of victims considered here, the divorcee and the unmarried mother. The divorcee is frequently blamed for losing her man because of infidelity (loose sexuality) or frigidity (over-controlled sexuality) or health problems, and her subsequent behaviour is judged by the same standard. Thus the divorced women studied by Nicky Hart (1976) claimed that they were objects of discrimination and derision, that they were blamed for losing their husbands, and expected to be sexually available to all-comers. They made comments like:

Widowed people get treated with sympathy and respect; there is a very different stigma still attached to the divorced and separated. p. 153)

Men think we are easy game. (p. 155)

When you are divorced, people think that there must be something wrong with you (p. 155)

[The neighbours] are watching me in case I step out of line; they talk about me enough already. (p. 166)

I am always frightened of doing something wrong; I know people would say 'You can see why her husband left her'. (p. 166)

Male neighbours think that you are so frustrated that you will sleep with anyone. (p. 182)

The unmarried mother is discussed in some details in Chapter 9, but she too is likely to be labelled as mentally ill (maladjusted) or overpowered by driving maternal instincts or uncontrolled sexuality. Adolescent girls in particular are not allowed to express any sexual drives they may have unless they marry, and if they show any signs of promiscuity they are likely to be locked up. The majority of adolescent girls who appear in court are there because they are 'at risk' – that is, sexually active – and therefore in need of care and attention (Wilson, 1978). Adolescent boys are not sanctioned in this way, but female sexuality is deviant outside marriage and brings disgrace on its performer. Adolescent girls are likely to have their sexual activity controlled for them, older women who are believed to have too little or too much sexuality are liable to become criminals or deviants or be treated as ill. Being considered 'ill' is actually a state of normality for women, as the final section will show, before we return to the working – and therefore deviant – woman.

IN SICKNESS AND IN HEALTH

In the nineteenth centry academic and public opinion in the middle and upper classes saw women as either sick or sick-making. Middle-class ladies were believed to be tender, delicate plants who were in constant danger of mental and physical collapse if they did anything unladylike. Learning Latin, Greek or algebra would give them brain fever, for example, and a career would cause physical breakdown. In contrast, the working-class women who undertook heavy manual work routinely were seen as carriers of disease and liable to infect their betters with VD, typhoid, cholera and diphtheria. While this very crude dichotomy between the sickly lady and the disease-carrying woman has vanished from medical journals and quality newspapers, the modern perspective on women's health is not so different. (See Duffin, 1978, for further discussion of Victorian ideas on women and health.)

Today women are regarded in a more unitary way irrespective of class, but *all* of us are regarded as perpetually ill or nearly ill, either mentally or physically or both. Psychiatry and psychoanalysis are still based on theories which regard men as healthy adults, but women as passive, dependent creatures who are fundamentally like children (Broverman *et al.*, 1972). The physical health of women is considered to be perpetually on a knife-edge because of the reproductive system. Women menstruate, get pregnant and have a menopause, and all these conditions are regarded both as *natural* and as dangerous threats to women's competence, both mental and physical. The medical professions have both neglected to treat these as illnesses which are painful and need treatment, and have used them as excuses or reasons for denying women top jobs, power, or even responsibility for their own lives. In part this is because all three processes scare and disgust men, especially menstruation, and partly because they are seen as 'natural'. Women are thus always seen as either 'ill' from one of these complaints, or likely to be 'ill' from one of them, and their mental stability as well as their physical robustness is seen as threatened by these processes. Both the medical professions and the majority of lay people and social scientists have accepted this view of women, so that pre-menstrual tension, menstrual pain, irrational behaviour in pregnancy, post-partum depression and menopausal 'madness' are all used as 'explanations' for women's irresponsibility, irrationality and incompetence, but at the same time women's psychological state is believed to aggravate or cause the *dysfunction* because the female processes are 'natural' in un-neurotic women. (See Judith Lorber,

1975, Leeson and Gray, 1978, and Barrett and Roberts, 1978, for elaborations and evidence on these arguments.) This 'double-bind' about women's health is summarised by Judith Lorber as follows:

Female patients are compounded deviants – they are defined as ill by virtue of their reproductive functions; they are also held responsible for whatever is disabling, difficult to manage, or disruptive about these functions; and finally they are blamed for reacting emotionally to their physical condition.

This leads to several common factors in the treatment women receive from the medical professions. First there is the lack of research into female complaints such as menopausal discomfort. Then there is the common practice of treating women's 'mental' problem with anti-depressants or tranquillisers rather than tackling their social situation or their physical symptoms. Finally there is the high rate of referral to psychiatrists, whose treatment usually consists of 'brainwashing' women into an even more rigid adherence to conventional sex roles. Carol Smart (1976, p. 149) has pointed out the absurdity of this treatment:

The treatment of women who are diagnosed as mentally ill or unbalanced is oriented towards their resocialization into their 'correct' social role ... It is ... a culturally imposed role which becomes increasingly inadequate and stressful as more women question their position in society. Resocializing women into a stereotyped feminine role which is no longer acceptable to many women is no solution to the stress that such a role itself manifests. It is after all quite conceivable that it is the untenable nature of the traditional feminine role ... that produces a high incidence of breakdown among women.

Smart (1976) analyses in some detail the argument that female deviance in Britain and the United States manifests itself as mental illness where males deviate by committing crime, and so this argument does not need discussion here. However, it is important to point out that the popular belief that spinsters are neurotic is incorrect, because mentally ill women are overwhelmingly married, and have been referred as 'sick' by their husbands for failure to perform domestic tasks. Just as the healthy woman is more at risk of death from pregnancy than from taking the pill or having abortions and avoiding all pregnancies, although this is not generally appreciated, so the people at risk of mental illness are not the frustrated spinster but the 'happily' married woman and the bachelor. The woman who chooses childlessness or not to marry is, therefore, at less risk of death and mental illness than the woman who takes the conventional path of marriage and motherhood. However, if a woman chooses to work at a career, she meets all the prejudice directed at the deviant, because she has avoided her 'natural' destiny. The man faces exactly the reverse prejudice should he choose fatherhood rather than his career, as we can see from this letter to *Woman's Own* (26 August 1978) from a maths teacher who had carried on working while her husband stayed home with their baby. She complains of being labelled a deviant:

> Since making this decision we have been subjected to a barrage of criticism from family and friends and to obstruction from officialdom.
>
> We consider it grossly unfair that a married woman may give up work and claim benefit from her husband's NHS contribution, while a married man who gives up his job voluntarily is denied the right to claim against his wife's contributions.
>
> We bitterly resent, too, the Inland Revenue's edict that there can only be one breadwinner in the home – the man – and that I am therefore taxed as a single person. This position, we are told, may be reconsidered. There could be a refund. But, with a baby, we need every penny we can get now.
>
> The attitude of our families has appalled us, too. Even though I took full maternity leave and breast-fed my child, I've been accused of breaking the mother–child bond. And I've been charged with forcing my husband to be dependent on me, so that he could not leave me – this, after seven years of good marriage!
>
> It has been implied that my husband lacks ambition, that he should feel the need to be the provider, even that he has forfeited his masculinity.

Thus the career woman is a deviant, and the non-working man is a deviant, and the working mother is the worst offender of them all, for all the accusations of deviant sexuality will be levelled at her, and the slightest sign of difficulty with any of her 'natural' functions will be a signal to confirm her deviance and for all around to try and force her back into 'natural' motherhood.

Chapter 7

Community and Class

The idea of 'community' is a complex one, in both its popular usage and its sociological one. Thus we hear that an old lady died of starvation because 'the community' did not look after her, that ex-prisoners need 'community care', that X is a 'community school', but in popular usages of this kind the word is hardly ever explained or defined. Sociological interest goes back at least to Tonnies, a German thinker of the last century, who first put the idea into serious academic discourse. Since the Second World War in British sociology the word community is nearly always used to refer to a particular set of research projects – called community studies – which were popular up until the mid-1960s but have now gone out of fashion. Two overviews of the genre are available, by Bell and Newby (1971) who deal with American and European studies as well as the British ones, and Frankenberg (1966) who concentrates on British life. While the lives of women in modern Britain are still focused on home and family the environment in which the home and family exist is an important part of their lives, yet most of the community studies are not very useful for charting the environment of the woman in modern Britain. There are three reasons why the information available is not very useful for this book.

First, the information collected in the heyday of the community study is now probably obsolete, for example, the farmers in Gosforth when Williams (1956) was there were only beginning to come to terms with farm machinery, some still refused to use even the tractor, and the production of, for example, eggs, was still totally unmechanised and unsystematic. Similarly the lives of fishermen operating out of Hull have changed since Tunstall (1972) studied them, and rural Wales (widely documented) has been affected by all kinds of changes. Many of the urban communities have been razed to the ground in slum clearance programmes. More recent data would be valuable.

Secondly, most of the community studies concerned rural areas, particularly in Wales, Scotland and highland or moorland areas in England, nearly all on the western side of the island. Information about the urban areas in general, and the crowded south and east of England in particular, is limited, although that is where most people live. This rural and Celtic bias in the studies is particularly remarkable when one realises that nearly all other areas of British sociology have neglected Scotland, Wales and rural areas for the study of urban problems.

Thirdly, nearly all the community studies were carried out from a structural-functional perspective, and a male viewpoint, even when the researcher was a woman. Frankenberg (1976) has recently castigated all the British studies, including his own in the Welsh border country, for their sexism – arguing that they adopted men's perspectives on the community and down-played women's – as well as for neglecting the class struggle. Thus, for example, women are described as 'gossiping' but men as 'discussing' in the accounts, and women's economic roles are frequently neglected.

Given these three major limitations of the *genre*, it seems hardly likely that any useful information about women's lives can be extricated from the community studies. Yet where women live, in terms of both the actual accommodation and the wider neighbourhood, is a central feature of their lives, because so many of them live and work in the same place. Living spaces are also crucially affected by the other factors which influence women's lives: class, because both housing standards and neighbourhood are class-segregated in Britain; region, because housing conditions and neighbourhood are very different in poor regions from rich ones; race, because the lives of women of different ethnic groups are very different in the different subcultures within Britain. Thus the life of the owner of Mallowfield Hall, Mallowfield, Buckinghamshire, is very different from that of the owner of 10 Acacia Avenue, Smalltown, Surrey, or the tenants of Flat 996, Attlee Court, Vast Estate, or 3 Back Lane, Dockside. Yet the last two will have more in common with each other than either has with the inhabitant of the crofter's cottage, shepherd's cottage, farmhouse or Gypsy caravan. And women in all these places may have more physical freedom than the Pakistani women studied in Bristol by Jeffery (1976) and in Bradford by Khan (1976, 1977), or the Sikh women studied by the Ballards (1977) in Leeds.

It is interesting that there are probably more data on Wales, and on ethnic minorities in large cities, than there are on England, and on 'native' lives in cities and suburbs. Certainly recent data on ethnic groups as diverse as the Poles, the Cypriots and the Chinese are more interestingly presented (Watson, 1977) than anything about the majority of city dwellers. Recent urban sociology in Britain has been more interesting about Sikh women than

'English' ones, and about deviant working-class males than conventional working-class women. This chapter looks at country women first, and then the towns and cities, but draws out common issues.

THE RURAL IDYLL

There has been a strong current of rural nostalgia or romanticism prevalent in British thought ever since the industrial revolution as Williams (1973), Davidoff *et al.* (1976) and Mathieson (1975) have chronicled. This romanticism for country life may have influenced the researchers who headed for rural communities to study them, although the intellectual influence of social anthropology with its developed methods for studying face-to-face societies was also considerable. Some of the studies also show signs of a strong desire to capture vanishing forms of life before they were swept away by the modern world. Whatever their inspiration, the studies of rural life by Arensberg and Kimball (1940), Rees and Davies (1960), Williams (1956, 1963), Littlejohn (1964), Frankenberg (1957) and Emmett (1964) provide fascinating reading, glimpses of a long-vanished past, and, more relevantly here, evidence about the power, economic and political as well as sexual, which can be wielded by women in Britain. This power of women, clear in the rural studies, is completely absent from much later sociology, to its detriment.

The work commonly cited as the first community study in 'Britain' was carried out forty years ago by Arensberg and Kimball (1940) in County Clare, Ireland. As this book is not about Irish women, the data from that classic are not included here. However, one of their central findings was that the farming areas were constantly exporting not only produce, but surplus labour, both male and female, to England. The lives of the Irish 'exiles' in the United Kingdom are not well documented, although myths and prejudices about them abound. The Irish women, married and single, led particularly 'secret' lives, concentrated in certain cities and often forming the backbone of the Catholic churches there. Mary Ciarain's (1973) work is the only systematic study I know. Based on interviews with Irish women living in Manchester, Ciarain found considerable differences in adherence to traditional beliefs, according to the age and the length of stay in England. Whether or not women adhered to segregated gender roles, were devout churchgoers and took jobs outside the home were three of the variables which showed differences between old and young, and long and short stayers. Younger women who had been brought up in Manchester were less likely to adhere to the traditional Catholic values of the rural Irish pattern described by Arensberg and Kimball, and more likely to want their daughters to have an 'untraditional' life. However, many of the women were still attached in important ways to rural Ireland, visiting relations there for all their holidays, and it was possible to find women who had never left Manchester except to travel 'back' or 'home' to Eire. Such women may never have left one particular area of Manchester where a strong Irish 'community' exists.

Given the importance of issues such as sex education, contraception and abortion in politics over the last decade, and the belief among pressure groups such as SPUC and LIFE that Catholic working-class women can unseat Labour MPs whose views on such matters are disapproved of, it seems high time some detailed work on the networks, beliefs and life-styles of Irish women in urban areas was undertaken. The adherence or otherwise of these women to the doctrines of the Catholic Church is actually a crucial political question for the Labour Party, and an interesting one for sociology.

Scottish women, in Scotland or outside it, have been largely unstudied, but the women of rural Wales have been better served by researchers over the years, although most of the data are now rather old. That collected in Herefordshire by Annie Whitehead (1976) in 1971 is more recent, if one can consider rural areas near the border as Welsh. The earlier studies, Alwyn Rees's, *Life in a Welsh Countryside* (1950), the four studies in Rees and Davies (1960), Frankenberg's *Village on the Border* (1957) and Isabel Emmett's *A North Wales Village* (1964) all contain data on women, although Frankenberg (1976) castigates them all for their sexism. The lives of the women in these 'communities' have much in common with women in other rural areas of Great Britain, but there is also a unique feature: the Welsh language and the culture associated with it, paralleled only by Gaelic in the Highlands and Islands of Scotland. (Emmett, 1964, writes feelingly of the centrality of Welsh and its culture.)

Indeed, whether or not Welsh survives may be in the hands of women, although this is not stressed in the Welsh community studies. There is recent research (Williams, 1978) which suggests that mothers play a crucial part in the continuation of the Welsh language. Whether or not children grow up fluent in Welsh and English in homes where Welsh is known seems to depend on a conscious decision by the mother. If she wishes it, the child speaks Welsh, if she is negative or indifferent, it does not. (This is not only a rural issue, of course, because women are crucial to the production of urban Welsh speakers too.) There appear to be two sets of values held by women which are associated with choosing to perpetuate the Welsh language. In the 'professional' classes the women value the intellectual aspects of the maintenance of Welsh, and keep the language alive, while in the unskilled working class Welsh is seen as the language of neighbourliness and lack of snobbery, and is kept alive for local reasons. The women of the intermediate groups seem not to value the cultural or the intellectual aspects of Welsh, and regard themselves as 'above' the Welsh-speaking *hoi polloi*. Here social class and values are more important than rural/urban divisions, although in other ways rural Welsh women may be more like other countrywomen than Welsh townspeople. It would be interesting to see how far the preservation of Gaelic in rural and urban Scotland is in the hands of women, and how far the cultural and linguistic traditions of Chinese, Greek and Turkish Cypriot and Asian families are in the hands of mothers.

Rural Lives

There seem to be seven themes which can be found consistently in all the studies of women's lives in rural areas, whether we examine work done in the 1940s and 1950s in the Cheviots in Scotland (Littlejohn, 1964) or in Cumberland (Williams, 1956) or in North Wales (Emmett, 1964) or the more recent work in Hereford (Whitehead, 1976) and the fenlands (Chamberlain, 1975). The seven themes which recur throughout all the rural studies are:

(1) The unremitting domestic toil
(2) The importance of agricultural work
(3) The shadow of the manor house
(4) The centrality of kinship ties
(5) The hostility to outsiders
(6) The hostility between the sexes
(7) The role of the women in maintaining respectability.

Domestic Toil.   While none of these points is necessarily restricted to rural areas, they are themes which predominate in all the community studies. For example, the older studies describe the endless hours of scrubbing, washing and home cooking which filled women's lives before electricity, mechanisation and convenience foods. The women of County Clare were first up and last to bed, in Llan many women were still cooking on coal or oil stoves, and in Gislea many of the women could still be found in cottages without mains drainage. An 83-year-old woman recalled:

> Life's much easier now for women ... They'd be washing all day sometimes. And the scrubbing. My hands used to be skinned often ... We had to knit father's socks. And make his flannel shirts ... We didn't get meat. My father had the meat ... and we had the onions and gravy. (Chamberlain, 1975, pp. 32–5)

Another of 51 recalled:

> Mum ... made runners and curtains from old sheets and she'd tear

them up and dye them... and we had an open hearth with a pot and a little oil stove ... half-way up was a well, where we got the water . . . Mum used to make rag rugs. And she took in washing too. And charring, the baker had a butcher's shop too, and she used to go up there and they used to give her a shilling ... And she'd have it in meat. (pp. 39–42)

These women were brought up in dire poverty, with the threat of the workhouse over them, but the toil associated with housekeeping was equally great for the more prosperous women. Only the wealthier farm people with servants avoided this kind of domestic labour themselves, and in their houses it was still done by women. The grind of cooking, cleaning, washing and mending would not have been so bad if it had not been for the fact that women also had to engage in a good deal of agricultural work, tasks particularly related to the rural scene. Thus Littlejohn (1964, p. 135) describes the division of labour between the sexes as follows:

the woman... does all the housework, rearing of children, feeding of chickens and milking of cows. The man does the heavy garden work, pig killing and curing as well as his paid job.

Agricultural Work. In Gosforth there was little hired labour on the farms, and where they were run by the family the farmers' wives and daughters worked in the fields during the two harvests, and frequently helped in the milking and in the preparation of food for animals. 'Generally, however, the activities of the women are confined to domestic duties and to the care of poultry and pigs' (Williams, 1956, p. 41). Indeed, Williams says that the eggs and poultry gave women considerable independence financially, although the wife was expected to clothe herself and the adult women of the family and maintain the house from the money. Rees (1950) reported something similar from rural Wales a decade earlier. Neither Williams nor Littlejohn says much about agricultural work done by poor women, although this was, and is, common in the fenland area studied by Chamberlain (1975, p. 93). A woman now in her fifties recalls:

Fourteen I was, when I left school. I won a scholarship to Ely High School, but couldn't go because mother couldn't afford it. Straight away I went to work for a man in the village, for two shillings a day. Weeding and picking flowers, potato-picking down the Burnt Fen.

Many of the older women in Gislea had spent hours gleaning as children, Chamberlain says (1975, p. 91):

Most girls left school early to begin their working life, often with several years' fieldwork experience behind them – gleaning, weeding and herb-gathering was the work of women and children. Several of the village women recall leaving school at the age of eleven, walking five or six miles to 'do' their acre . . .

Chamberlain argues that mechanisation has taken over the men's work on the land, so that men plough, sow, reap, thresh and bind by machines, often all alone. In contrast, she says, the traditional work of women:

has not changed greatly. Flowers for Covent Garden are still grown and have to be weeded and picked by hand. The celery still has to be harvested and the beet cut and singled where a single seed is not used. This type of work is considered 'woman's work' and is poorly paid, seasonal and backbreaking.

In Gislea it is mainly the older women who still do this labouring in the fields, although two younger women Chamberlain interviewed took active parts in rural work. One woman of 23 works on her parents' farm: (1975, pp. 107–8)

In the summer I grow flowers, so in the spring I have to set them, by hand. We have a drill, but it doesn't work very well . . . They need weeding and hoeing. Winter time is taken up by the cattle. I'm in charge of about fifty head . . . I'm solely in charge of the cattle and the flowers, so I don't get any help. But I do other jobs in between, if I have a spare day or two, like picking potatoes and putting them in bags, setting celery plants and weeding them, and I used to single sugar beet . . . In the summertime I have been up at a quarter past seven in the morning . . . and gone out . . . again till it's dark at night . . . We had a field . . . that hasn't access to water . . . and you need to pump it every day. A 150-gallon tank which all has to be pumped out of the ground, so I do it first thing in the morning and then if it's hot I have to go back and do it again in the afternoon . . .

This farmer's daughter loves her farm work. Another fen woman works with the flowers:

We're in partnership with my brother-in-law over the flowers and we take it in turn to pick them, share the work. But that's hard work in the summer, though in the winter I've nothing to do, apart from my own work in the house . . . Summertime, I'm working till ten or eleven at night . . . the weekend we set these dahlias, we start on a Saturday morning at about ten o'clock and it takes us the whole weekend until Sunday evening . . .

The fenlands are largely devoted to arable crops. The other rural studies come from livestock rearing areas, and we do not know if the women of the Cheviots, Cumberland and rural Wales have been stripped of their farm work by mechanised milking parlours, hen batteries and intensive rearing. One would imagine that machinery has made livestock rearing a male preserve, but we do not know about what has happened to the egg money, although Littlejohn (1964) says the practice was declining in Westrigg.

The Shadow of the Manor. The interrelationship between domestic toil and farm work is closely tied in with the 'shadow of the manor'. Nearly all the rural communities studied describe in graphic detail how in the recent past, or even in the 'present', the local upper classes dominated the whole village, but especially the women. In Gosforth, Williams says, 'the older residents of the parish today' could remember the 'opulence' of the mansions, and the deference expected of ordinary people. He quotes one villager: 'When I was a laal lad like, ivverybody had to do their honours to Miss Senhouse and that mak o'folk' (1956, p. 117).

There could be unpleasant economic consequences for the worker who did not conform. Because the gentry controlled work and housing, the 'rude' family could be sacked, evicted and reduced to living on 'haver-meal poddish' (oatmeal porridge). When Williams lived there, Gosforth's big houses had lost their power. Yet the underlying attitudes had not changed. He attributed this to the 'large percentage of adults' who had been 'employed as servants in the "big houses" at one time or another', (p. 119). The most famous part of Williams's analysis of the present-day effects of the 'shadow of the manor' is his study of the leadership roles in the many local activities. He found that the top social class 'led' almost all organisations, men's and women's. One occasion for deference was the cleaning of the church for harvest festival, when eight working-class women did the heavy work while two unmarried 'ladies' decorated the pulpit with flowers. One of the cleaners told Williams later:

It's all very well for them class folks to say the Church needs cleaning, but they make damn sure they don't come and do it themselves . . . That'll be the day when I'm up there draping them flowers all over t'place and them two . . . are scrubbing out. (pp. 103-4)

The volunteer scrubbers had come forward, apparently, because 'they thought people would talk if they didn't' (p. 104).

The real importance of the manor in the past was twofold: the majority of men were employed on the land and the women were employed in domestic service. Thus in Gislea Chamberlain says (1975, p. 20):

> until forty years ago the village was largely controlled by the Coatesworth family. They owned virtually all the land in the village and what local industry there was . . . Most of the work in the village was in agriculture: working for the Coatesworths . . .

Women not in agriculture were probably in domestic service, as they had been in Westrigg (Littlejohn, 1964). Here domestic service had been the only occupation open to girls, and Littlejohn says they were frequently taken from school at 12 to enter service. Westrigg was in the estate of the Duke of Garvel – a pseudonym for one of the wealthy dukes who still own the Scottish borders – who owned all but three of the farms at the turn of the century. As the landlord he was powerful (p. 51):

> The landlord played an active part in farming . . . he could terminate the lease of any farmer . . . The Duke wielded considerable influence in local affairs . . . informants could never give instances of what exactly they meant by saying that 'the Duke was the law up here' or as one put it 'he strode like a lion through the place'.

The power was symbolised in the church where the Garvel pews were reserved 'so that even in the Duke's absence Garvel was always present' (p. 50). The minister was 'a power in the land second to the Duke' (loc. cit.). Deference had to be shown not only to the duke and the minister, by everyone, but the labourers had to show deference to the wealthier farmers. A middle-aged working-class woman told Littlejohn (p. 74):

> When I was a girl we used to curtsey to the ladies, the big farmer's wives. Some of them were just . . . I wan't say what, and I made up my mind if ever I had children I'd never tell them to curtsey to the likes of them.

Yet deferential styles of behaviour by farm workers and their families have not gone from Britain, for Newby (1977a) observed them in Suffolk in the early 1970s. He lodged with a farm worker who lived in a tied cottage and worked for an archetypal 'English Country squire' (Newby, 1977a), as he had done for thirty years. The colonel ran his farm with ten workers and a manager, and was busy with public affairs such as being a magistrate. Newby says that the colonel:

lived in a 'big house' nearly a mile from the Hectors' cottage. Doreen Hector . . . had worked for Mrs. Todd as a domestic before she was married. Both her father and her two brothers worked for Colonel Todd, and they all lived in tied houses nearby.

The colonel was a benevolent employer and his wife gave Christmas gifts to the workers. Although a union man, Newby once 'observed Jack Hector touch his forelock and Mrs Hector bob a quick curtsey' when Colonel Todd was around. The 'paternalism' even included a cricket match between a colonel's eleven and one made up of the farm workers, in which the gentry wore whites, caps and blazers and the workers wore flannels. The shadow of the manor was still looming large in men's and women's lives.

Gislea differs from Newby's part of Suffolk because the Coatesworth family were gone, but the old days were remembered – days when:

A few girls were able to get a 'position 'in the village, either with the Coatesworth family at the Hall or the Red House, or at the Vicarage. But most of the girls . . . had to leave the village. (Chamberlain, 1975, p. 91)

Later Chamberlain quotes an 83-year-old widow who had been in service at the Coatesworth's (p. 99):
Everybody that lived in the village was subservient to them. They got to be . . . They were the owners of the village, really . . . We had good food . . . But we worked hard . . . up at seven o'clock. We had to go to bed at nine, and worked all the while . . . They had wooden stairs from the kitchen up to their landing, what they called the servants' stairs, and they were wood, they got no carpet or anything on it, and I had to scrub those all down, with whitening, to make them white, and she came in one day as I was doing them, and she said, 'You haven't got it out of the corners'. And she made me go and do them all over again, with hot water and a wooden skewer and go in all the corners of the stairs to get them clean.

If the shadow of the manor house, the coming of rural factories, the farm and the home form an economic nexus covering women's labour, the other important feature of their lives is interpersonal relationships. Here the role of kinship ties, the hostility of insiders to outsiders, the hostility between the sexes and the crucial role of women in maintaining respectability form a net of values and beliefs which organise women's lives. The depth, spread and importance of kinship ties has been emphasised in all the rural studies, where the villagers can trace all kinds of links among themselves and use them for all kinds of purposes.

Kinship Ties. In Gosforth, for example, Williams (1956, pp. 74–5) reported a farmer with sixteen close relatives living in other households in the parish, and nine more distant ones, and a woman with blood ties to twenty-seven other households. The farms were nearly all worked by families with little paid labour. 'Neighbour' and 'kin' were overlapping categories in Gosforth, but 80 per cent of householders had relations elsewhere in the parish. Williams points out that the neighbouring person who is *de facto* kin, however distant he really is, is more important than the close blood relation away from Gosforth. The ties of kinship and neighbourhood are used by the men to lend farming equipment, and by the women to mind children and help with shopping. It is, of course, impossible to separate kinship from neighbourliness here, and the important solidarity is 'Gosforth folk' versus 'outsiders'. Similar accounts of the importance of kinship links in social and economic life can be found in all the rural communities, so that in Westrigg, although relations between employer and employee were more 'industrial', the people were bound together by links of mutual obligation and kinship.

Most commentators have suggested that this network of kinship ties is, if not a good thing in itself, a functional part of country life. Whitehead (1976) has rather a different view. In the Herefordshire village that she studied 'male kin form a source of mutual aid and exchange (for tools, garden seeds, shopping for these items, job information, etc.) as do female kin'. Whitehead argues that women are more dependent on these ties than men because they have no workmates, cannot go to the pub and are isolated in their homes. About 25 per cent of the women did not have kin of the same age living near, and these people told Whitehead they were lonely. Although the kinship links were useful for friendship and for domestic help, such as babysitting or coping with the husband while having another baby, Whitehead argues that they have negative connotations for women's lives. While other authors have argued that the network of women acts as a social force to fight male oppression and reinforce women's solidarity, Whitehead doubts this, and argues instead that the women's kinship networks actually reinforce the system of social control over young women. The newly married, and those with young children in particular, have little else but kinship links to rely on, but 'while they may welcome the support and interest in domesticities which the female kin network apparently provides, wives will find its moral censure the more trying because they are more confined within it'.

Whitehead's view is far more negative than those of all the other authors of community studies, who stress the positive aspects of kinship in rural areas. For Williams, Gosforth is given stability and continuity through its kinship system, while in Llan, Emmet (1964) argues that it forms one of the ways in which villagers combine against outsiders. This too is an important part of 'community' studies, the solidarity of the insiders against the wider world.

Hostility to Outsiders. In Frankenberg's Petrediwaith, the Welsh border village, feeling against outsiders was strong. His classic analysis of factions in the village showed how the outsiders were used as scapegoats by the villagers to take unpopular actions and shoulder the blame for 'trouble', quarrels and failures. Littlejohn (1964) reports a somewhat similar event in Westrigg although he analyses it in class terms. There were two branches of the WRI in the parish (Scottish equivalent of the Women's Institute in England and Wales), and in the smaller, breakaway group the following procedure is adhered to (pp. 84–5):

> The members are, like the main one, mostly working class. Every year they elect the same working class woman as president, she invariably refuses office ... They then elect another working class woman, a relative newcomer to the parish, who accepts. The rest openly jeer at her efforts to control the affairs and meetings ... Meanwhile the middle-class secretary 'really' runs the branch.

In Gosforth, Williams found considerable hostility to outsiders, particularly officials from the Ministry of Agriculture and such like. He does not distinguish this hostility's effects on men and women, and all his examples concern men, except one farmer's wife who said no one spoke to her, but all knew her business. Families of incomers without kinship ties who flouted the village's class norms were *socially* invisible, and this must have been much harder for the women than their husbands. The popularity of illegal cock-fighting has something to do with being suspicious of strangers, but Williams does not say whether the women collude in concealing the sport from authority.

In Llan, Emmett (1964) analysed the feuds in local organisations to see if Frankenberg's analysis held true there, and concluded that the position was somewhat different. She argued for an all-consuming Welsh/English hostility, which embraced country/town, worker/boss, insider/outsider and other polarities under the cultural and linguistic label. That is, hostility to outsiders was always expressed primarily in Welsh versus English terms rather than those of class; for example, Emmett says that the villagers of Llan 'saw their troubles in terms of foreign oppression rather than class war' (1964, p. 82) and felt like a colony smarting under economic, linguistic and cultural oppression. The resistance to outsiders was expressed not so much against individuals in the manner Franken- berg describes, but by the poaching of salmon from the rivers 'owned' by the rich English. Emmett says (1964, p. 69): 'anyone who is Welsh goes poaching. When I say anyone, I mean men only, of course.' The women may not actually fish the salmon out of the rivers but the account of poaching shows that women are an important part of the 'poaching culture'. First, the women support the activity, both by eating the fish, and by forming part of the local grapevine which watches all the time for police and bailiffs and records all suspicious movements of the forces of English law and order. Women, as much as men, observe and report their observations. Emmett sees salmon poaching as part of the general anti-English, anti-government, anti-official attitude held by Llan people who adhere to traditional values. She summarises this atti- tude (p. 72):

> If it were forbidden by the Government to grow asparagus, and the chapel were fairly indifferent to the ban, North Welsh people would grow it although few have even heard of, never mind tasted, asparagus; few know it is thought of as a luxury food and probably no one would like it.

The parallels with salmon are obvious.

In Gislea today the attitudes of the fen people about outsiders are equally strong – they are untrustworthy and to be regarded with suspicion. Chamberlain reports (1975, p. 20):

> The villagers were feared...as a tough and unmanageable bunch. Fights and feuds were common and the villagers built their homes with doors that could not be opened from the outside. A few still exist today. Hostility was not reserved for neighbour- ing villages, but was a welcome given to many. For with unem- ployment so high, poaching became a major village occupation and a stranger often meant the law. It took a brave policeman to stop a fight or arrest a man for poaching...

Apparently, too, there were shopkeepers who kept their doors locked, only opening to clients they knew. The village is less iso- lated than it was, although it is hard for the women to leave as public transport is virtually non-existent. For the women left there day after day, the isolation and hostility faced by strangers is con- siderable. Chamberlain says (1975, p. 158):

> There may, in some cases, be a class or regional barrier, but more often than not it is due to the fact that there are very few

places or activities for the women to meet each other unless they are religious.

In fact Gislea has a considerable number of American service families renting houses, but they are socially invisible. They are 'never mentioned'. Even the village girls express no interest in the servicemen (p. 158). Chamberlain quotes 'outsider' women such as Pat Stevens, 'You can feel welcome for a long time and then suddenly you feel you are a stranger' (p. 169). And Laurie Delf who says she 'never belonged' (p. 162). Yet both these women served the village, Pat Stevens in the post office and Laurie Delf in the health centre. Barbara Holman says the women of the village resent her – 'they resent newcomers without a doubt' (p. 166). The wife of the Anglican vicar, Christine Elsegood, has been in Gislea twenty-three years, but says (pp. 119–20):

When we first came here . . . there was a lot of hostility to us, and for the first two years I think I cried almost every night.

The classic example of the active hostility to outsiders and their ideas in Gislea is the affair of the playgroup. A pre-school playgroup started by an outsider ran into trouble with the powerful clique of the old women in the village who tried hard to kill it by a mixture of political power (pressure on the hall committee and parish council) and kinship links (forbidding young kinswomen to take their children to it).

This playgroup issue is unusual in that most of the 'troubles' concerning outsiders discussed in community studies are men's business. The salmon poaching, use of incoming men at the football club in Frankenberg's village and the cock-fighting in Gosforth are all men's work. Yet if Whitehead is correct in her argument that the kinship network serves to exercise social, that is male, control over women, maybe the hostility to 'outsiders' serves the same function? The Gislea women clearly feel their 'stranger' status more than their husbands, and the attacks on the playgroup certainly *serve* to control the young village women although spearheaded by women, not men. But, as Whitehead argues, the older women may collude with the male values because they have a more realistic knowledge of the consequences for 'errant' women. Certainly the hostility between the sexes reported from all the rural areas has harsher consequences for women. They get beaten up, bear the pregnancies and suffer the isolation, while the men do the beating, enjoy the sex and socialise in the pubs. The young female stranger is likely to suffer most from the anti-'outsider' feelings and the hostility between the sexes.

Hostility between the Sexes. Whitehead (1976) describes being on the receiving end of male hostility when living in an isolated cottage outside the parish. One evening:

> in the gathering dust, I received a visit from a group of young men in a van, who shouted and made animal noises and menacing gestures from the track across the stream . . .

The appearance of her father caused them to vanish, but she was later harassed in a more subtle way. An anonymous phone call brought the police to her gate to check on an illegal vehicle, a false charge as it happened. Such anonymous phone calls to the law seemed to be one element in a wider sex war in the parish, used by women against male drinking as well as by men.

Whitehead sets these incidents aimed at her in the context of the general efforts made by young men to control the manners and morals of the parish, and especially its young women. One young mother was 'controlled' although her only 'sin' was taking her children for walks in the woods! A male clique acting as an anti-vice squad had been reported thirty years and more earlier by Alwyn Rees in central Wales, and elaborated later by others. In one case a widow's affair with a younger man was forcibly broken up by a series of vicious acts, such as dropping vermin into the house. The young men in Emmett's (1964) part of Merioneth seem to have lived their leisure time in a similar 'pack', but Emmett only mentions them in the context of visiting sexually available women who have 'a reputation for allowing easy access' to their beds (p. 107). It would be fascinating to know if the widow's affair was resented because she ceased to be available to other members of Rees's village!

In Emmett's village, the sexes lived largely segregated lives, and courtship was kept private. She does not emphasise sexual antagonisms, but says that the men 'have been reluctant to marry' (p. 110), although 'I cannot extend this reluctance to marry to women' (p. 111) suggests a divergent set of perspectives between men and women. The existence of separation and divergence is also apparent in the chapter on law and order in Llan. While Llan men are very unwilling to take each other to court, or even invoke legal sanctions against one another, women did take legal action over paternity against men. This, in an area where the law is in the hands of the 'colonial' English power, suggests considerable hostility between the sexes, or desperation, or the existence of two separate worlds. Another hint of sexual antagonism in Llan is found in Emmett's discussion of women's collusion in salmon poaching where she argues (1964, p. 69) that:

> They would rather their men came in excited from an evening's

sport than lethargic or quarrelsome from an evening's drinking.

In other words, poaching is better than the pub.

The women in Whitehead's village would have understood that only too well, for in that area the men drank in pubs that ignored all the licensing hours and came home unpredictably drunk, quarrelsome and aggressive. The husband's absence from home was the main source of women's dissatisfaction. Many men worked long hours, and while both sexes thought some time in the pub was a man's right, it frequently grew to an amount of time regarded as unreasonable by the wives. Whitehead says:

> Some husbands confined their drinking to the evenings after they had been home . . . to have tea. Others had a drink on the way home, and this could easily turn into an evening's drinking. For some men . . . hours of 'work' not taken up with working were spent in the pub . . . Some young wives found that the marriage they dreamed of . . . turned out to be a succession of evenings spent alone with the television and the baby and the husband's dinner drying up on a plate over a pan of simmering water.

Whitehead goes on to analyse in considerable detail the forms and causes of marital discord and other kinds of sexual antagonism in the village. While 'new' marriages were fraught with public conflict, Whitehead points out that they lasted, in that divorce or permanent breakdown was unknown. (Although it looks as though the women have nowhere to go, because their mothers reinforce the men's customary rights to behave as they like.) The couples whose rows were most visible were those in which the women wanted to see more of their husbands, or go out by themselves. Both these were blows to a man's self-esteem. Whitehead says that as long as the man 'won' quarrels, by staying out, giving her orders and beating her, he was high status, but if the wife started rows with him, succeeded in getting him to babysit, locked him out or did not cook for him, he lost face. The 'troubles' in these young marriages were actually aided and abetted by the clique of men in the pub, and the landlady. For example, she organised darts matches on bingo night, thus provoking severe rows in several homes. The women were quite unable to organise any cohesive efforts against the drinkers, but rather sided with the male value system to force errant women back. The women had no jobs, indeed many had never worked, and so were totally dependent, and were expected to stay home being good wives whatever their men did.

The only other community study which revealed similar structural, or at least deep-seated, hostility between the sexes was the work on a mining town, Ashton, carried out in the 1950s by three men. This study, *Coal Is Our Life*, is still one of the steady best-selling books in social science, although now very out of date. The three men fell into the trap of adopting the perspective on women of the men in their sample rather than actually studying the women themselves. Thus, Dennis, Henriques and Slaughter (1957) see the women as trivial beings who splinter class loyalties and force men to go underground. Frankenberg (1976) summarises this major fault in the research 'The relations of production at work are lovingly and loathingly described; the relations of production in the home and community are ignored with equal determination!' Certainly incidents recorded in Ashton suggest that there is a strong tradition of all men combining to keep women in their place – out of the pub, the club and the betting office, just as Whitehead reports it for Hereford.

Yet, while the hostility between the sexes is so strong in Ashton – or at least the three men say it is – a clear male/female hierarchy is obviously present in the other studies. Thus, of Westrigg, Littlejohn says (1964, p. 127):

Within the working class, male dominance is exemplified in numerous details of social life. For example, husbands sometimes censure wives in front of children. Visitors . . . are usually offered the fireside chair the wife normally occupies while the husband stays put in his. If other men are in the house, the wife must either remain silent or join in the men's conversation which always centres round male topics . . .

Littlejohn thought the gap between the sexes was narrowing 'and the male is becoming less dominant' (p. 135). This suggestion opens up the wider debate about changing patterns of family life, which are discussed further in this chapter.

Williams reports that in Gosforth women have 'inferior status' in 'many farm families' and illustrates this as follows (1956, p. 150):

The patriarchal organization found on so many farms permits the farmer and his sons to leave home every night without question: the farmer's wife, who is too busy for social calls during the greater part of the day, would not think of asking her husband to take care of the house and the younger children while she went out in the evening, except in such circumstances as a neighbour's illness.

Yet later Williams says that 'elements of conflict' have been introduced into such families because farmers' wives and daughters have met townswomen at the WI, whist drives, and so on. It would be interesting to know if the antagonism related by Whitehead grew up in Gosforth too. Certainly the drinking existed, and as an all-male activity for Gosforth people: 'most folk don't like lasses in pubs, and they don't go' (p. 135). Women may drink at home, but avoid the pub. Williams says drinking has declined since the 'good old days', but the pubs have the same kind of male age groups attached to them as the one described by Whitehead.

Whitehead argues that this sexual antagonism in Herefordshire is only a *local* manifestation of the oppression of women by all men in all areas of British life. Whether or not one wants to accept this, all the community studies in areas of Britain where women's labour is not essential as a provider of food show the segregation and mutual suspicion between the genders. The recent study of farm workers (male farm workers, that is) by Howard Newby (1977*a*) found that in Suffolk, although over 70 per cent of his sample were married, only 20·6 per cent of the wives were working in regular employment (p. 353):

> Notwithstanding their occasional employment as casual labour on farms for fruit-picking, potato-lifting, etc., most wives were therefore economically dependent upon their husbands.

Newby links this lack of work for women outside the home to a range of factors, including a patriarchal family structure. He points out (p. 355) that:

> Those workers living on patriarchally run farms therefore tend to move back and forth between one patriarchal institution and another, the difference being that in one he is exercising traditional authority, while in the other he is subjected to it.

The women, in turn, are rarely free of such authority structures, and are *always* subordinate members of them. Those women who had jobs outside the home were predominantly in domestic service (41·2 per cent), in shop work (14·7 per cent) or food processing (14·7 per cent) or in agricultural labour (11·8 per cent): all occupations which reinforce traditional subordination of women (see Chapter 6).

The source of hostility between the genders seems to be partly the economic dependence of women – hostility because women are unskilled and unable to support themselves – and partly male fears about control over female sexuality. However, even in subcultures where suspicion and hostility between the genders is common, there is a complicating factor in the relationship between men and women based on women's role in reproducing labour power. Several recent commentators such as Gardiner (1976) have argued that complex industrial societies *need* domestic labour to refresh and refurbish workers, as well as women to bear and rear a new generation of workers. Women's domestic work is seen as essential to keep complicated societies functioning. At the level of individual families, the woman's role in home maintenance produces a 'peculiar' male dependence on women.

Maintaining Respectability. Throughout many of the community studies, the researchers show that it is the women who are crucial in maintaining respectability. The dividing line between 'rough' and 'respectable' working-class homes is a Maginot line personed by housekeepers and mothers. This is captured most vividly by Littlejohn (1964, p. 123) when he says of Westrigg:

> The wife can have ... a great deal of responsibility for maintaining [the family's] status and can be responsible for its downfall into the non-respectable 'slum class'. A consideration of the criteria which mark off the two classes makes this clear, for the differences between them concern only household economy, which is largely the wives' affair. In the working class the family is expected to use a table cloth or oilcloth and not always eat off bare boards; to use earthenware and china dishes and not enamelled tin ones; to have at least one cooked meal a day; to have a clean outfit of clothes for public appearances; and not to get into debt with tradesmen.

Littlejohn says that there could never be more than one or two families of the rough kind in the parish at any given time, but when one fell into the 'rough' style of life, it was recognised by everyone, and could well be blamed on the wife. He quotes an example of Westrigg censure (p. 124):

> She was an awful creature. They left as she owed too much all round ... She used to be after everybody here. She'd ask for anything – clothes, money, food ... she used to send the bairns for them ... oh it was terrible, every time you looked out the window and saw one of the bairns you sat quaking. She never cooked anything ... bread and jam it was, just bread and jam.

Littlejohn amplifies this by saying that the neighbours reckoned her husband a pleasant man with moderate habits; 'it was her expenditure on cigarettes and beer for herself that left the family so badly equipped'.

The control of women over family finance, and particularly payments to tradespeople, is characteristic of marriage where the gender roles are kept separated, with each spouse having his or her own responsibilities. For example, Isabel Emmett found that in Llan the men gave women their 'housekeeping' money, and family finances were left in their care, especially shopping and paying the mail order 'clubs'. Thus in Llan too, presumably, a thriftless woman can run her family into debt, as in Westrigg. Much more recently Howard Newby spent six months living in a Suffolk farmworker's home of the 'respectable' variety, where the next-door neighbours were 'decidedly rough ... compared with the respectability of the Hectors'. The house was much more sparsely and poorly furnished and considerably less clean and tidy (Newby, 1977b). However, in this case the family had been impoverished by the man's drinking rather than Mrs Davies's poor management. For when arguing that the difference between a comfortable and respectable working-class home and an uncomfortable and rough one is dependent on the woman's skills and budgeting, it is important to remember that this is only so when the wage packet is coming into the home regularly. As Leonore Davidoff (1976) has acidly pointed out, a woman who has no male breadwinner, or a man who does not provide any money, cannot maintain respectability however 'good' a house-keeper she may be.

However, if we accept Davidoff's point, it is still the case that, given constant amounts of money coming into a home, the woman maintains its respectability. This has been argued for North American urban homes by Dorothy Smith (1973), and a similar point can be made about the urban sociology of Great Britain. Certainly, as we move from truly rural material towards the urban data, studies in small towns such as the mining community of Ashton (Dennis et al., 1957) show this phenomenon. In Ashton the women have responsibility for budgeting expenditure on food, clothes and furniture, and a comfortable, debt-free home for a miner is only possible if he hands over a reasonable sum and she uses it wisely. The same pattern is found in the studies of 'real' urban areas, whether the old inner city neighbourhoods or the newer estates, and this role for women provides one continuity in women's lives which transcends the 'urban'/'rural' distinction.

This role for women, common to town and country, is paralleled by continuities in other areas of women's lives. If we reconsider the seven themes used to examine women's lives in rural areas, most of them can equally be said to apply to the lives of urban women. The themes of unremitting domestic toil, the importance of kinship, the hostility to outsiders, the centrality of class and the hostility between the genders can all be found in the urban studies. This is because many aspects of women's lives in modern Britain are not fundamentally affected by the rural or urban setting, because they are more firmly bounded by domestic ideology and social class. This will become clear as we turn to the lives of urban women.

URBAN LIFE IN BRITAIN

Much of the available data on urban life in Britain is as badly out of date as the rural material already discussed. The studies of housing estates are at least twenty years old, those of slums (Paneth, 1974; Kerr, 1958) are older. More recent work in urban sociology has neglected women completely, as Lofland (1975) has argued. The material we do have has been collected mainly in the London area, mainly on the working class or on immigrant groups, and mainly on men and their work. Thus a typical study of urban life published recently, Hill (1977) on the dockers, studied London dock workers and focused on their work lives. Their wives were not included, so the data on home lives was given only from the male perspective. The only work done recently on urban women has been carried out by women in studies of housework (Oakley, 1947a and b) and outwork (Hope et al., 1976), with the exception of Young and Willmott's *The Symmetrical Family* (1973).

Making use of *The Symmetrical Family* is a hazardous proceeding. The book has been castigated by professional sociologists such as Runciman (1973) Frankenberg (1976) and Bell (1974), Firth (1974) and Harris (1974), although the non-specialist press received it warmly enough. While accepting the sociological criticisms of the book, I want to make some use here of the data, because they are relatively recent, focus on women, and deal with urban slums, suburban areas and commuter towns. It is not easy to detach these data from the Young and Willmott theory, nor to know how far they could be applied to areas of Britain other than the south-east of England, such as Cardiff, Manchester, Glasgow, Aberdeen, Newcastle or Leeds. Before using any of the data it is necessary to examine the theory of the book and the criticisms of it, so that the data can be seen in perspective.

Young and Willmott centre their argument on something they call the principle of stratified diffusion. This is a theory that innovations in social and family life-styles found among the upper-middle class today will be gradually diffused down to the lower orders. Human social history can thus be seen as a procession marching past fixed landmarks, with the upper-middle class as the vanguard and the lower classes at the rear. A significant change in life-style, whether possession of a washing machine, or the decision to have a small number of children, or go to wife-swapping parties, thus begins with the vanguard, but will eventually become normal among the people at the rear. This is rather like the argument found in the mass media that what is happening in California in 1979 will be happening in Wakefield in 1999, and because it is pure futurology it is very hard to prove or dismiss. Young and Willmott are very keen on their principle, however, and apply it particularly to changes in gender relationships in the family over the last two hundred years. Briefly, they suggest that the family has gone through three stages and is now about to evolve into a fourth stage which is appearing now in the vanguard of the great procession. Stage One was usual before the industrial revolution, when the family was extended rather than nuclear and served as a unit of economic production as well as consumption. Stage Two came with the growth of factories, and took adults and children out to paid work and destroyed the extended family. Stage Three took women out of the workforce back into the home, put children into schools, and produced a couple who spent some time together inside the home. Stage Four, a newly emerging pattern, consists of women returning to careers, while men became even more home-centred. In Stage Four, the symmetrical family, each adult has two careers, one in paid work and the other domestic.

Thus Young and Willmott are arguing that their new kind of family – the symmetrical Stage Four – will soon spread down the social hierarchy to become a common pattern. The symmetrical family of Young and Willmott has affinities to the 'dual-career family' studied by the Rapoports (1976), yet there are differences. The Rapoports have actually found some examples of dual-career families to study, yet make no such sweeping claims for the future dominance of the form; Young and Willmott have failed to find any symmetrical families in their study, yet claim not only that it exists, but that it will sweep Britain! Critics of the Young and Willmott thesis have not only queried the theory, and the findings of the survey on which the book is based, but have also suggested that it is sexist as well (Frankenberg, 1976). While all these serious criticisms are amply justified, there are useful and usable data about the lives of urban women in the south-east of England buried in the book, which can be extracted and reinterpreted. Indeed, using the themes already mentioned at the opening of this section – the centrality of class, the unremitting nature of domestic toil, the importance of kinship and hostility to outsiders and between the genders – the data provided by Young and Willmott do not support the growth of symmetry within the family but the reverse!

Of course, Young and Willmott are not entirely blinded by their optimism about symmetry, and even they found that class differences were large, and affected all areas of work and domestic life. Most of the examples they give refer to men, however, as in this typical passage about relations between class and space allocation. They collected information on the space controlled by a machinist, an accounts clerk and a manager in one London furniture company (1975, p. 43).

The manager had a London house of about 4,600 square feet, a cottage in Sussex of 2,500 and an office of 600 (or 900 if his secretary's suite was added in), making some 8,000 square feet whose entrances and exits he controlled. An accounts clerk had a suburban house of 950 square feet, and an office 'space' of 150, making 1,100 in all, while a machinist had a flat of 550 feet and a workspace of 150, or 700 in all. Judged by this ready reckoner, the manager had seven times more prestige than the clerk or eleven times more than the machinist.

While this is an interesting, concrete, example of class differences in the London area, it is also very sexist. Note that the secretary is treated as a possession of the manager, and that none of the men's wives and children is apparently a joint controller of any of these spaces. Man is truly a territorial animal here!

Class is a central factor in the lives of urban women, not because there is still the shadow of the manor hanging over them, but because class considerations determine where they live, how much they live in, how long they live and how far they have any control over their lives. Thus Young and Willmott's interviewers found in Deptford 'Miss [sic] Fernando from Trinidad'. She lived with three children on £12 per week, paying £4 rent for two rooms in a house shared with three other families and fourteen single men. Her only heating was an oil stove, and she was too disabled ever to leave the building (1975, p. 60). An English-born couple in Acton were little better off. Forced back from Harlow New Town by unemployment, they lived in four rooms over a shop. They had no bathroom, and one room was unusable because 'You can smell the damp as soon as you go into the room'. (1975, p. 63.) With four children under 11 this woman was unable to work, and her husband brought home £18 a week. In complete contrast are the lives of the sample drawn from the Institute of Directors. Here no wives were actually seen by the researchers, but some idea of their lives can be gained from data provided by their husbands. This sample of 190 men all earned £5,000 per annum or more, whereas less than 2 per cent of the main sample did. Eighty-eight per cent 'of the wives had servants, living in or out, and practically all had had some help when their children were young' (p. 258). Only 10 per cent of these women worked outside their homes for money, but all lived in comfort. Many had two or more homes, and there were boats, swimming pools and tennis courts in the family. These women did not, however, have their husbands. Most were away for twelve hours in the day, and often away on trips. These wives were in positions similar to the wives of trawlermen studied in the 1950s by Tunstall (1972) where they had to become used to frequent absences.

Between these extremes were many families in which women

had tolerable accommodation and plumbing, but nothing approaching luxury. In her research on housewives in the London area, Ann Oakley (1974*a* and *b*) suggests that average living conditions for a working-class woman are of the following order:

> Joan Hubbard, an ex-shop assistant married to a toolmaker. She has two children aged four and two years, and lives in a privately rented unfurnished flat. It has two bedrooms, a kitchen, a bath and inside lavatory, and one living room, and is within five minutes' walk of the shops. The Hubbards have access to a small garden, but they have no running hot water . . . Joan Hubbard has a single tub washing machine . . . a vacuum cleaner and a fridge.

The middle-class women were likely to be better housed and equipped, and Oakley mentions one housewife with three children in a four-bedroomed, centrally heated house. This woman had a wide range of domestic tools, a daily help and use of a car.

Domestic Toil
The social class of the woman also affects a whole range of other aspects of her life, which are detailed in the other chapters of this book. Here I want to move from the class differences in housing and living conditions on to consider the theme of unremitting domestic toil which, like class, unites the urban and the rural woman. The omnipresence of domestic work is already apparent from the material on class differences already presented on urban women. Whatever class women are in, they seem confined by *responsibility* for running the home. Even the rich wives of Young and Willmott's 190 directors were responsible for child-rearing and housekeeping, and they received little practical help from their husbands. While servants might do the work of house and garden, they were expected to supervise, maintain high stanrards and cope with any problems. 'I haven't time to think about domestic things' (p. 258) and 'you had to have a woman who could cope with her business' (p. 259) were typical male comments. The *Observer* (4 June 1978) carried a discussion of such women, and interviews with some of them. Katherine Whitehorn commented that such women:

> are, in fact, a living contradiction to their label which says they are dependent. They cope alone, they get used to making all the decisions from house plants to play schools . . .

Of course, comparing such women with single-parent families such as the Trinidadian mentioned earlier shows clearly that the responsibility is very pleasantly cushioned for the rich woman. Oakley (1974*a*) points out that even among the Rapoports' dual-career families the *responsibility* for housework and child care is firmly located as the female's, and in ordinary families the women are even more rigidly locked into domesticity. In Oakley's sample the amount of housework ranged from forty hours per week to over a hundred hours, and men did very little. Oakley found only six husbands who took a large part in housework (two working class and four middle class), and ten who had high participation in child care. In contrast, twenty-four men took little part in housework, and eighteen little in child care. Oakley points out that the very language used by her sample to describe their husbands' participation in housework – typically 'he *helps* me with *my* work' – shows neatly where the responsibility lies.

Oakley's sample were nearly all full-time housewives. Such women are increasingly rare. By 1977, 50 per cent of married women were working or seeking paid work outside the home (*Social Trends, 1977*). We lack accurate data on how far women in paid work are given more domestic help, or how far hours of housework are reduced. Young and Willmott (1975, p. 111) found that women with full-time jobs put in more hours of work (domestic plus paid) than women with part-time jobs, who in turn put in more hours than men. The men worked longer hours outside the home than anyone else, but did far less domestic work than women, who put in three hours a day in the week and five on Saturdays and Sundays when in full-time work, and five and six hours if in part-time work. However, they found that full-time housewives averaged only 45·5 hours' work in the home, which seems very low compared with Oakley's findings, so one may doubt their category 'work'. Meals, for example, were not included, although feeding children is actually part of child-rearing, and so on.

Young and Willmott's sample included a good many women engaged in part-time work (320) of whom many were mothers of children under 16. These women included several outworkers, and some on shiftwork of various kinds. Working part time was frequently possible because of help from kin. Thus, an office cleaner got up at 5.10 a.m., worked from 6 a.m. to 8.30 a.m. and then fetched her daughter from her mother to take her to school, and a part-time secretary leaves her children with either her mother or mother-in-law. This economically essential child-minding service is one of the central ways in which the ties of kinship are important in urban areas.

Kinship Ties
Young and Willmott (1957) brought to public attention the importance of kinship ties in an urban area in their study of Bethnal Green in the 1950s. Their main sample of forty-five couples had, on average, thirteen relations within the borough, and the family

network was used to get work, and houses, as well as forming the most important group for leisure activities. In particular, Young and Willmott made great play with the mother–daughter tie, particularly when the daughters were married with children. Marriage and child-bearing segregate the sexes and reinforce the ties between women. While generations of subsequent commentators have accepted this analysis, few have pointed out that the mother–daughter solidarity may have an economic base. Where there are very restricted child care facilities, a mother who needs to work must be able to rely on kin to care for her children. Even after they are at school, they may need to go to Gran's for tea after school, and anything other than close relations with Gran could cause economic as well as emotional disruption for many women. The family is a unit of production – children are produced – and kin are an important part of that production process. This solidarity for women with other female members of their families has been reported more recently than Young and Willmott in Swansea (Rosser and Harris, 1965; Barker, 1972) and in the London area by Oakley (1974a). The existence of female kinship group solidarity has been widely accepted as a fact of working-class life.

Two sorts of women are seen as deprived of this female kin support in urban areas, the geographically mobile middle-class woman and the dweller on the new housing estate. Studies of middle-class families are rarer than those of working-class life, but Bell's (1968) work in Swansea on middle-class lives would suggest that kinship links are strong, but not so sex-segregated. The dual-career families in the Rapoports' work were as dependent on family members for child care as anyone in Bethnal Green, but until we have more systematic information it is hard to know how far middle-class women are without support of female kin available to working-class women. If they do lack such support, they may also be freer, for Whitehead (1976) argues that the young women were kept in order by older female kin, who refused to support them if they rebelled against traditional patterns. Women's lives on estates are slightly better documented than middle-class women's but not much.

When Frankenburg (1966) reviewed British community studies there were $3\frac{1}{2}$ million British householders on council estates, and an unknown number on private estates. Frankenberg discussed several studies of life on estates in Liverpool, Sheffield, the midlands and outer London. The general pattern was for traditional kinship links to break down, or change their character, because of the physical distance between the new estate and the old neighbourhood. Where kin can be reached, it is usually only at weekends in a formal way, where constraints on dress, behaviour and time operate very differently from the rules governing 'popping in'. What we have on estates is very limited, and now very dated, apart from popular journalism about depression in housewives, vandalism and attacks on the vulnerable old, ill and alien. Data are needed on old-established estates to see if neighbourhood and kinship links have developed, and on newer estates to see if the isolation of the 1950s is being repeated in the 1980s. Until we have them, it is hard to know how far urban women's lives are lacking in 'community spirit'.

There is an equivalent lack of data on women's perceptions of 'outsiders' in urban areas, which are far less well understood than such feelings in rural Britain. Data are urgently needed on such questions as the extent to which women reject people of other races, colours, creeds and classes, or are merely suspicious of strangers. There are probably anti-English feelings in Welsh cities as strong as those in Emmett's Llan, and equally strong feelings in Scotland. Who and what constitute an 'outsider' to the various subcultures in Britain is an uncharted territory.

The hostility between the genders highlighted by Whitehead (1976) is probably as strong in many urban milieux as it is in rural Here-fordshire, but again we lack data. The Young and Willmott thesis of increasing symmetry is obviously incompatible with such segrega-tion and mutual suspicion, so the issue really turns on how far sex roles are becoming more symmetrical. Oakley (1974a) argues strongly that Young and Willmott are misguided, and prefers to follow work by Barbara Harrell-Bond (1969). Harrell-Bond suggests that male and female roles in marriage cannot be seen as segregated or joint in a simple one-dimensional way, but need to be viewed separately in four areas of the marriage: money, leisure, child care and housework. This makes far more sense of contradictory data, but analysing the information in various surveys shows that there are still many women living in segregated relationships. Once attitudes and actual behaviour are also separated, the vision of the symmetrical family vanishes. While many couples believe that the man *would* do domestic tasks, they do not actually undertake them. Oakley found that half her working-class women had husbands who took little part in child care or housework, and occupied very dif-ferent, and highly segregated spheres. Hostility and incomprehension between the genders as acute as anything found by Whitehead is equally common in Oakley's London sample. For example, one woman was so heavily responsible for financial matters that she had to make 'payment for her husband's driving fines, and these have amounted to £114 over a two year period' (1974a, p. 144). This is a far cry from Young and Willmott's world, where no one actually incurs fines, and the withholding of money from wives is seen as a legacy of the long-vanished Stage Two family.

Invisible Women
In the absence of data from urban Britain about the changing roles

of men and women, it seems sensible to suspend judgement on the extent to which gender roles are becoming less segregated in any of the four areas. Hill's (1977) data on London dockers argue they are, Oakley's (1974a) on housewives that they are not. However, the real problem is the invisibility of women in urban sociology, which has resulted in a chronic lack of recent data. Lyn Lofland (1975) has produced a major indictment of American urban sociology which is equally true of the British work. Lofland suggests that the portrayal of women in urban sociology is akin to the image of the butler in the classic detective story. Just as the large country house has an efficient butler as part of the scene, who may discover the body and take some part in the plot, so urban sociology has women as essential but passive and subsidiary characters. Such characters are part of the stage set, but not really part of the action. Thus in urban studies women are commonly described as reflecting the dominant culture, but *never* as creating or determining it. So, for America, Lofland says: 'There is nothing in urban sociology on women quite comparable to the finely textured, close-grained, empirically loving portrayal' of male worlds in such books as *Tally's Corner* (Liebow, 1967) or *Street Corner Society* (Whyte, 1955).

Lofland argues that the treatment of women as part of the scenery rather than as actors can be traced to the sex of the researchers, the policy of funding bodies and the emphasis on 'community' studies in urban sociology. The first of these three points is simply made: most researchers have been men. In many of the urban subcultures studied it is simply not possible for a male researcher to talk to, spend time with and observe women. Lofland quotes researchers who found that it was not possible to interview women in their homes without endangering the good reputations of respectable wives, and those who found they just did not have the ability to engage in formal conversations with women. Further, there are subcultures where no women could be alone with unrelated males under any circumstances, such as the Muslim families studied in Bristol by Jeffery (1976) and in Bradford by Khan (1976), among Turkish Cypriots, and probably also among many Catholic groups. No accurate knowledge about the lives of women in urban milieux is likely until women researchers study them. For example, researchers on male urban adolescents such as Parker (1974) and Willis (1977) have been forced into relating to women in the same manner as the males they were studying, because any other role and perspective would result in physical aggression and the abrupt termination of the study. The perspective of the women in the same areas cannot be obtained by a young man living with the neighbourhood males, but only by a young woman living with them.

On the issue of funding, Lofland argues that the fund-givers are usually interested in male troublemakers, particularly black males, juvenile delinquents and skid-row alcoholics, and hence research into these groups is funded. The only women in urban areas who are seen as 'trouble' are prostitutes, and the American urban studies of women focus on them, and on families headed by women. 'Ordinary' women are not a social problem, and so not worth studying. The same points can be made about British funding agencies, in that they too are likely to be interested in social problems, rather than the normal, invisible woman.

Lofland's third point is perhaps the most interesting, and certainly the least obvious. She argues that the ambiguities of the term 'community' have led to the social invisibility of women. Briefly, Lofland argues that when the early American researchers in urban areas, who had *expected* to discover social disorganisation and a 'breakdown' of 'community', found organisation, rules and tightly knit neighbourhoods, this blinded them to other salient factors. Thus 'like good bloodhounds, armed with the scent of the community model', male urban sociologists went out researching in environments which supported the community model. Thus, Lofland argues, the fact that three of the most famous studies were done in traditional Italian-American areas with rigidly segregated sex roles has passed without comment. In these Italian areas women are likely to be unemployed, and confined to housework – invisibly contained indoors. There is a distinct lack of work on women who do go out to work, and on those public places where women congregate. We have ethnographies of bars, street corners and billiard halls, but not of shops, beauty parlours, coffee and tea rooms, or bingo halls. Lofland actually argues that the lives of affluent women in suburbs are less geographically restricted than their husbands', who shuttle between home and work, because the women move more widely around their neighbourhoods. This last observation seems particularly American, because life is certainly not *perceived* in this wide-ranging way by British suburban women; but we have no studies to confirm or deny Lofland's case. The invisibility of women is, however, acutely observed.

Chapter 8

Power, Politics, Leisure and Religion

Rocking the Cradle or Cradling the Rock?

> *Plaid* and Liberal mothers seem to have had more political influence on their children than Liberal and *Plaid Cymru* fathers. (Madgwick *et al.*, 1973, p. 223)

The grouping of topics in this chapter may, at first, seem bizarre. There are two good reasons for discussing politics and religion together, especially in a book on women. First, there was a traditional link in British politics between party and religion, which has vanished from much of England, but still holds in the Celtic regions. Until the 1930s Anglicans were Conservative, Nonconformists were Liberals, and the Labour Party was associated with atheism. Political and religious beliefs were entwined in ways which make discussing them together very sensible. Secondly, the political and religious systems in modern Britain systematically deny women power officially, yet rely heavily on the labour of women, given voluntarily and in their 'free' time, to continue functioning. This use of female leisure to sustain a political and religious order from which they are otherwise excluded leads naturally into a discussion of the relations between leisure and power in modern Britain. This chapter opens with a demonstration of the *powerlessness* of women in modern Britain, and then moves through discussion of the political and religious systems to an analysis of leisure.

The chapter begins with a discussion of what groups in Britain are powerful, and what groups form the British elite. Women are shown to have little formal power, in that they control little wealth and are not part of any of the elites who control British life. Indeed women have not only been excluded from the corridors of power in the past, but are considered fundamentally unworthy to join them in the future. In addition, the chapter shows how the absence of women members of, or recruits to, powerful and elite groups in Britain has not been noticed, far less commented upon or explained, by researchers studying elites, politics, law or religion. Yet, as the chapter goes on to argue, the British woman who is active outside the home spends much of her time and effort sustaining the political and religious order by her voluntary effort. Thus women form the backbone of the systems of social control in modern Britain while they are quietly but firmly excluded from participating in them at any but the most lowly levels. This chapter looks first at elites, wealth and power in Britain; then at the political system; then the religious order; and finally at how women use their leisure.

ELITES AND POWER IN BRITAIN

Sociologists have generally devoted far more time and energy to studying the poor, the deprived, the criminal and the downtrodden groups in society rather than the rich, the well endowed and the successful. This is partly because of the historical development of the subject, with its concerns of preventing social upheaval and promoting social welfare, but also because the powerful are less accessible for study. Rich, powerful people can protect their privacy and refuse to be studied in ways that the poor cannot. There is also a peculiar brand of inverse snobbery among social scientists which regards all research on middle- and upper-class groups as 'irrelevant' or 'self-indulgent'. Thus it is considered more important, or respectable, or correct, to study working-class groups. This means we know more about working-class boys than public school boys, more about coal miners than members of the National Coal Board, about dockers than members of the National Docks Board, and more about farm workers than large land-owners. Yet, as Giddens (1976) had cause to point out in an article on 'The rich', the most traditional elite group – the aristocracy – still control not only great wealth but large areas of land and hence enormous numbers of houses, farms and tenancies. Giddens began his article with the engagement between the Duke of Roxburgh and Lady Jane Grosvenor (a daughter of the Duke of Westminster). The groom inherited 60,000 acres of Scotland as part of an estate valued at £2½ million, while the Grosvenor family controlled 300 acres of central London and a £300 million fortune. These two young aristocrats (aged 21 and 22) had considerable power, both directly controlling land and indirectly via the property market. Yet the Duke of Roxburgh's Scottish estate is relatively small. John McEwan (1975), writing in *The Red Paper on Scotland*, says that no accurate register of land-ownership in Scotland has been produced since 1874, when 106 people owned half Scotland. He has attempted to do a survey of acreage and ownership and concludes that 6½ million acres out of 9,985,300 are owned by 340 private companies or families; 140 individuals or private companies own half the Highlands and Islands; four people each own half a million acres, ten own 1 million, fifty-six own over 3 million. He has produced a list of large land-owners in the five countries of the Highlands and Islands, Sutherland, Ross and Cromarty, Inverness, Argyll and Perthshire which included the following large estates: the Wills family (tobacco), 193,700 acres; Duke of Atholl, 130,000; Duke of Sutherland, 123,800; Duke of Westminster, 120,800; Cameron of Lochiel, 97,600; Vestey family (meat), 93,100; Earl of Seafield, 86,600; Col Whitbread, 80,000; Lord Lovat, 80,000; and the Duke of Argyll, 73,400. This, being based on the Highlands and Islands, does not take into account the large holdings in the Scottish borders, where the Dukes of Roxburgh, Buccleuch and Hamilton have large estates. McEwan's list is interesting, though, because it shows how some of the largest land-owners are families who made money in industry and commerce who have opted to 'invest' in a very traditional manner, in grouse moors and deer stalking. In such ways, as Giddens points out, do the newly rich in Britain become assimilated to the life-style of the traditional aristocracy. He comments on the desire of those who make money to acquire the life-style of the traditional elite:

> Here we find the strength of the Achilles heel, according to one's point of view, of the wealthy in Britain: the traditional search to attain the public esteem and the social honour that the accumulation of wealth alone cannot bring.
> This is how the life-style of the country gentleman comes to be sustained without serious signs of disintegration. The old money still for the most part absorbs the new, and still normally at one generation removed.

Sociologists have paid very little attention to this traditional way of life among large land-owners. Howard Newby's (1977a) study of land-owners in East Anglia is the only sociological account of the country lives of the rich, and we have no parallel studies of their urban lives. One is thrown back on to accounts drawn from public sources – such as reference books and newspapers – which are often produced by the rich themselves and are therefore not an unbiased source of data. The lives of the women are less well known than those of the men, who are, conventionally, active in the City or the House of Lords, and may make public pronouncements. Except in times of family crisis, such as the Argyll divorce case, the women live very private lives, and no sociologist has bothered to try to collect data on them.

Woman (3 July 1978) offered a rare glimpse into the lives of aristocratic British women when it followed up the six women who had been maids of honour at the Coronation in 1953. The magazine commented that 'some had lived quietly, others have been unable to avoid the headlines', and it is the former who typify the invisible life-style of the large land-owning families in Britain. The six were Lady Jane Heathcote-Drummond-Willoughby, Lady Rosemary Spencer Churchill, Lady Mary Baillie-Hamilton, Lady Moyra Hamilton, Lady Anne Coke, and Lady Jane Vane-Tempest-Stewart. They were respectively daughters of the Earl of Ancaster, the Duke of Marlborough, the Earl of Haddington, the Duke of Abercorn, the Earl of Leicester and the Marquis of Londonderry. All but one of them have married, all have country houses and several London homes as well, and most are described as fond of riding and hunting. Two married men with fortunes from industry or commerce (one a brewer, the other from shoes and property), illustrating the way in which the aristocracy has brought in money from respectable newly rich families. None is described as active in any charitable or political field, and only one in a commercial enterprise. *Woman* would not want its readers to envy such wealthy women, or wonder why the Drummond family own a fortune 'running into millions', so we are told of endless tragedies in all their lives, with dead brothers, divorces, suicides and drug-addict children, to show that the rich are not happy. It is, however, a serious criticism of British sociology's neglect of women that there are no academic data on women such as these.

If the aristocracy, and the very wealthy who live similar aristocratic lives, have not been adequately researched, the situation with regard to other groups of powerful people in Britain is little better. There is a shortage of adequate academic information on the elites in the economic, religious and educational spheres, as well as the landed gentry. Indeed, sociologists have devoted so little attention to powerful groups in Britain apart from the political parties that there is little or no consensus about who is to be considered 'elite' and who is not. Giddens (1974) drew together a series of relevant writings and suggested a range of elite groups in contemporary Britain, together with their administrative support and their recruitment sources. The basic categories of elite and their pools of recruits are shown in Table 8·1, which is adapted from Giddens. It is clear from the table that Giddens is distinguishing several spheres of British life with different elite groups, some of which overlap, but others do not. Thus the religious elite may overlap with the 'active' peers, but the armed services elite are not allowed to, for generals, unlike bishops, cannot sit in the House of Lords. Giddens separates the economic sphere, the political system, the judiciary, the civil service, the trade unions, the military, the religious sphere, the mass media and the educational elites. He does not go into any detail about the reasons behind his choice, so that we are not told why only the Anglican Church in England is considered elite and the Moderator of the Church of Scotland, for example, is not. However, the categories in Table 8·1 probably encapsulate a common view

Table 8·1   *Elite Groups and Their Potential Recruits*

Category	Elite	Recruits from
Economy		
Largest industrial firms	Directors	Senior management
	Large shareholders	
Large banks,	Directors	Other elites
insurance,	Large shareholders	
finance houses		
Nationalised industry	Directors	Other elites
	Board members	
Political System		
Monarchy	Monarch	Royal Family
House of Commons	MPs	Candidates
House of Lords	'Active' peers	'Passive' peers
Judiciary	Judges	Barristers
Civil Service		
Home	Under-secretary	Administrative
	and above	clans
Foreign	Officials, grades	Officials, grade 5
	1 and 2	and above
Trade Unions	TUC Council members	TUC delegates
Military	General Officers and	Colonels and above
	equivalent ranks	+ equivalent ranks
Religious	Church of England	Assistant bishops
	archbishops and	and suffragan
	bishops	bishops
Mass Media	Directors, large	Members of
Newspapers, IBA	shareholders,	elites
and BBC	board members	
Educational	Vice-chancellors;	Professors and heads
	Masters of Oxbridge	of departments
	colleges, headmasters	
	of Clarendon schools	

of who are the powerful people in British society, and they are used here to demonstrate how men have a monopoly of positions in some of the spheres, and an overwhelming predominance in the rest.

Table 8·1 includes one elite group which is entirely male, and may well remain so for the rest of the twentieth century, namely the Church of England. (Even if women were to be ordained as parish priests tomorrow there would not be women bishops for many years, if ever, and at the time of writing the idea of the female vicar is so controversial as to be remote.) The upper strata of the armed services and the foreign and colonial service are also effectively male, and likely to remain so. Indeed, this is so taken for granted that Otley (1973) who writes at length about the grammar and public school backgrounds of army officers does not bother to say that he is ignoring the officers in the WRAC. There are, therefore, several elites in Britain which women cannot join, or have so far not managed to join. However, even in those elites which have been open to women for fifty or even a hundred years, elite women are scarce. Education is a good example of this. It is about a hundred years since women were permitted to enter universities, since sound academic schools became available, and since colleges of education were founded for ladies. (See Delamont, 1978.) Most of these institutions began as single-sex ones, with women principals in the female establishments and men in the male ones. Gradually since the Second World War many have become co-educational, and women have lost control of not only the co-educational institutions, but also of the single-sex ones. Thus Lady Margaret Hall, Oxford, and Roedean School have male heads. It is not clear whether Giddens would include the heads of the Oxbridge women's colleges in the elite with the 'masters' of the men's colleges, or the heads of the girls' public schools with the heads of the Clarendon (boys') schools. As we have yet to see a Mistress of Balliol or Trinity College, or a headmistress of Harrow, the positions Giddens mentions are all held by men, and comparing six women college principals at Oxbridge with the fifty-plus men would hardly give women an equal footing as the elite. Leaving aside the Oxbridge colleges and Clarendon schools, the proportion of women in the rest of the educational elite is tiny, even if we draw our net wider than Giddens's. Table 8·2 shows the gender distribution in authority positions in education provided by the DES in 1973. The table shows a severe under-representation of women in all these educational institutions. The recruitment potential is not great, either, for only 2 per cent of university professors are women, and women in senior posts in polytechnics and colleges are equally rare.

The judiciary is equally a male preserve. While women are about a third of the lay magistrates in England and Wales, and about half the members of juries, and are thus well represented in the *unpaid*

Table 8·2 *Women in the Educational Elite, 1973*

Post	Total	No. of Women
University vice-chancellor	44	0
Polytechnic principal	28	0
Medical school principal	24	1
Agricultural college principal	44	0
College of education principal	172	72
Member of the UGC	21	2

parts of the legal system, they are scarce in the paid parts of it. No woman has yet been appointed Lord Chancellor, Solicitor General or Attorney General, nor has any woman yet sat in the Court of Appeal or on the Judicial Committee of the House of Lords. Only ten of the two hundred and fifty circuit judges are women, and only four of the seventy high court judges. No government concern has ever been expressed about these low percentages, and the recent Royal Commission on the legal system/profession does not have gender imbalance among its terms of inquiry. The small number of women judges is directly related to the recruitment of the judiciary from barristers *only*, for the barristers are even more thoroughly male than the rest of the profession, the solicitors. In the early 1970s only 7·5 per cent of the practising barristers were women (252 out of 3,368) and only 1 of the 250 Queen's Counsel, the barristers who have 'taken silk' and can prosecute for the Crown. Although the Sex Disqualification (Removal) Act of 1919 forced the legal profession to admit women, the majority of chambers of barristers had never recruited a woman as a pupil in 1973 (*The Times*, 1 January 1973). By 1976 8·1 per cent of barristers were women, but only 4 out of 370 QCs, and half of all chambers had still never recruited a woman. However, even if judges were to be recruited in future from solicitors, this would not widen the scope for women judges. In 1974 about 6 per cent of qualified solicitors were women, but only about 4·5 per cent of those actually practising.

Nor do women fare any better in gaining positions of authority in the more 'informal' areas of the legal order – the various national and local tribunals. Table 8·3 shows that few of either the chairpeople or the members of local tribunals are women. The Industrial Tribunals are the arena for cases under the 1970 Equal Pay legislation which came into force in 1975. The lack of women on these tribunals seems particularly unfortunate, for it shows that the government is not practising what it preaches. Una Kroll (1975) claims that only 11 per cent of the 1,350 members of all government tribunals were women.

Table 8·3   *Women on Tribunals (1973)*

| Tribunal | Chairpeople | | Members | |
	Women	Total	Women	Total
Rent	17	250	90	500
Pensions appeals	0	16	6	34
Industrial injuries	0	27	2	250
Industrial	0	44	7	400

Giddens divides the economic sphere into three categories: the nationalised industries, the financial sphere and the productive industrial sphere. Just as the government has not put women on to tribunals, it has not put women on to the boards of the nationalised industries and equivalent bodies which are in its gift. The government has considerable patronage because there are a great many lucrative jobs in these QUANGOs (quasi-autonomous national government organisations). Melville Currell (1974) says that in 1973 there were no women on the boards running the gas, electricity, coal, atomic energy, railway and aerospace industries, nor on the Post Office Board. In 1971 only 5 of the 425 people on such public boards were women. In 1977 there were nineteen QUANGOs in Wales, and only one was headed by a woman (*Hansard*, December 1977, pp. 701–2). If the government has not put women on the boards it controls, perhaps it is not surprising that only 1 per cent of the members of the Institute of Directors were women in 1975 (400 women out of 35,000 members). Of course, these 35,000 members of the Institute of Directors include many people who are too insignificant to form part of Giddens's financial and commercial elites, but the overall gender balance is probably much the same in the elite sphere.

Giddens argues that the elite in the financial and commercial spheres is based on the directors and the large shareholders. These two categories may overlap, of course, as directors may well have shares in the companies they direct. Shareholders of any kind are rare in Britain, for Westergaard and Resler (1975, p. 158) say 93·4 per cent of the population own no shares at all. Our data on the wealthy are, however, far from complete, and we know little about who is wealthy, or where the wealth is. Richard Whitley (1974) studied the directors of large companies, comparing the top fifty industrial concerns in Britain and the main financial institutions such as clearing banks, merchant banks, insurance companies and the Bank of England. He used the published self-report data on these directors, and his sample included over 500, but he gives no figures on their gender. Presumably they were all men? Certainly they were predominantly educated at boys' public schools and belonged to all-male London clubs. In the same volume Pahl and Winkler (1974) report a study of directors sampled via the Institute, and also fail to mention gender. Stanworth and Giddens (1974) present a profile of company chairmen, in the same volume, based on 460 chairmen who had held office over the past seventy years. Again they compare financial and industrial enterprises, and again make no mention of gender. The analysis is made in terms of boys and men, sons and grandsons, Clarendon schools and Oxbridge, so we assume that all the chairmen were men. All three papers show that the financial institutions are more closely tied to traditional elite values of public school, Oxbridge and connections to the aristocracy and landed gentry than the commercial concerns. The close ties between banking and the aristocracy in Britain were plotted in a pioneering paper by T. Lupton and Shirley Wilson (1959, reprinted 1973) which examined the background to a scandal about a Bank Rate leak in 1957. They showed how Conservative Cabinet members, senior civil servants, and Directors of the Bank of England, of the 'Big Five' banks, of leading City firms and of insurance companies were knitted together by kinship *and marriage*. Thus the daughters of the Ninth Duke of Devonshire provided links between many of the key figures in the scandal. This paper by Lupton and Wilson is unique in the two recent collections on power and elites in Britain edited by Urry and Wakeford (1973) and Stanworth and Giddens (1974), in that it actually mentions women, even though they are only wives, daughters, nieces, daughters-in-law and aunts of the elite males. Otherwise all the material on financial elites is *apparently* about men only.

It would not be so easy to assume that all the owners of wealth are men, and so when one turns to two papers on wealthy Britons one might expect to find some discussion of women. Harbury and McMahon (1974) studied the chief wealth-leavers in Britain by tracing men who left £100,000 or more. They left women out of their research because of the difficulty of tracing them when they change their names! Rubinstein (1974) presents a parallel study, 'Men of property', based on all those who left estates in the twentieth century valued at over £500,000. Rubinstein says that 675 people have left estates worth over a million pounds since 1809 of whom about 50 were women and 25 foreigners. However, he excludes both the women and the foreigners from his analysis and says in his footnotes:

I mean no slight towards women here. In the entire nineteenth century, there were fewer than a dozen women's estates worth £500,000 or more; in 1971–2 alone, there were 25. The increase in the number of women to inherit property absolutely is arguably the most important change in Britain's wealth elite during this century.

If this is so, one wonders why neither he, nor any other researchers, have studied this important change in the wealth elite! Rubinstein says data on the women are hard to find, and so leaves them out.

Data on regional distribution in wealth patterns are not commonly presented in such accounts of Britain's wealthy people. John Scott and Michael Hughes (1975, 1976a and b) have published data on Scotland's wealthy people, but a similar analysis needs to be done for Wales. However, Scott and Hughes write about how much of the economic power in Scotland is centred on an elite of sixty men and do not even bother to state whether they mean sixty males or sixty people. We assume the former, because the presence of a woman among them would probably have been worthy of note! So even a pioneering study of a regional economy does not correct the imbalance of the other studies concerning gender.

Thus the most recent, consolidated research on wealth and the power associated with wealth has either failed to mention whether women are included in its analyses or has deliberately excluded them. We therefore have no data on Britain's wealthy women, and very little on women who have been successful in industry or commerce (Fogarty *et al.*, 1971). The failure to notice the gender inequalities in wealth and power is perhaps the most disturbing feature of this whole area, exemplified in Urry's introduction to his collection (Urry and Wakeford, 1973) where he mentions racial inequality but ignores gender. To summarise, so far we have seen that women are completely excluded from the elite Church of England posts and from the armed services, form an insignificant part of the educational elite and the judiciary, and are apparently without economic power and noticeable wealth. Turning now to the more clearly *political* spheres of British life, we can see that women are under-represented in the mass media, the TUC, the civil service and in politics itself.

Giddens suggests that the elite groups in the media are the boards of directors and large shareholders of the major newspapers and independent television and radio, and the boards of governors of the IBA and the BBC. Women are non-existent in most of these spheres. Katherine Whitehorn pointed out in the *Observer* (July, 1978) that 'the newspapers of Fleet Street . . . have no woman on any of the boards at all' because the one woman director of IPC had gone to manage a business.

The TUC General Council is overwhelmingly male. There are two seats reserved for the representatives of the women's conference and these are the *only* women on the Council. In 1975 a survey of sixty-two unions showed that there were 2,259 full-time male employees but only 71 full-time women employees (*Financial Times*, 1 November 1975). Thus the recruiting base for the General Council is heavily biased towards men, and no steps are being taken to correct this. The predominance of males among full-time workers is as characteristic of unions representing mainly women workers, such as the NUT and the shop workers' union USDAW, as it is in unions representing 'male' occupations like printing. As the position of women in the trade union movement has already been mentioned in Chapter 6, there is no need to talk further about it here.

Women gained equal pay in the civil service after a long struggle in 1962, but they are under-represented in the higher echelons. Mackie and Pattullo (1977, pp. 86–7) discuss how in 1971 an enlightened report on women in the civil service was produced, which recommended changes in the rules to allow women to raise families and pursue careers. Although the intentions were good, in 1974 in the upper echelons of the civil service (under-secretary and above) there were 24 women and 793 men. The administrative section of the diplomatic service had 1,100 men and 43 women, 1,083 male assistant secretaries and 53 females, at senior principal level 514 males and 16 females. Mackie and Pattullo point out that it is the recruitment figures which are most important for the future – and while the proportion of women applying to train for the administration rose, the recruitment stayed still at 33 per cent between 1971 and 1974.

Women in Parliament
Finally, we come to the political sphere itself. This is better documented than the other areas mentioned so far in the chapter, being discussed in Brookes (1967), Currell (1974) and Mellors (1978). Their documentation reveals a depressing picture. Women have never managed to hold 5 per cent of the seats in the House of Commons, and the women life peers are an equally insignificant part of the total membership of the Upper House. A thorough study of the women life peers and their activities has yet to be written, so the analysis here focuses on the House of Commons. Between 1918 and 1974 just over 1,000 women stood for election to Parliament, compared with over 22,000 men (Currell, 1974). The Labour Party had fielded 444 women candidates and the Conservative Party 269, the remainder standing as Liberals, nationalists or independents. The number of women candidates and of women elected has risen gradually since 1918. In 1918, seventeen women stood and one was elected; in 1929, sixty-nine and fourteen; in 1945, eighty-seven stood and twenty-four were elected; and in 1966, eighty-one and twenty-six. A number between twenty and thirty has been standard in most Parliaments since the Second World War, and there are no signs of it rising higher. About a hundred

different women have sat as MPs, some for long periods but others for only a very short time. The majority have been Labour members (forty-eight), with rather fewer Conservatives (thirty-nine), four Liberals, and the rest mainly nationalists. Mellors (1978, p. 106) concludes that 'of all socio-economic groups, women are the most under-represented at Westminster'.

Mellors found that women MPs were more likely than men to be over 40 when elected, and more likely to have local government experience, but less likely to be fighting their first election. In 1967 Pamela Brookes calculated that the average age of women MPs on election up to 1966 had been 45, and that between 1918 and 1966, the majority of the women MPs were married (forty-four) or widows (thirteen), although a substantial number (twenty-six) had been single. It was noticeable, though, that only seventeen of the women MPs had had children of school age, while twenty had had childless marriages. The majority of women MPs had received a secondary education, and many were graduates, but no girls' school or groups of schools predominated as the major public schools do in studies of male MPs. The girls' school which has so far sent most women members to the House is St Paul's, and the two leading universities are London and Oxford. Mellors (1978, p. 110) summarises the educational backgrounds of women MPs compared with men as follows:

> The most prominent features of the educational backgrounds of women MPs have been the large proportion who received a secondary education and the relatively small proportion who were educated at a public school . . . Working class women are almost wholly excluded from election.

Melville Currell (1974) has surveyed all the women MPs still alive who sat in the Commons from 1923 to 1974, and has also carried out two studies of women *candidates* who stood in 1964 and were adopted in 1973. She shows how growing up in a politically active family is important in the socialisation of the future woman politician, and also reveals that many women who entered both Houses were regarded as substitutes for a husband who had died, or been made a peer. Several women MPs took over a seat vacated by their husbands, even when they were not primarily interested in parliamentary politics. Such substitution is one way women can avoid the difficulties of getting selected to fight a seat in the first place. There is agreement among practitioners and commentators that getting selected as a *prospective* candidate is the hardest part of becoming a woman MP. Thus Barbara Castle says in *Woman* (2 October 1976), 'I'll always say the toughest fight I ever had was getting on the shortlist for selection as a candidate'. Statistically this is probably true, for Currell has calculated that 'once selected for a constituency, then the chance of the "average" woman candidate has, over the past decade, come to equal . . . that of the "average" male candidate' (1974, p. 27).

Although getting shortlisted and adopted for a seat may be the hardest part of the political process for a woman, if elected to the Commons her chances of office and power are small. Between 1918 and 1974 there had been nine women parliamentary secretaries, three under-secretaries, four women ministers outside the Cabinet, and three Cabinet ministers (Margaret Bondfield, Barbara Castle and Margaret Thatcher). Barbara Castle (*Woman*, 2 October 1976) has argued that Harold Wilson was 'more pro-woman than any other person' she knew and quotes him saying 'Isn't it wonderful? . . . I've just appointed the first woman chairman [*sic*] of such-and-such.' He apparently lured her into several jobs by saying she would be the first woman to do them and 'undoubtedly went out of his way to see if there wasn't a woman who could do a particular job'. Castle contrasts this with Callaghan who 'is a bit of a male chauvinist. He is not one to give women opportunities.' The success of a woman MP in gaining office is, of course, closely related to the patronage of the male Prime Minister, and those women who have been chosen for offices have been concentrated in the fields of health, education and Scottish affairs. Jean Mann (1962, p. 39), herself an MP for many years, has argued that women were often given offices when nasty jobs had to be undertaken, so that Margaret Bondfield had Labour during a period of high unemployment in 1931, and Edith Summerskill had Food during the acute food shortage of the postwar period. Harold Wilson's choice of Barbara Castle to pilot his bill to restrict trade unions would be a modern example of using a woman to tackle unpopular issues.

The woman MP also suffers a good deal of difficulty and criticism by virtue of her gender. There are practical problems, such as the shortage of lavatories, and the lack of changing facilities, which can hamper efficiency in the new MP and in the minister. Barbara Castle says (2 October 1976), 'One of the problems when a woman becomes a Minister is that there is unlikely to be any provision lavatory-wise for her. What's more there are no facilities for changing her clothes either . . . when I first went to the Department of Employment . . . they had to turn all the men on the ministerial floor out of the gentlemen's and put them elsewhere!' Apart from poor physical facilities, the woman MP or minister is excluded from much of the informal colleagueship of what is essentially a male club, and is thus barred from much of what happens. Then she is likely to face a barrage of criticism, for if she is married she is neglecting her family, if single she is out of touch with family life. If she campaigns on feminist issues she is accused of neglecting her constituents and trivialising politics; if she does not, then she is neglecting to serve the women of the country. Her clothes, speech, hair style and behaviour are subject to constant appraisal, and her private life has to be above reproach. In short, the woman in the political elite suffers all the disadvantages of any professional woman, with none of the compensations of power and authority which might soften the hardship.

This section has shown how the role of women in the wealthy, powerful and elite groups in Britain is a minute one. The next section shows how the political order is sustained at the level of ordinary British people.

POLITICS IN MODERN BRITAIN

The academic study of politics in Britain has been as much be-devilled by sexism as the other areas of academic inquiry. Murray Goot and Elizabeth Reid (1975) have published a devastating critique of all the studies of voting behaviour, which casts serious doubt on all the so-called established findings on women. Similar points are made about the American research in Jane Jaquette's *Women in Politics* (1974). Goot and Reid raise serious doubts about the sampling, the design of research instruments and the conclusions of the researchers about women's political behaviour. Thus they make us think twice about a quote from a basic textbook on women and politics such as that by Dowse and Hughes (1972, pp. 192-3):

> One of the best researched findings in British politics is that women participate less and declare lower levels of interest than do men . . . Women are less likely to vote than men. In general, women are more conservative politically and are usually less politically interested than men.

Dowse and Hughes go on to suggest that this finding has also been confirmed from countries as dissimilar as Mexico and Japan, as well as in Scandinavia and the United States. Yet if one examines the kinds of criticisms levelled at the vast edifice of research by Goot and Reid it turns out that the whole edifice is built by piling one sexist assumption upon another. Indeed, if the apolitical nature of women is the finding which is the best-established one in the subject, then the subject must be in a poor way for findings. However, before embarking on a detailed critique of the supposed findings on women, it is necessary to know something about the political attitudes, knowledge and behaviour of the British public as a whole.

The most important thing to realise about political behaviour in Britain is that it is a very insignificant part of almost everyone's lives, men's as well as women's. The only political activity in which most people are involved is voting for the House of Commons about every four or five years. Eighty per cent of adults make this gesture, but it only occupies a few minutes six or eight times in the adult's life. Only about half the adult population vote in the more frequent local elections, and only one person in every fifty takes an active part in political campaigning.

The *average* British adult apparently takes little interest in the workings of the political system at national or local level. Although over 90 per cent of adults identify themselves with a particular party, most people cannot name their MP or local councillors, do not recognise photographs of members of the Cabinet, and frequently say that opposition members are in the government. Thus Enoch Powell is often believed to be in the Cabinet, while actual ministers are unknown. People may feel strongly about *issues*: trade unions, pay, the health service, comprehensive schools, council housing; but they do not know much about what is actually happening in the government.

Most people, too, have little sense of the meaning of many terms used by the minority who are interested in politics, and by the mass media. Butler and Stokes (1974, pp. 329–33) tried to discover whether people understood, used, or identified with the terms left and right wing. While politicians and journalists thought that between 60 and 90 per cent of the general public would find the terms meaningful, only 21 per cent of their sample of the public said that they ever thought of politics in this way. Only a quarter of the respondents said they thought of themselves as right or left wing or in the centre, and one in five could not rate the existing political parties on the right-wing–left-wing dimension *at all* – that is, the terms were so meaningless to them they had no idea how to use them. Only 39 per cent 'correctly' identified Labour as left wing, although the majority could identify Labour with the working class rather than the middle class. When those who claimed to use the terms were asked to elaborate, only two in a hundred people could offer a thorough account, such as this one from a London Transport supervisor:

> To the left means increased social and welfare benefits, the elimination of private wealth, and nationalization. To the right means the preservation of private wealth and the reduction of expenditure on social benefits.

About fourteen people in a hundred merely said that Labour was left and working class. Conservative was right and middle and upper class. However, a good many of the people who said they thought of the parties in terms of left and right wing had no clear idea of any underlying rationale. Thus many people thought the

Conservatives were right wing because they had the right – that is, correct – ideas. A man in Sheffield said:

> Well, when I was in the Army you had to put your right foot forward, but in fighting you had to lead with your left. So I always think that the Tories are the right party for me and that the Labour Party are fighters.

The reader should note that this a man talking. Commentators who argue that women are peculiarly ignorant about politics should perhaps reconsider their ideas about the level of sophistication present in men.

The majority of adults are not, therefore, very involved in the political system, except to vote for a governing party, and identify in a rather unfocused way with a party for much of one's life. The particular party is generally that associated with the person's social class, but age, religion, region and education have an effect too. However, as Butler and Stokes (1974, p. 155) are at pains to point out, the association between politics and class is relatively recent. They say:

> At the start of this century the basis of politics was very different. The Labour Party scarcely mattered and religion was at least as important as class in shaping partisanship.

Until about fifty years ago the main political division was between Conservatives who were Anglican, and Liberals who were Non-conformist. Many working-class people only got the vote in this century, and women have only had the vote for fifty years. The two-party, class-based system centred on the Labour and Conservative parties may also be coming to an end at the time of writing, and so may only have existed for half a century before vanishing again. As yet it is not possible to know whether there is to be a permanent Liberal revival, a continuing nationalist vote in Wales and Scotland, and a substantial political role for the National Front.

This book does not have space for a detailed analysis of the political attitudes and behaviour of British people in general, or of gender differences in such behaviour. It is necessary, however, to examine the supposed gender differences, to see how far women in Britain really are uninterested in politics and conservative in their attitudes. Goot and Reid (1975) provide a detailed critique of this supposedly solid finding about gender differences, which can only be summarised here, but the implications are clear. They argue that gender has been neglected in many studies, that the received wisdom on women and politics is wrong, and that much of the research is conducted in a highly sexist manner, at the level of both research methods and the discussion and conclusions. The authors show how women are discounted by political scientists who talk cheerfully of 'democracies' which deny the vote to women. This sloppy thinking is typical of much of the research and discussion on women and politics.

Goot and Reid go on to examine some of the most commonly the research instruments used. They point out that many studies ask questions about the party which suits 'the man who has high ideals', or whether 'the ordinary man' should be active in community politics. While the researchers probably meant man/human, Goot and Reid point out quite reasonably that women answering such questions may well think the question refers to man/male. Even well-constructed interviews which use 'people' most of the time sometimes slip up over this. Butler and Stokes (1974, p. 479), for example, in a question about trade union officials, refer to such people as 'he', and Madgwick *et al.* (1973, p. 252) ask questions about 'Welshmen' and 'Englishmen', rather than Welsh people.

Goot and Reid go on to examine some of the most commonly cited 'findings' about women's role in politics, and demolish the evidence which is supposed to support them. They focus especially on the idea that children take their father's politics, that wives defer to their husbands' beliefs, that women are conservative, fickle and lack interest in politics. All of these so-called findings turn out to have little data behind them, and rest on dubious assumptions. Thus, a careful re-examination of the data on parental influences on voting preferences shows that the politics of the mother are just as important as the father's. The issues of women's deference to the men in their families, their conservatism, their lack of interest and their fickleness are far more complex, and are all closely inter-related. The difficulty of disentangling the facts from the prejudices of the researchers, and of sorting out family pressure, conservatism, fickleness and lack of interest, is considerable. Many researchers and commentators also say contradictory things about women, apparently without noticing. Women are frequently accused of being too conservative and unwilling to face change, yet are also accused of being fickle in politics, constantly changing their preferences in an irrational way. Underlying such unremarked contradictions in the literature is a more fundamental confusion about women. Political scientists view women as damned whatever they do. If they behave and believe like their husbands they are accused of being sheep-like, lacking interest in politics, and being deferential and dependent. If they vote or have attitudes which differ from those of their husbands – which usually means attitudes which do not 'fit' their husband's social class position – they are accused of false consciousness, ignorance or innate conservatism. Thus women *never* have political ideas of their own in the literature, they are either dependent or misguided. No one ever examines whether women's beliefs are rational, understandable or worthy of study in their own right. Even feminist commentators have taken the 'findings' as if they were true, and tried to explain them in feminist terms.

It is important, therefore, to understand how far the various so-called findings are real, and how far sheer prejudice. Goot and Reid re-examined the idea that women are less interested in politics, and concluded that this was *only* true if one accepted a narrow definition of 'politics'. For example, one study which 'found' girls to be less politically involved than boys based this on a finding that when girls were asked to name the social reform they would most value they overwhelmingly opted for a non-political reform. Thus girls were not as politically involved as boys. Yet girls had voted for the elimination of crime and criminals! Somehow the researcher thought this was not a political issue, although one would have thought that 'law and order' was a central topic in several recent campaigns. When studying adults, many researchers have offered lists of 'political' topics to respondents to gain some idea of how important they are to voters, and what attitudes people have to them. Butler and Stokes (1974, p. 454), for example ask about 'the Queen and Royal Family, unofficial strikers, the BBC, the EEC, social class, London, the USA, comprehensive schools, the police, the SNP, and coloured immigrants among other topics'. The lists used do not include those issues on which women's political campaigns have been focused since the full granting of the suffrage in 1928. Reading history or politics, one would never know that there had been female campaigns, but there have been a great many in the last fifty years, and they might reasonably be included in a researcher's definition of what constitutes politics. Yet they never are. Nor do the lists include any of the issues of particular concern to women as a whole.

Since the 1920s when women first entered Parliament, there have been women's campaigns on equal pay, on various aspects of sex discrimination, on nursery schools, on family allowances, on the rights of divorced women, on taxation, on contraception, abortion and women's health, and on consumer protection of various kinds. None of these ever figures in lists or definitions of political issues. Yet the women in the Labour Party and in trade unions fought vigorously for contraception to be available for working-class women between the wars, women in the civil service and teaching campaigned for equal pay from 1945 until 1956, and more recently there was a massive mobilisation of women from all over the political spectrum to defend the principle that family allowances should be paid to the mother. Most recently, a campaign by women has been directed at the Inland Revenue's practice of writing to

men about their wives' tax. Women have been central to the recent
political activity over abortion, both in the anti-abortion groups and
those who wish for a woman's right to choose. It is likely that a list
of political issues which was made up of day nurseries, abortion,
epidurals, rape, battered women's refuges, home childbirth, family
allowances, free contraception, equal pay, taxation of women's
wage packets, wages for housework and unit pricing of groceries
would show men less interested and informed about politics than
women, but no such research has ever been done. Politics is defined
as a set of issues about work, not about day care and family allowances.

Feminists have argued that men have deliberately fostered the
notion that politics is about war and work and foreign policy so as
to stop women from meddling, but this seems too simple. Rather
the researchers' ideas of what is political has been too narrowly
focused on a small list of topics within a wider spectrum. The researchers need to investigate attitudes to politics with a wider
working definition of 'the political' before arguing that women are
not interested or uninvolved. No one argues that a man who is
more interested in the relationship of the TUC to the Labour Party
than in EEC fishing policy is not interested in politics, yet, effectively, researchers have condemned women on grounds as illogical
as these.

Thus I would argue that women's lower levels of interest and
knowledge in politics are not proven. Goot and Reid spend considerable time on the more vexing question of women's conservatism.
This has been reported from both national surveys and more intensive local studies such as Margaret Stacey's two projects in Banbury
(Stacey, 1960; Stacey et al., 1975). The commonest finding which
supports women's conservatism is that women with husbands in
working-class jobs are more likely to support the Conservative
Party than men in working-class jobs. Such women are seen as
working-class voters who have failed to understand the 'proper'
voting pattern for them – that is, failed to appreciate their 'true'
class interest – and are thus deferential to authority. There are
substantial numbers of working-class men who vote 'wrongly' of
course, because if they did not no Conservative Party could ever
get elected as the working class is 70 per cent of the electorate.
However, women who hold 'traditional' attitudes and vote for the
Conservative Party are seen as particularly misguided. Their 'incorrect' voting pattern is associated with age, religion and the role
of the family in society. Older voters are more likely to support
the Conservatives, or maybe Conservative voters live longer because
they are in healthier occupations, and women have longer life
expectancies. Also people who are regular churchgoers in England
are more likely to be Conservative, and women go to church more

than men. It is, in fact, very hard to separate age, religion and gender in voting behaviour. Margaret Stacey (1960, p. 47) suggested that women in Banbury, who rarely worked outside the home, were alienated from the Labour Party because it was associated with the trade unions, with whom they had no contact.

Goot and Reid (1975) offer a rather different hypothesis for the greater conservatism of women, which they argue has in any case been greatly exaggerated and oversimplified by researchers. They suggest that women's understanding of their social class position may not be the same as those used in research. Researchers classify women into social classes on the basis of their husbands' occupation, or that of the male head of the household. Goot and Reid argue that this may not be either the class in which the woman's own job would place her or the class in which she feels herself to be. In addition, they argue that the relationships between class and party may be rather different for women in ways that have not been properly explored. Going beyond this, I would argue that no one has yet examined the possibility that women's political beliefs may be *rational for their lives as women*. Everyone assumes that working-class women are misguided in voting Conservative, but it is possible that they have correctly perceived they will have better lives under a Conservative government. Thus Madgwick *et al.* (1973, p. 27) say blithely 'women tend to be less radical than men and have stronger Welsh cultural sympathies' and add that this shows most strongly on the issue of Sunday opening of pubs, where women are more hostile to opening than men. Now the researchers may equate dislike of Sunday opening with conservatism, but a reader can legitimately say that not wanting the men to vanish drinking on Sundays is hardly irrational, and scarcely conservative. Once one is prepared to accept that the conservatism might be rational, because women have other things in their lives than the occupation of their husband, the whole question of women's conservatism and traditionalism needs new research and conceptualisation.

Finally, we need to consider the ideas that women's political ideas and behaviours are fickle, and heavily influenced by their husbands or other men in the family. The attribution of fickleness to women's changes of political line seems to be largely prejudice on the part of the researchers. Men are seen as changing for rational reasons, women are not. But the question of husbands' influence over wives is worthy of further consideration. Goot and Reid point out that no one has actually studied husbands and wives as married couples, and followed the process of political attitude development and the emergence of voting intentions. Most of the research has been done by interviews of men in some households and women in others, not of couples together. Goot and Reid point out that, given the female gender of most interviewers, the pressures .on male and female respondents are very different. Men are unlikely to admit to women interviewers that their wives form their political judgements, whereas women can make a reverse claim with no loss of face. Thus, Goot and Reid say, research will only show male influence on women, not the reverse, if it occurs. A study of the process of political attitude formation in marriage is obviously needed. Researchers have also failed to appreciate the lack of autonomy available to women in certain kinds of marriage, where physical force may coerce women's behaviour. Women who claim it is 'more than their life's worth' not to vote a certain way may not be joking.

There are many gaps in our knowledge of political attitudes and behaviour. More data are needed on political views in Wales and Scotland, and there are several areas of gender differences which badly need researching. What is even more important than more data is a change of attitude on the part of researchers and commentators, so that women are not viewed with prejudice, but dispassionately. It would produce an important change in political research if women were classified into classes by their own occupations, treated as rational, and given credit for the political activities in which they are engaged. With such a change of attitude might come some novel insights into the received wisdom that women are traditional, family-centred, religious, conservative and love the Royal Family. The relations between religion, politics and leisure for women are especially interesting, and it is to religion in Britain that we now turn.

RELIGION IN BRITAIN

In many ways religion is a very difficult subject to discuss in a book such as this, because there may well be an enormous gap between religious behaviour (such as churchgoing), religious beliefs and religious prejudices. Thus while a lower proportion of the population goes to church regularly in 1978 than did in 1908, it is impossible to know whether people are less likely to believe in a god, or whether they have abandoned entrenched hostilities to other sects and denominations. Nor is it at all clear whether it is the behaviour, or the private beliefs, or the entrenched hostilities, which are socially significant in modern Britain. Thus a vague feeling of anti-Catholicism may be more socially significant in a population than a positive belief in Protestant theology or regular attendance at church on Sundays, but we have little information on the social context of belief in modern Britain. It is noticeable that religion is not considered important enough to rate a census question outside Northern Ireland although race and nationality at birth have been included, nor does the government collect data on religion in other surveys.

Social Trends, 1977 has only one table on religion, and that is based on data provided by the churches themselves about their 'members' – a difficult concept to use. Table 8·4 shows the data provided by *Social Trends* rearranged to show the churches in descending order of number of adherents.

While this table shows some very interesting things about membership of different religious groups in Britain, especially the extent to which Britain is now a pluralist country in religious terms, two things about religion are not apparent from such a table. Such a table cannot show the beliefs of people not counted as members by anyone – and that is the largest section of the population of Britain – and it masks tremendous regional variations in membership patterns. In this section I want to examine the importance of 'passive' religious belief, then the data in Table 8·4 and then look at regional variations, before turning specifically to women. Almost by definition the latent or passive religious adherence is not measurable, but it shows up clearly in the differences between people's labelling of themselves and the figures for church attendance or membership.

Table 8·4 *Church Membership in England, Wales and Scotland, 1970 and 1975*

Church	Membership (thousands)	
	1970	*1975*
Roman Catholic	2,219	2,108
Episcopalian	2,398	2,078
Presbyterian and Congregational	1,629	1,465
Other Trinitarian	526	574
Methodist	612	552
Muslim	250	400
Baptist	293	256
Jews (heads of households)	113	111
Sikhs	75	115
Mormons	88	100
Hindus	50	100
Jehovah's Witnesses	62	79
Spiritualists	45	57
Buddhists	6	21

Source: Adapted from *Social Trends, 1977* (pp. 219–20)

Thus Butler and Stokes (1974, p. 156) say that 69 per cent of their sample in England said they were Church of England in 1970 when asked their religious affiliation, while in 1970 the Church only claimed 2 million members in England when the population was about 46 million. The Church of England is therefore a 'residual' adherence for many people who are not members of it in any active sense. Butler and Stokes (1974, pp. 156–7) quote a telling incident to illustrate this point. One man interviewed answered 'none' to their question on religious affiliation, but when asked whether he was an atheist or an agnostic asked the interviewer to explain the two terms. On hearing her explanation he said: 'You had better put me down as Church of England.' The Anglican Church in England probably has many such residual adherents.

Related to this pool of residual adherence is the question of the decline in church attendance, and the use of church ceremonies at marriage, death and birth. While church attendance and the use of church ceremonies have declined dramatically during the twentieth century, it is not at all clear that this represents a decline in belief. Attendance at church was not only essential for social respectability in many circles in the past, but was also enforced on servants, tenants and other dependants by their superiors. Squires and mill-owners who sacked and evicted non-attenders ensured large church attendances, but it is arguable whether those pressed into attendance believed in what they heard. It could even be argued that the core of truly devout believers has always been small. Thus falling church attendance may have more to do with lessening social pressures than any change in private beliefs.

The data on church membership given in *Social Trends* are, however, interesting. While the total number of church members is well short of the total population (just over 8 million out of 54·4 million), the proportion belonging to some religious body is still quite large. Protestant varieties of Christianity still claim the largest body of adherents, but the Roman Catholics are the largest single denomination. They are closely followed by the Episcopalian (Anglican) churches, and then by the Presbyterians and Congregationalists. No other church has a million members. It is also noticeable that there are now more Muslims than Baptists in Britain, as well as considerable numbers who adhere to other 'Eastern' religions. It is significant that there has been a *decline* in membership of the main Christian churches – Catholic, Episcopalian, Presbyterian and Congregationalist, Methodist and Baptist – while the 'Eastern' religions – Buddhism, Islam, Hinduism and Sikhism – have gained members, as have the Mormons, Jehovah's Witnesses, Spiritualists and the Orthodox churches (Greek, Russian, Armenian, and so forth). The number of Hindus in Britain doubled in five years, apparently, while Buddhism saw a rise of over 300 per cent. These figures tell us both that Britain is increasingly a pluralistic religious culture, and that patterns of immigration have changed the religious face of Britain. However, gross figures for Great Britain can obscure considerable regional variations, and it is to these we now turn.

Region and Religion

Religious adherence in Britain is closely related to regional differences. The people of Wales and Scotland have different religious affiliations from those usual in England, the distribution of Roman Catholicism is highly uneven across Britain, and there are concentrations of Judaism and the 'Eastern' religions in some areas while they are almost unknown in others. Thus we expect Catholics to be found where there are Irish, Poles and Italians, and mosques to spring up in Bradford rather than Oban or Penzance. What is less well known is the tremendous variation between different regions of Britain in their adherence to varieties of Protestantism, and these regional variations include religious affiliations which are an important element in feelings of 'Welshness' and 'Scottishness'. It is also true that some British churches draw their strength from one region more than others. Thus Scotland with 1,042,000 members of the Church of Scotland provides the majority of Presbyterians in Britain. Wales has long been the home of Nonconformity, and in 1975 there were 59,000 Baptists, 94,000 Presbyterians and Congregationalists, 77,000 members of the Union of Welsh Independents outnumbering the 133,000 members of the Episcopalian Church of Wales.

The Welsh community studies show how deeply religion is embedded into 'Welshness' and Nonconformity into opposition to Englishness (e.g. Rees, 1950). Historically there had been an identity between landlords and the Episcopalian Church on the one hand, and the tenants and Nonconformist chapels on the other. By 1940 Rees could argue that 'the traditional poor, together with the richer members of the community, predominate in the Church, while people of intermediate status form the majority of chapel congregations' (p. 157). By 1940 the old alliances in politics of Liberals and Nonconformists versus the Conservative churchgoers had largely vanished, because, Rees said, there was no longer any need for them. However, Madgwick *et al.* (1973) found that there was still a significant number of Nonconformists active in Cardiganshire politics, and Chapel membership was still an important feature of local life. In rural Wales there is still a consequence of the Nonconformist heritage in the 'dry' Sunday when the pubs are closed – for Temperance, speaking Welsh and chapel membership go together to make up a set of values to which many people still adhere.

Scotland is a great stronghold of Presbyterianism, for the Church of Scotland had over a million members in 1975. There are also 309,000 Roman Catholics in Scotland, reflecting the Irish immigration in the industrial cities of the west coast, and 78,000 Episcopalians. Roman Catholicism has a stronger hold in Scotland, with 16 per cent of the population, than it does in England and Wales, where 10 to 14 per cent of the population are Catholics. The greater

Glasgow area has Catholic/Protestant hostilities as intense as those found in Northern Ireland, complete with Orange lodges and street violence; and the two football teams, Celtic for the Catholics and Rangers for Protestants, meet in symbolic conflict on the field to the accompaniment of religious insults. In rural Scotland the extreme Protestant sects enforce joyless puritanism and Sunday is kept as a solemn Sabbath. However, even in the urban areas it can be argued that the Church of Scotland has a stronger hold on its members than the Church of England does: sixty-one in every hundred members of the Church of Scotland roll actually made a communion at least once in 1974, compared with only eighteen in every hundred English Anglicans.

The Anglican Church in England has seen a sharp decline in all forms of religious observance during the century, but a decline with considerable regional variations. Perman (1977) says that in 1910 69 per cent of all babies born in England were baptised Anglicans, 43 per cent of adults had been confirmed and 10 per cent had made their Easter communion. By 1973 only 47 per cent of babies were being baptised and only 20 per cent of adults had been confirmed. Yet this steep decline in key religious ceremonies was not distributed evenly across dioceses. The large industrial areas such as Birmingham and Sheffield have seen a far more general Anglican decline than more rural dioceses, together with a rise in other religions and Roman Catholicism. There are regional variations in other Christian churches across England, and the strength of the congregations of other religions will also vary according to the nature of the population. Roman Catholicism is strong in industrial cities where Irish, Poles and Italians have settled; Islam where there are Turkish Cypriots and Pakistanis; and the Greek, Russian and Armenian Orthodox churches where there are Greek Cypriots, Lithuanians and Ukrainians, and Armenians. Similarly areas of West Indian settlement have produced Pentacostal churches, Sikh areas have Sikh temples, and Jewish areas have synagogues. A detailed religious ethnography of a multicultural area in a large city would be fascinating to read.

The role of women in the religious life of Britain is imagined to be considerable, in that they are believed to be the main churchgoers in all the major Christian churches at least. Yet women are under-represented in the leadership positions in nearly all the Christian sects, both in the ministry and on the committees and councils of lay people. In the Church of England Una Kroll (1975) claims that women are 60 per cent of the active church members, yet form a tiny minority of office-holders as well as being excluded from the ministry. Kroll says that in 1974 the General Synod had 10 per cent of women, the House of Laity 23 per cent, the Board of Finance 5·8 per cent, the Standing Committee 6 per cent, and women constituted only 2·5 per cent of the Church Commissioners who control the wealth of the Church. While the Nonconformist churches do allow women into their ministries in many cases, their governing bodies are equally male-dominated. The Roman Catholic and Orthodox churches exclude women rigidly from all authority positions, except in convents. Yet these other Christian churches are equally dependent on women to make up their congregations, and to keep their churches clean, funded and fed.

The role of women in the religious life of Britain has to be seen in three distinct parts: their presence in the congregations, their definition by the theology and the openness or otherwise of the ministry itself. Surveys, both national (Butler and Stokes, 1974) and local (Stacey, 1960; Stacey et al., 1975), show that women are both more regular in their church attendance than men, and make up the bulk of congregations in Christian churches. I know of no systematic data on gender differences in religious behaviour among Sikhs, Muslims, Hindus, Buddhists or Russian and Greek Orthodox members in Britain, and so cannot discuss these further in this section. When the researchers in Banbury did a survey of church attendance on a Sunday in 1968 they found that in all denominations but the Roman Catholic women were 60 per cent of the congregation. Two thirds of the Banbury respondents who said they belonged to a religious organisation were women, many of them widows and spinsters (Stacey et al., 1975, p. 32). Women are not only the largest part of the congregation, their labour is often crucial in fundraising and other tasks. Perman (1977, p. 126) says pointedly that:

> most churchmen have been content to regard women as the perpetual Marthas of the churches – as nuns, Sunday School teachers, ladies who do the flowers and make the tea, or as the dutiful wives and mothers of the male hierarchy.

This was certainly the religious role of the women in the community studies of rural areas. Thus, in Gosforth, Williams (1956) showed that it was women who cleaned and decorated the church for the festivals. Much more recently Chamberlain (1975) has shown that the same pattern of Martha-dom prevails in the religious life of the fen women of Gislea. Religion is still important in Gislea, and the women play an important part in sustaining the religious order.

Gislea is divided into Church and Chapel factions, with two Baptist chapels feuding among themselves as well as opposing the Anglicans. Chamberlain says attendance at services is much higher than the national average, and 'the ministers' wives uphold the Christian ideal of the family . . . and provide much of the social life for the women of the village' (1975, p. 118). Thus one Baptist minister's wife describes a range of women's clubs she runs, including prayer meetings, and has been very active in the Girls' Brigade. The Anglican minister's wife describes the role of women in the Church (p. 121):

> Us women share the cleaning, we all have a part of the church to clean. We have a rotary flower guild so that the church is always kept with flowers... women do indeed play a large part in the Church of England. They help with the flower guilds, the cleaning guild, manning the stalls at the garden fetes and catering on various occasions.

Women are thus relegated to the scrubbing brush and the tea urn when they are not actually worshipping. There is apparently excellent theological juistification for keeping women as lay people with only menial tasks to perform within Christianity. There is no room in a small book of this kind to examine the theory behind the subordination of women in all Christian sects, but Clara Henning (1974) has analysed Catholic canon law for the interested reader. It is clear from her data that the Catholic Church is extremely hostile to women compared with many of the Noncomformist churches, which allow women to preach and become ministers. The Anglican Church in England is beginning to look unusual in its continued refusal to ordain women. Laurel Walum (1977, p. 132) summarises the relative positions of the genders in the Christian religious world as follows: 'The church, then, tends to be a social organization controlled by men to service women.' Whether the Bible (and the Talmud) were ever intended to provide a structure for men to control women, rather than to regulate the lives of men and women, is not clear, but that is what they have effectively become.

Women's greater devotion to religious observance when they are denied any power in the system, and when the theology of Christian churches is so deeply imbued with women's sinful, polluted and polluting nature, is a mystery. Yet women's 'leisure'-time is frequently devoted to sustaining institutions in which they have no formal power and whose theories treat them with scorn or pity. The leisure hours of British women are often, in fact, full of hard work, very often of the domestic and caring kinds with which their working hours at home and in employment are occupied already. Women's 'leisure' is frequently a continuation of their housework and paid work, and not a mental or physical change or rest at all. This paradox will be examined in the final part of this chapter.

LADIES OF LEISURE

Although there have been many utopian claims about how leisure is going to increase dramatically with high technology, and everyone will be freed from drudgery to take part in hobbies and sports, most of the emphasis behind such comments is in fact on men. Little is said of the likelihood of *women* having increased leisure, and the research on existing leisure patterns is heavily biased towards male pastimes. Thus *New Society* publishes a pamphlet, *Leisure and Lifestyles*, based on twelve articles published between 1973 and 1975. Only one article is about women and that concerns the underwear they buy; the discussions of leisure are all focused on men. A similar bias informs Young and Willmott's (1975) discussion of leisure, despite their claim that families are becoming symmetrical and male and female roles more equal. We know more about football clubs and mountaineering than we do about the women's clubs and organisations across the land, but it is possible to extract some information on what women do when not working from published data. *Social Trends, 1977* (p. 179) says that adults in Britain have about 26 per cent of their time available for leisure pursuits, after work, sleep, eating and travel to and from work. Given the large amounts of time women in paid work spend on housework, one wonders whether this average covers enormous imbalances between the genders in 'free' time, but *Social Trends* does not break down figures by gender. Leisure-time needs to be considered in two categories, holidays and time free during the rest of the year. Holidays will be covered first, before other forms of leisure activity.

In 1976 60 per cent of British residents had some kind of holiday (*Social Trends, 1977*: 179), but there were clear class differences in the number, length and type of holidays taken. Thus 50 per cent of those people in skilled or semi-skilled occupations and those dependent on welfare benefits took no holiday at all in 1976 and a third of them had only one holiday. Among the two top social classes 50 per cent had one holiday and another quarter two or more. The majority of people still take their holidays in July or August, and, contrary to the impression of mass overseas travel, almost all holidays take place in Britain. Thus in 1961 31 million British residents took their holidays in the United Kingdom and 6 million abroad, in 1976 38 million had home holidays and 7 million foreign ones (*Social Trends, 1977*, p. 180). Those people who do go abroad nearly all stay in Europe. Table 8·5 shows the destinations in Europe visited by the highest percentages of British residents in 1966, 1973 and 1976 as shown by *Social Trends, 1977* (p. 180).

The types of holidays people have at home and abroad are rather different. Over 50 per cent of foreign holidays are spent in hotels, but in the United Kingdom in 1976 only about a quarter of holidays involved hotels, while a quarter were spent camping or caravanning,

Table 8·5   *Most Popular Holiday Destinations in Europe*

	1966 %	1973 %	1976 %
Spain	22	35	29
France	14	11	12
Italy	17	8	10
West Germany	7	4	5
All European destinations	94	86	86

and a quarter with friends or relatives. The cynic might well conclude that the growth of self-catering holidays in Britain has reduced women's leisure, compared with the hotel, boarding house or holiday camp where meals were provided. However, we need data on the division of labour between the genders on holiday to be sure that this cynical view is true.

The majority of the population only have one holiday if they manage a break at all. The rest of this chapter is devoted to a consideration of all the forms of leisure activity other than holidays; that is, the things people do apart from their paid employment and domestic work. There are relatively few data on women's leisure, but is is possible to use some of those available on married men because these often involve family and, hence, women's leisure. There is a table of leisure activities of adults (over 16) in Britain in *Social Trends, 1977* (p. 183) which is based on a large sample, and deals with activities done at least once in the four weeks preceding the survey in 1973. The categories are so broad that very little can be learned from the table, but there are gender differences in leisure, so the main findings are reproduced in Table 8·6. This shows that men are more involved in outdoor and indoor sports as spectators and participants, while women are more involved in social and voluntary work and clubs. It is also clear that some activities are common to both sexes, particularly open-air outings, TV-watching and visits to cinemas, and so forth. The information provided is not detailed enough, however, to get any picture of what leisure actually involves for most people.

Young and Wilmott (1975, pp. 212–16) are interested in leisure, and the relations between increased leisure-time and the equality of gender roles in the family. However, they only provide detailed data on the pursuits of married men, not their wives. The main findings adapted from several of their tables are shown in Table 8·7 which gives those pursuits mentioned by more than 10 per cent of their sample of 591 men in the London area. Their data are shown broken down by social class, and there are clear class differences in leisure activities. Television and the pub are the major leisure activities of semi-skilled and unskilled workers, apparently, and it

Table 8·6   *Main Leisure Activities in 1973*

Activities	Percentage of Sample	
	Women	*Men*
TV, radio, playing records	94	94
Going out for meal, drink, dancing, bingo	50	63
Gardening, DIY, needlework, hobbies	46	50
Betting, gambling, games of skill	22	33
Open-air outings	21	21
Social and voluntary work, clubs	21	17
Cinema, theatre, opera, concerts	18	17
Active outdoor sports	11	24
Watching sports and games	5	16
Active indoor sports and games	6	14
Visiting buildings, museums, zoos, etc.	9	9
Amateur music and drama	3	3
Sample size (100%)	12,472	11,197

Source: Adapted from *Social Trends, 1977*, p. 183.

is clear that only middle-class men attend church or do voluntary work in any numbers. Money obviously affects many of the pastimes, for car ownership and eating out are commoner among the more affluent. Housing conditions also relate to leisure use, for the more affluent are more likely to have a garden, and to own a house to decorate and maintain. Many of the more popular activities for men look as though they might also involve wives, such as TV viewing, outings in the car, eating out and dancing. Yet Young and Willmott see leisure as a male preserve, for the only thing they say about women (1975, p. 217) is:

Most wives were less engaged in sport, as spectators or players, they knitted or sewed more often than they did anything else except watch television... and in all, outside the house, they did less things than men... Those who worked went to restaurants, pubs, cinemas and theatres more than those who did not.

Perhaps the working women had more money! Although Young and Willmott say that married men spent much of their time at home, and when out they were mainly with their families, they also found that 25 per cent of professional and managerial class men and 27 per cent of those in clerical jobs said their families interfered with their leisure. So much for the symmetrical family which they claim to have found!

Table 8·7 *Leisure Activities of Married Men by Social Class*

Activity	Professional and Managerial	Clerical	Skilled	Semi-skilled and Unskilled	All
	%	%	%	%	%
Watching TV	95	99	98	95	97
Gardening	70	62	66	50	64
Pleasure trips in car	62	51	62	49	58
Listening to music	65	70	52	44	57
Home decorating and repairs	52	55	56	45	53
Going to pub	51	42	54	58	52
Cleaning car	55	44	51	35	48
Walking	56	63	41	36	47
Reading books	67	63	33	28	46
Car maintenance	30	25	38	25	32
Eating out	48	31	25	23	32
Swimming	34	25	20	8	22
Attending church	22	20	12	7	15
Cinema	16	20	8	13	13
Collecting stamps and other objects	14	24	11	8	13
Voluntary work	19	10	8	5	11
Dancing	12	14	10	12	11

Note: Total in sample =· 591.
Source: Adapted from Young and Willmott, 1975.

Young and Willmott's male sample showed that middle-class men had more leisure activities than the working class did, and that throughout the sample one leisure activity tended to lead to another, so that active people got drawn into more and more things. Middle-class men were also more likely to hold offices in things they belonged to, or perhaps to take their leisure in ways which involved organisation and office-holders. The other major class difference concerned seeing friends and relations, for while the working class saw more relations and fewer friends, this was reversed for the middle class. Young and Willmott's (1975) research therefore confirms the pattern of their earlier work that leisure in the working class is closely tied to seeing kin.

While Young and Willmott's data do not allow us to say much about women's leisure except by inference, they do show how class differences have an important relation to leisure. The two studies of Banbury, a small town near Oxford, carried out by Margaret Stacey and her colleagues (Stacey, 1960; Stacey *et al.*, 1975) show how class and gender segregate leisure patterns, and actually give reasonable data on women. In addition, because the two surveys took place twenty years apart, there is evidence on changing leisure patterns and enduring ones, which is lacking in other studies. In 1950 Stacey found that religion, politics and leisure were closely entwined. Anglicans and Conservatives belonged to one set of clubs for sport and leisure, Nonconformists and Liberals belonged to another set which only overlapped slightly with the Anglican one because the Liberals were mainly teetotal. The Labour Party people were not religious, and were segregated in another set of organisations. The Anglican/Conservative area included sporting clubs, for bowling, rugby, cricket and tennis especially and the 'business' organisations such as the Chamber of Commerce, Round Table and Rotary Club. The Nonconformists/Liberals were less sporting, but did meet the Anglicans/Conservatives in some of the 'business' organisations.

All the women's organisations found in 1950 were in the Anglican or Nonconformist areas except the Co-operative Women's Guild which was Liberal/Nonconformist only. There do not seem to have been any clubs for Labour women in 1950, but the Anglican and Nonconformist women had the Inner Wheel, Townswomen's Guild and the Business and Professional Women's Club, as well as religious and social service groups to go to. Most women's groups met during the day, mid-week. Stacey said (1960, p. 79) that ' very few women go out in the evening or at the week-end on their own, whereas it is expected men will do so'. The Business and Professional women were the only group to meet at night. Charity work divided the Labour people off from the other activists in 1950, for they were only involved in statutory social services, while the Anglicans and Nonconformists were active in charitable work through voluntary bodies.

When the researchers carried out a further study of Banbury's voluntary associations in 1967, the Anglican and Nonconformist groups had merged, and the Labour people had become involved in some non-statutory charities. Otherwise the class lines and gender lines were drawn in much the same places. Women's horizons had widened slightly in that there were more evening meetings, and more women were involved on the committees of mixed societies. Nonetheless, in 1967 more men (two-thirds) than women (half) belonged to things, and men still had a wider range of activities and ran more societies. However, there seems to be a major definitional problem in Stacey's categories of voluntary association which serves to confine women's leisure, which must be discussed before these findings can be understood.

Stacey divides voluntary associations into the following categories: sports, hobbies, cultural, social, social services, charity, mutual and occupational. She then argues that clubs for sports and hobbies are predominantly male, while women's organisations were mainly in the religious, social and social services categories. I would argue that, in fact, Stacey's categorisation actually makes the women's activities look more restricted than they are, because it classes as 'social' clubs which have much wider functions than that. The Townswomen's Guild, for example, is classified as 'social', yet it could be called a 'hobbies' club, a 'cultural' club and a vehicle for social services if one classifies what the members *do*, and it was founded as a vehicle for political education by the women's suffrage societies when the full vote was won in 1928 (Stott, 1978). Many women's organisations are multi-purpose, and so women are seen as unduly restricted by a classification such as Stacey's. A rugby club is unambiguously sporting, but women's societies are multi-faceted. The only thing that does seem to be clear about women is that the majority do not, given choice, want to spend their time running about muddy fields chasing pieces of plastic, nor swilling gallons of beer after such chasing. The sports they prefer are clean, non-violent and played without large teams.

There does, however, seem to be a tendency for women to spend their leisure in socially responsible ways. Chamberlain (1975, p. 144) summarises the social consensus about women's leisure as follows:

> Social activities for women must do and be seen to be doing something for the improvement of the community or of themselves as well as providing, incidentally, a social outlet. If you are a woman, you must wait for the Over Sixties before you can join a club for amusement.

Chamberlain is writing of Gislea, where women have a branch of the Women's Institute, of the Mothers' Union, a Young Wives Fellowship and a Meals on Wheels service, plus the women's prayer meetings. Men in Gislea have soccer, cricket, fishing and bowls clubs, and the pubs into which women can only go with an escort. Gislea's leisure is a miniature of Banbury's, and Chamberlain's comment applies to Banbury, and to Britain. Men work, and so men can have *pure* leisure, women do not, in society's view, do real work, so they have not earned the right to real leisure, they must be earnest and worthy. Women are thus only allowed leisure if it supports them in their roles as wives and mothers, or improves society for the less well endowed. Whether leisure is organised in

Rotary Clubs and rugby playing, or disorganised in pubs and neighbourhoods, only men are free to enjoy it as genuine relief from toil. When women become involved in leisure activities which are not an extension of their domestic roles, they are subject to scorn, ridicule, discrimination and even violence.

Much male leisure involves sport, either participating in indoor or outdoor sports or watching them 'live' or on TV. Yet women are not supposed to play sports themselves and are popularly believed to dislike it on television. A woman who does engage in sporting activities is subject to an amazing double-bind, where she is either a 'masculine' harridan or so sexy and feminine that her sporting achievement is subordinated to her sex appeal. There is no good British book on women and sport to compare with Thomas Boslooper and Marcia Hayes's *The Femininity Game* (1973) in which they explore this double-bind in the American context. Boslooper and Hayes challenge the prevailing American message that 'feminine' women aren't supposed to take any form of strenuous activity' (p. 42). They claim that denying women true participation in sport is also harmful to non-sporting men and actually claim that 'American society cuts the penis off the male who enters dance . . . and places it on the woman who participates in competitive athletics' (p. 45). What they say about particular sports is very American but the underlying message is true in Britain (p. 51):

> Swimming, golf, and riding are considered graceful (and therefore, appropriately feminine). Baseball, track and basketball are more closely competitive, sweaty, and 'awkward' . . . the feminine sports all require a certain amount of money to pursue – they are traditionally upper-middle and upper-class sports. The others, while more easily accessible, bear not only a masculine, but a class and cultural stigma.

Boslooper and Hayes provide detailed statistics on how women's sporting facilities are chronically under-financed in the United States compared with men's: for example, male sports coaches at UCLA earned $408,000 a year in 1973 while women's sports coaches were volunteers, and there were no sports scholarships for women students. Equivalent research on women's sporting expenditure in Britain needs to be done, to see if the same economic injustice is present here. Indeed, the only academic writing on women in sport in Britain is by Critcher (1974), who examines the contradictions between the role of sport in Britain and the role of women. Critcher discusses press coverage of women in sport, and shows how media usually either emphasise the woman's sex and neglect her sport, or emphasise her role as wife and mother and neglect her sport.

Foreign athletes in contrast are denigrated as 'masculine' and ugly. This attitude leads to headlines such as 'Housewife climbs Everest', 'Mother of two runs 3,000 metres' or 'Grandmother to captain England'. The Montreal Olympics in 1976 offered the press plenty of room to criticise foreign women athletes as 'masculine', for the most successful women on the track and in swimming were not only muscular (urgh!) but also communists (i.e. brainwashed puppets of cruel masters). Jill Tweedie, writing in the *Guardian* (8 August 1976), discussed this issue and argued that 'to wholly admire these female athletes one must appreciate them visually and to do that means readjusting a web of preconceived notions of feminine beauty and worth'. This is obviously something the mass media in Britain are not yet prepared to do, so coverage stays fixed on saying women in sport are feminine and beautiful, or that they are good mothers. Thus the *Observer* (21 August 1977) says that Tessa Sanderson, the best woman javelin thrower in British history, 'is an extremely attractive girl . . . hairdo like a blackberry, taut boilersuit and a wide magenta-lipsticked smile'. The *Sunday Times* (7 September 1976) writes up Beryl Burton, the greatest woman cyclist the world has ever seen, by stressing her home baking, her knitting and her happy marriage, and covers the dismissal of Rachel Hayhoe Flint (24 July 1977) from the England cricket captaincy by saying she is five years married, and 'a spiffing mummy'. If the best sportswomen in the world are assumed to be 'really' wives and mothers, or too masculine for comfort, it is little wonder that amateur sport does not thrive among women.

If sport is out for the majority of women, TV, radio, reading books and magazines and going to the cinema are socially respectable in most circles. Feminists have been heavily critical of mass media and their image of women, especially advertising, and a collection of papers edited by Josephine King and Mary Stott (1977) makes these criticisms clearly. However, the papers written by feminists attacking the sexism of the mass media do not tell us what they mean to women, and what use women make of them. Dorothy Hobson (1978) argues that mass media are an important part of the everyday lives of the full-time housewives she studied, and that they are *not* leisure for the housebound woman. She goes on (p. 95):

> Television and radio are never mentioned as 'spare time' or leisure activities but are located as integral parts of everyday life. To take radio as an example, Radio 1 and local radio are listened to during the day while the women are engaged in domestic labour . . . they see the radio disc jockey as another 'person' in their privatized world. Phone-in programmes are also important in counteracting isolation . . . These programmes not only provide

a contact with the 'outside world; they also reinforce the pri-
vatized isolation by reaffirming the consensual position – there
are thousands of other women in the same situation, a sort of
'collective isolation'.

Hobson's sample were very socially and geographically isolated,
seeing no friends and, apparently, no kin either. Perhaps their
dependence on the mass media is an extreme case, but we do not
know. Ann Oakley's (1974b) London sample mentioned use of the
radio 'for company' and one, at least, planned her working day
round a soap opera on TV, but watching is is also a social event.
Patricia Andrews is 24 with two children, and in describing her day
she says (p. 108):

> I never sit down in the morning; I never even have breakfast. I
> don't sit down till half past four when I watch *Crossroads* . . .
> My friend comes up or we go down there and have coffee and
> watch *Crossroads*.

The use of mass media to structure and punctuate the day is probably common, but without more detailed data of this kind we
will not know why women watch, read and listen as they do. It is
also important to know how far TV and radio are seen as 'leisure'
activities by women, for it is possible that men, and male researchers, have seen them in this way, but women do not. This
may be one paradox of leisure, that leisure for men is essential for
women, while women's leisure involves them in voluntary work, in
which they engage 'for company'. A discussion of voluntary work
may illuminate this point.

Although a minority of women are involved in voluntary work
and formal organisations, such groups are an important social
phenomenon, and one that is badly under-researched. No good
social science research has been done on the large organisations for
women, such as the Women's Institutes (WI), Townswomen's
Guilds (TG), Women's Royal Voluntary Service (WRVS), Citizen's
Advice Bureaux (CABs) and Mothers' Union, nor on the large
youth movements run by women, such as the Girls' Brigade, Guides
and Brownies, YWCA, and so on. There are more data on the
voluntary movements of vociferous minorities such as the National
Viewers' and Listeners' Association than on the true mass movements. Yet the mass movements are the leisure activities of millions
of British women. Mary Stott (1978) says there are 3 million women
in all-female organisations in Britain, and *Social Trends, 1977*
(p. 182) that there are over a million girls in organised youth
movements, most of whose leaders are women. There are nearly
100,000 girls in the Brownies and the Guides, for example, and that

means a great many Brown Owls and Guide Captains involved in the movement. However, all we know about most of these voluntary movements is that they exist, not what they mean to their members. The voluntary groups can be divided into those which are clearly charitable or 'do-gooding', such as the WRVS, St John Ambulance, Red Cross and CABs; those which mix social and philanthropic aims such as the Inner Wheel, WI and TG; and those which are primarily social, such as the National Housewife's Register. The distinctions, though, may be entirely phoney, for women may actually be active in Oxfam, or the Red Cross, because it is a socially respectable way of meeting friends and going out. Without studies of participants we cannot know the meaning that these organisations have for them. Indeed, given the lack of data on women's leisure, we are thrown back on to journalism and statements by the organisations themselves. Some of the examples which follow show how hard it is to disentangle 'selfless' from 'selfless' motives in women's voluntary group participation.

Women are central to many of the charities in Britain, collecting on doorsteps, staffing the shops, selling flags and organising coffee mornings, jumble sales and dances. Such work is very time-consuming, and can only be done by women volunteers who are leisured enough to have 'free' time. The *Sunday Times* (21 May 1978) featured twelve women in Swindon who had collected £101,000 for cancer research over the previous twenty-five years. This sounded like pure charitable work, with doorstep collections and so forth, but the committee also ran several fashionable social events to cement the committee and attract new members, so obviously this charity was also a social club. At a more official level one can see how the rise in the number of Citizens' Advice Bureaux from 416 in 1961 to 710 in 1977 has *de facto* involved more and more women in their work. In 1976/7 they handled 2,890,000 inquiries (*Social Trends, 1977*, p. 218) which represented a great many woman-hours. Presumably the volunteers make friends among themselves and look forward to the company, or they would not do it, but we do not know this. The WRVS was founded in 1938 and according to the *Observer* (21 May 1978) has 200,000 members of whom nearly all are women. They are famous for meals on wheels and hospital work, but here, too, one imagines the members enjoy friendship and social contact. It is cases like these which make Stacey's categories inadequate, and the inadequacy is reinforced by an examination of further women's organisations.

Two of the most famous women's organisations are the Women's Institutes, founded in 1915 for rural women, which had 440,000 members in 1978; and the Townswomen's Guilds, founded in 1928, with 250,000 members in 1978 (Stott, 1978). Both these are multipurpose organisations: social, charitable and educational. More recent groups are the Pre-School Playgroups Association and the National Housewife's Register which, founded in 1961, had 20,000 members in 1978. While there is evidence that many women are not reached by any of these organisations, those who are members gain both self-confidence and new skills from them. Mary Stott's official history of the TGs includes the following poem which sums up what members of such organisations feel about them (p. 38):

> A spinster, a wife and a widow
> All lived in a street in our town.
> The spinster was shy
> The wife she was young
> And the widow was lonely and 'down'.
> And none of these three knew the others;
> Their days were imperfectly filled –
> Till somebody had an idea
> And started a Townswomen's Guild.
>
> The spinster, the wife and the widow
> All went to the meeting and soon
> What a different life they were leading,
> To each one the Guild proved a boon.
>
> The first went to classes in drama
> And even took part in a play,
> The second got help with her cooking –
> Ideas galore came her way.
> The third found good friends all around her
> To help her along in her pain
> And all three were busy and useful
> And life was worth living again.

Madgwick *et al.* (1973) report that the WI served a similar function in Cardiganshire for newcomers and women who were not attached to chapels. Welsh-speaking women in Wales also have Merched y Wawr, founded in 1967. This organisation has all its proceedings in Welsh, and in 1970 there were eleven branches in Cardiganshire with a membership of 800. This organisation may well be very important in maintaining the Welsh language, if it is the mothers who actually decide whether children are reared as Welsh-speaking or not.

On the whole the larger women's organisations have avoided many political issues, if one takes political in its narrow sense. The issues upon which the women's organisations have coalesced into a political force fall mainly into the category of issues which men call trivial, although they have importance for women. In the early 1960s the respectable women's organisations combined to campaign for the removal of turnstiles from public lavatories. Stott comments that 'this battle may have a faintly comic ring now but the campaign did show how much persistence is needed to remove a grievance which affects only the female sex' (1978, p. 162). The women did win, and turnstiles have vanished from women's lavatories. More recently, a coalition of all women's groups across the political spectrum fought for child benefits to be paid to the mother, and again won. These coalitions are rare, and the major women's organisations have stayed away from controversial issues and campaigns.

In complete contrast to the non-controversial pattern of the majority of women's organisations, it is important to remember that a minority of women are devoting their leisure to campaigns of a highly controversial nature. On the one hand there are the women members of the revolutionary political parties and the various groups based round women's liberation, while on the other there are the campaigns to restore national 'purity' by curtailing pornography, abortion and other features of the 'permissive society'. The various left-wing political groups such as the International Marxist Group, International Socialists and Workers' Revolutionary Party all depend heavily on female members, but their lives are relatively unknown. The many manifestations of the contemporary women's movement are also relatively undocumented, but across Britain many women are devoting their leisure to establishing refuges for battered women, rape crisis centres, feminist newspapers, lesbian communes, free contraception and abortion advice centres, radical day care centres and feminist therapy groups. A glance at the periodicals *Spare Rib, Women's Report, Red Rag* and *Women's Voice* reveals the wide range of activities, but it is hard to estimate how many women are involved in such movements.

Sociologists have directed more attention at the conservative groups, most of which are mixed but depend heavily on women's work to survive. We have studies of the National Viewers' and Listeners' Association (Wallis, 1975) and of the Festival of Light (Wallis, 1976) but the anti-abortion groups SPUC and LIFE have not yet been properly researched. While such groups are absorbing the energies of some women only, they could have far-reaching effects upon the lives of the rest if any of their campaigns were successful. The vast majority of women, however, have one leisure activity which is a far cry from either meals on wheels, running a rape crisis centre or campaigning against pornography, and that is visiting kin. The role of the web of kinship in women's lives is the subject of the next chapter because kinship visiting is closely tied to parenthood and family life.

Chapter 9

The Mother, Grandmother and Widow: Parenthood and Old Age

66   I am by nature very active, and during pregnancy had
     very good health, and was able to look after my home
     and family up to the time of confinement. My con-
     finements have not been what would be called bad
     times. (Wages £1·50 to £1·80; 4 children.)

150 I have not got one healthy child among my five . . .
     they are suffering through the past generation . . . The
     fifth is now nine years old, and suffers from malnutri-
     tion . . . I was always ill, right through my married
     life till now, I have done child-bearing, and am now
     in better health than I can remember. (Wages £1·65
     to £2·25; 5 children.)

(from Llewelyn Davies, 1915, pp. 98 and 156)

Motherhood is popularly supposed to be women's natural destiny,
and at the same time the most honoured and exalted role. (Hence
the motto: 'The hand that rocks the cradle rules the world.') All
women are believed to have an instinct, a biological urge or drive,
both to become mothers and to nurture children. Motherhood
therefore provides women with both personal satisfaction and social
approval, and satisfies their biological urges. These ideas are widely
held by men and women in modern Britain from all walks of life,
and are used as the justification or rationale for a whole range of
other attitudes, beliefs and prejudices. Thus both Ann Oakley's
(1974a) London housewives and Margo Galloway's (1973) students
in Scotland believed that woman's maternal instincts meant she was

destined to rear the children, and to stay home doing housework, as well as implying a whole range of temperamental characteristics. The idea of this chapter is to examine the social meaning of parent-hood in modern Britain, which should throw some light on how far these popular beliefs have any basis in fact or logic; and then to discover how the roles of wife and mother lead inexorably towards the roles of the older woman in British society, grandmother and widow.

The generally held belief that woman's biological structure and her drives towards motherhood are her main purpose in life leads to a whole range of other beliefs and practices. For example, the opposition to women vicars in the Anglican Church typically either points out the awful possibility of the pregnant vicar or mentions darkly that menstruation renders women unclean. (An idea common in many 'primitive' cultures with which British bishops might hesi-tate to identify themselves, fear of menstruation is discussed in Mary Douglas's excellent *Purity and Danger*, 1966.) Yet when one ex-amines the dominant ideology in Britain about motherhood it turns out to be much more complex, and less straightforwardly related to biology, than at first appears. For while the popular belief is that all women are destined to be mothers, have uncontrolled, un-controllable and socially desirable drives towards maternity, and because of this cannot be given responsible jobs, training, advanced education, or any other material advances in society, the actual situation is much more complex. In fact, not only is the evidence for a maternal instinct in humans very poor but the popular beliefs about the maternal instinct are, in reality, structured in accordance with social conventions which are rarely examined by either the general public or social scientists. The latter point is the focus of the first part of this chapter, for the 'biological' or otherwise nature of maternal feelings in women is outside the scope of this book.

Sally Macintyre (1976*a*, 1976*b* and 1977) has demonstrated quite clearly how the beliefs of the general public, the medical profes-sions and sociologists about women and maternity in Britain are based on an unexamined assumption. For the dominant reproduc-tive ideology (a useful phrase of Joan Busfield's, 1974) in Britain is not only a belief about sex and gender: all women have a natural urge to be mothers; rather it is also a belief about *marriage*. The dominant ideology of reproduction actually states that while *all* women want to be mothers, they really want to be *wives* and mothers. That is, no sane, well-adjusted, rational female wants to be a mother outside marriage. This leads to two interlocked beliefs: (1) all married women want to fulfil their natural destiny so that once they are wives, motherhood is a desired next step; but (2) motherhood is undesirable for single women. This dominant ideo-logy is captured in the famous 'doctor' joke:

Doctor: Well, Mrs Brown, I've spendid news for you . . .
Patient: It's *Miss* Brown.
Doctor: Miss Brown, I have terrible news for you.

In summary, all rational, adult women want to be mothers in wedlock, so all married women want babies and no unmarried women do. This basic belief leads to a series of correlated ideas, so that the 'problem' of the unmarried mother is 'solved' if she marries; that married women who do not want children are 'unnatural' or 'ill' or 'selfish'; and, socially most crucial, that because women are 'driven' to maternity by biological urges, all offspring of married women are 'really' wanted.

There is no equivalent ideology about fatherhood, in that men are seen as having a *sex* drive, but not a paternity urge. Interestingly the sex drive is held to be present in men irrespective of their marital status, and can be used to justify crimes such as rape and indecent exposure, as well as supporting prostitution. Sociologists have given little or no attention to fatherhood as a role in men's lives, and indeed, very little data have been collected on fathers' attitudes to, or hand in, child-rearing, childbirth or family planning. In popular belief, the only males who seem to be recognised as having a strong desire for fatherhood are those with substantial assets to pass on, such as Henry VIII or King Hussein of Jordan, who seek fresh wives in a desperate search for sons. Ordinary men may well desire children, but sociology has had very little to say about them and their wishes. Because this is a book about women, nothing more is said in this chapter about fatherhood, but research on married and unmarried men's attitudes and behaviour towards fatherhood as an ideal and as practical behaviour is urgently needed.

In this chapter the biological facts about motherhood or potential motherhood (pregnancy, miscarriage, abortion, infertility and childbirth) are separated from the social facts of being a wife or not, a parent or not, a rational human being or not, and so on. The social role of 'mother' is not necessarily related to biological issues, because one can adopt, foster or otherwise acquire a child by legal means, or become an 'instant' mother by marrying a man with children. Such a separation of social facts from biological ones is normal sociological procedure, but has not characterised the sociology of fertility or motherhood so far. Rather, as Macintyre (1977) shows, sociologists have unconsciously adopted the perspective that marriage and babies 'belong' together, while unmarried mothers are deviant in some way.

Sally MacIntyre also shows clearly that the medical professions' treatment of biological facts is totally determined by the social facts. Indeed, she summarises the medical view by saying: 'At its crudest, this leads to the position that maternal instinct only operates in married women, and not in unmarried women' (1976a). This social construction of the biological facts leads to a set of opposed beliefs about appropriate medical treatment for married and unmarried women, which Macintyre summarises as follows:

Married Women
(1) pregnancy and childbearing are normal and desirable, and conversely a desire not to have children is aberrant and in need of explanation
(2) pregnancy and childbearing are not problematic, and to treat them as such indicates that something is wrong
(3) legitimate children with a living parent should *not* be adopted
(4) childless couples should present their 'problem' to the medical profession for diagnosis and treatment
(5) it is sometimes clinically advisable to tell a woman to have a baby
(6) the loss of a baby by miscarriage, stillbirth, or neonatal death should be an occasion for distress and grief.

Unmarried Women
(1) pregnancy and childbearing are abnormal and undesirable, the desire to have a baby is selfish or aberrant and needs explaining
(2) pregnancy and childbearing are problematic and need to be treated as such
(3) illegitimate children should be adopted
(4) unless marriage is imminent, diagnosis and treatment of infertility are not relevant
(5) it is never appropriate to advise childbirth
(6) loss of a baby should not produce grief, but rather relief.

These differences in basic treatment, both medical and personal, were revealed in Macintyre's research on the pregnancy careers of twenty-eight women in Aberdeen in the early 1970s. Very similar conclusions came from the research carried out in Ipswich in 1969/70 by Joan Busfield (1974). It is important to stress that all these 'medical' beliefs are not grounded in biology, but in social consensus, a set of beliefs shared by much of the population, and most powerful people in modern Britain.

At earlier periods in Britain's history the beliefs would have been different, and several ethnic groups in modern Britain do not share them today. The West Africans in London studied by Esther Goody and Christine Groothues (1977), for example, hold very different ideas about parenthood from the medical and judicial professions in Britain. Similarly there is considerable evidence that in rural Britain illegitimacy was high, and carried little or no stigma, and that marriage normally followed proof of the woman's fertility. In other words, a woman had to prove she could become pregnant before she was marriageable. Gill (1977) has discussed this for Scotland and there has been a controversy about the economic basis of illegitimacy in Scotland in the *Scottish Journal of Sociology* (1976, 1977). Thus it is important to bear in mind throughout the discussion of parenthood that the relation between social and biological facts is not a constant one, but changes over time. Women whose own beliefs are at variance with prevailing orthodoxies must not, therefore, be condemned as 'irrational', or 'mad', but as members of minorities with different perspectives on the relations between sexual activity and marriage. Bearing this in mind, we can examine the main facts about parenthood in modern Britain and how it affects women.

The major difficulty with this approach – trying *not* to assume that married women want children and single ones do not – is that the extant research has not been carried out on this basis. Researchers have almost always been so blinded by the dominant reproductive ideology that they have restricted their sampling, their questions and their conclusions to within its basic premises. Thus only married couples are asked about their family building plans, and whole projects are established to examine the 'problem' of teenage pregnancies (Murcott, 1980). The published research available for this chapter includes recent work on family building intentions of married couples only (Busfield, 1974; Cartwright, 1976), on illegitimacy in Scotland (Gill, 1977), on single women with children (Marsden, 1973), childless couples (Humphrey, 1969; Owens, 1979), women involved with abortion (Horobin, 1973), and the pregnancy careers of young women in Aberdeen (Macintyre, 1976*a*, 1976 *b* and 1977). It is, however, sometimes rather hard to reconcile the findings of these disparate studies because of the different assumptions upon which they are based.

However, all the available data on parenthood in Britain have to be seen against the demographic background; that is, in the context of the changing population. The best-known thing about the population of Britain is that it is not growing at the rate expected in the 1960s. In 1964 government forecasts were for a population of 75 million by AD 2000, but a dramatic fall in the birth rate took place, so that recent estimates have been much lower; *Social Trends, 1977* (p. 41) now suggests that the population of England, Wales and Scotland will only be 56 million in AD 2001. As the editors point out, the fall in the birth rate over the last ten years either means that some or all of the people are both *choosing* smaller families and attaining their choice, or that more people are managing to have the number of children they want. There is, of course, a third possibility, mentioned by Jeremy James in the

Listener (27 January 1977), that is, increasing proportions of in-fertile or subfertile couples, who are not managing to have children they want. In his article he quotes a consultant gynaecologist – since famous for producing the first 'test tube' baby – who 'is certain' that 15 per cent of married couples are 'medically infertile'. What-ever the cause, the birth rate has fallen rapidly since 1966, as *Social Trends, 1977* (p. 47) shows. Table 9·1 shows the number of live births per thousand people in Great Britain since 1951. This table shows that the birth rate rose after 1951 to a peak in 1966, from

Table 9·1 *Live Births Per Thousand People*

Year	1951	1961	1966	1971	1976
Live births	72·5	90·0	91·1	84·2	61·0

which it has declined to a level lower than anything known since the depression between the two world wars.

An examination of the figures for births in more detail shows several factors which account for the fall. The editors of *Social Trends, 1977* say that the important factors have been the halt to the dropping age of marriage (i.e. brides are older on average than they were), that within marriage the first child is longer delayed than in the mid-1960s, and that the number of third and subsequent children, especially among manual workers, has declined markedly. However, it is also clear from the figures that while married people are choosing, or producing, fewer children, the single women of Britain are choosing to have, or 'falling for', a higher *proportion* of Britain's babies. Thus the family building intentions and achieve-ments of the married are slightly less significant for predicting birth rates and populations than they were, and the family building intentions and achievements of the single women more significant. As these illegitimate births have generally been seen as 'accidents', however, no serious work has been done on the family building intentions of single women. Table 9·2 shows the illegitimate births in Great Britain as a percentage of all the live births. For England and Wales alone, illegitimate births were 9 per cent of all live births in 1970, and 10 per cent in 1976.

While the proportion of illegitimate births has been rising, the proportion of children conceived before a marriage has been falling. Some of these children will have precipitated 'shotgun' weddings, some will have been conceived in the period preceding weddings already fixed, and it is hard to know – without a detailed study of their parents – how far such children were 'wanted' or not. Certainly a great many teenage brides go pregnant to their weddings:

Table 9·2   *Illegitimate Births as a Percentage of All Live Births*

Year	1951	1961	1966	1971	1976
Percentage	4·9	5·8	7·7	8·4	9·2

Source: Adapted from *Social Trends, 1977,* p. 47.

Cartwright (1976) says two-fifths; *Social Trends, 1977* (p. 47) offers the figures shown in Table 9·3 for live births within eight months of marriage to brides under 20.

Table 9·3   *'8 Month Births' as Percentage of Live Births to Women under 20*

Year	1951	1961	1966	1971	1976
Percentage of live births	55·1	56·8	54·9	56·8	50·6

These two trends seem to be running counter to one another; a higher proportion of illegitimate babies, but a slightly lower one of premarital conceptions. Research into these two categories of pregnancy, unhampered by beliefs about their social appropriateness or otherwise, is needed. The lack of knowledge about these births is in contrast to our information about the falling 'legitimate' birth rate. The falling numbers of third, fourth, fifth, sixth and subsequent children in marriages is clearly shown in *Social Trends, 1977* (p. 55). Not only are the absolute numbers of births declining, so too are the proportions of third and subsequent children. Thus, comparing 1972 with 1976, there were 262,200 first children in 1972 and 211,200 in 1976; 223,900 second children compared with 195,100; 93,600 third children to 64,400; and 12,200 'fifth and subsequent' children in 1972 compared with 5,900 in 1976. If we use the data collected by Ann Cartwright (1976) on about 1,500 people from all over England and one area of South Wales in two surveys in 1967/8 and 1973, we can see how these demographic changes relate to people's intentions and desires.

Ann Cartwright's two surveys show that between 1967/8 and 1973 both desired family size and actual family size declined. She summarises her findings (1976, pp. 165–6) as follows:

In 1973 parents were intending to have smaller families than they were in 1967/68.... The trend is to less variation in family size ... the stereotype of the two- or three-child family is becoming more and more common.

Cartwright found in 1973 that 78 per cent of mothers already were happy with, or wanted, two or three children. The main distinction between wanting two or three children was due to their sex. Twenty-six per cent of those with two children of the same sex wanted a third child, while only 17 per cent of those who had one of each already did. However, as her sample were recent parents of a legitimate child, they cannot tell us anything about the increasing proportion of childless married women. *Social Trends,1977* shows that an increasing proportion of married women are deferring their first child, either from choice or because of subfertility, and a growing proportion are staying childless for five years or more. In 1975 over 20 per cent of the women who had married in 1970 were childless, and 70 per cent of those who had married in 1973. It seems possible that two quite different patterns of childbearing are developing: one group bearing children in their teens inside and outside marriage, while another set defer childbearing until several years of marriage have passed.

However, it is important to point out that the available data show British women are not in control of their own fertility for a whole variety of reasons. Single women are still under pressure not to have children, and married women to have them, and both groups face problems over implementing any decisions they may make. If we consider first the case of the married woman, and then the unmarried, certain similarities will appear.

CHILDLESS BY CHOICE?

Ann Cartwright (1976, p. 21) suggests that only about 4 per cent of married couples intend to remain childless, but stresses that intentions about family building are fluid and not static. Her own data show that 4 or 5 per cent of *mothers* report that they had not wanted *any* children when they married, while a further 11 to 20 per cent had uncertain views about having some or any children. Table 9·4 shows her figures in 1967/8 and 1973 on this question for both fathers and mothers. Several things need to be said about this table. First, by the time Cartwright questioned these people they were parents of at least one child, and it is hard to know how much reliance we can put on their recollections of intentions at marriage years before. Some people may feel embarrassed at confessing they did not want children if they have had one or more, while others may have forgotten what they wanted, never thought about it at the time, or even be claiming now that they 'never wanted' children causing them problems at the time of the survey. However, from Table 9·4 we can see that men were less likely than

Table 9·4 *Percentage of Parents 'Uncertain' about Children and Wanting No Children at Marriage, 1967/8 and 1973 Samples*

	1967/8		1973	
	Mothers	Fathers	Mothers	Fathers
	%	%	%	%
'Uncertain' about parenthood	11	15	20	20
No children wanted	4	3	5	2

Source: Adapted from Cartwright, 1976, p. 20.

women to say they had not wanted any children – although men who resented their children may have refused to participate in the survey. It is clear, though, that a substantial number of women reported that they had no clear commitment to a *particular* family pattern, and a small proportion that they did not want any children. Yet even in a period with legal abortion and NHS contraception all these women had had at least one child. This needs to be explained – perhaps more than the high illegitimacy rate does – although that has produced a government report (Court, 1976).

The married woman who does not want children has, in modern Britain, to be steadfast and determined if she is going to achieve that aim. She has perhaps twenty-five years of fertile marriage in which to avoid conception and/or childbirth, and she must do so against a range of difficulties. Although contraception has improved significantly since 1945, sterilisation is still the only 100 per cent safeguard and, together with all the more reliable contraceptives, is firmly in the control of the medical professions. Apart from sterilisation, there is no totally effective, medically safe contraceptive to suit all women; for all known methods have side-effects, and *can* be ineffective. The Pill can be rendered useless by gastric upsets, for example, even if taken conscientiously. Even if there were such a contraceptive, the medical professions would probably try to hold it back from married women. Sally Macintyre (1976*a*) reports a 29-year-old married woman who had attended a clinic for the Pill for six years and 'after a period of cues and hints she was finally directly informed that she ought to have a baby'. Macintyre also heard a gynaecologist lecture a medical audience and tell them that for married women 'if she gets pregnant it doesn't matter very much'.

Apart from such direct control and influence over fertility being vested, not in women themselves, but in a predominantly male medical establishment, the married woman who wishes to stay childfree faces a wide range of pressures from other sources. Family, distant relations, neighbours, the mass media, and all agencies, such as employers, building societies, insurance companies, trade unions and architects, for example, all assume the married woman will sooner or later choose motherhood or be overcome by her 'natural' maternal instinct. The pressures can be seen from accounts of both deliberately childfree couples and those with subfertility problems, who complain of the cruelty of such pressures when they are unable to comply with them. (An uneasy alliance between childfree and childless to resist such pressures was struck with the establishment of the National Association of Non-Parents, but the alliance did not survive and the two groups split apart.)

A major source of pressure on the married woman to have children is the potential grandparents. From the perspective of the would-be grandmother this is quite understandable, as we shall see later in the chapter, but it can be hard to bear for the childfree or subfertile woman. *Woman's Realm* (29 July 1978) carried this letter on its problem page from a would-be grandmother:

Unfortunately, neither I nor my husband get on very well with our daughter-in-law – she always seems to be searching for something to quarrel about. A few weeks ago, when I made a casual remark about how we were looking forward to having grandchildren, she turned nasty, and said she didn't want babies. My son loves children – I know he would like a family – and I feel I want to talk to her, and tell her how rewarding children can be . . . How can I go about this tactfully?

Note that this woman does not ask whether she should put pressure on her daughter-in-law, only how to do it. She was advised to say nothing, but what evidence we have suggests she is unlikely to obey. In a study of 216 couples who had been investigated for possible infertility at a hospital, Michael Humphrey (*New Society*, 13 March 1969) reported that these 'simple country folk' were acutely sensitive about their childlessness. Only half the women said their relatives were sympathetic to the problem, while the rest reported that kin assumed they did not want children. Neighbours and friends were equally hostile, and Humphrey wrote that 'social difficulties were frequently mentioned, and one woman went so far as to declare "you are social outcasts" '. Indeed, three-quarters of the women reported 'wounding insinuations' that they did not want children, and these produced 'considerable distress' in a quarter of them.

More recent studies on married people with children show that those people without are seen negatively. Joan Busfield's (1974) data from 340 married couples in the Ipswich area show that the idea that children are necessary to 'complete' a family is widespread. This sample said that children 'made' a family, providing the parents with security in old age, richer emotional lives, a focus of pride and achievement, and that children stabilise a marriage. These couples saw childless women as wrapped up in themselves, childish, neurotic or ill. Similar comments were made by the housewives and mothers in Ann Oakley's (1974a) study, who typically made comments like (p. 178):

> I think children make a home really, I see people who are married and don't have children who are quite miserable.

There is, of course, a contradiction here. Subfertile couples suffer from accusations of selfishness and worse because they are believed not to want children, when they are often desperate to have them, while the married woman who is genuinely against motherhood for herself is disbelieved, and if she does conceive, is unlikely to be allowed an abortion. Beliefs about the naturalness of motherhood lead to two distinct groups of women being made miserable by relations, friends, neighbours and, if they are public figures, the wider society. The vehemence of accusations levelled at women known or believed to be *choosing* not to have children can be seen in the following letters to the *Sunday Times* (10 March 1969). Irma Kutz had written an article saying she did not want children, and there was a large correspondence. The 'letters editor' commented that 'not all disagreed with her views', which clearly implied that all correspondents had been expected to attack her. However, the strength of feeling among those who disagreed with her was tremendous, and was only equalled by the lack of logic in their arguments. Irma Kutz was, in one letter, accused of going against nature; an accusation which cannot but be meaningless. If all women have a natural urge to motherhood, Irma Kutz would have it; if she does not, then it cannot be *universally* natural. Two letters were particularly vitriolic;

> I hope the mother of Irma Kutz did not have the misfortune to read her daughter's article. She is already disappointed by not having been presented with any grandchildren. When so many women . . . will go through all sorts of embarrassing questions and examinations to achieve their goal, surely the writer can see that it is adverse to nature not to want a child?

What a pity Irma Kutz's mother did not think like her. If she had we would be without one very bitter person who is desperately fighting for a substitute for love.

Note also here the correspondents' emphasis on the potential 'need' of Irma Kutz's *mother* to be a grandmother.

Faced with both ineffective contraception (or lack of knowledge about contraception) and social pressures, it is perhaps not surprising that so many married women 'give in'. While some genuinely change their minds and choose motherhood, others claim to have been trapped by circumstances, or to have been coerced into giving birth. The available data suggest that women who are hostile to childbearing at marriage postpone their first child for longer than those who want children when they marry. Ann Cartwright shows that a quarter of the 'anti' group at marriage had been married for four years or longer before their first child, compared with only a tenth of the 'pro' group at marriage. Cartwright asked these women what had led them to change their minds about having children, and two-fifths of the 'anti' groups said they had not done so. A third of them said that they had come to regard children as an integral part of marriage: that is, they had fallen into line with the majority sentiment. The two-fifths who said they had not changed their minds made comments such as (1976, p. 21):

I didn't change my mind, but my husband thinks you can't be happy if you haven't got children so I agreed.

Well, I was unlucky and got caught.

We didn't plan, I just conceived – but I had no maternal longings.

It was unplanned. I didn't change my mind – the baby was a mistake.

These comments show women caught in unwanted motherhood by either a 'failure' to manage contraception and pressure from husbands. Ann Oakley's (1974a) study of forty London housewives showed similar reasons for pregnancies among women who had not wanted children at marriage. Thus one woman said 'if I'd known then what I know now, I wouldn't have had any of them' and another 'After we'd been married about two and a half years, my husband said we really should have a baby. I wasn't too keen.' The Newsons' research in Nottingham (1965) also revealed unwilling mothers, such as Mrs Lievesley, an engine driver's wife, who had five children. She had 'had to get married' nineteen years ago, and she had not wanted her recent baby either (p. 18).

We didn't want none of 'em, come to that. They was all accidents. But we was *really* surprised to see Vicky, because we was using something before her.

Once a woman has one child in wedlock, the pressure to have a second is almost as strong. 'Only' children are regarded as unlucky or spoilt, and the ideal family has two or three children, including at least one of each sex (Cartwright, 1976; Busfield, 1974). However, after three children, social pressure slackens, until the woman with a great many children is considered 'odd'. The lack of control over their own fertility experienced by British women even in 1973 is clear from Cartwright's data on the joy or otherwise with which over 1,400 pregnancies had been greeted by her sample, and it shows that, just as women have little 'choice' about a first baby, so too many have little control over subsequent conceptions either. Table 9·5 shows these data from Cartwright (1976, p. 15), and it is clear that any pregnancy a woman has may bring her face to face with becoming or remaining a mother against her will.

Table 9·5   *Mothers' Initial Attitudes to Pregnancy*

	1976/8 %	1973 %
Sorry it happened at all	15	13
Rather it had been later	17	14
Rather it had been sooner	7	10
Pleased	61	63
Total in sample	1,473	1,461

Source: Cartwright, 1976, p. 15.

At first sight, it may seem odd that so many women have unwanted babies. Three findings seem to 'explain' why so many married women become unwilling mothers of first or subsequent children. There is research evidence that knowledge of contraception is often non-existent or faulty, that contraception techniques known are not always effective, and that the medical profession takes a large part in determining married women's fertility in ways they do not want. First, many women are not knowledgeable about contraception and conception. Jane Hubert (1974) interviewed fifty-four women attending an antenatal clinic for their first birth and found that two-thirds of the thirty-four married women and all but one of the twenty single women had not planned their pregnancies.

None of these women with unplanned pregnancies had used any contraceptive method but withdrawal, and none of them knew anything useful about contraceptive methods. Hubert collected a fine range of erroneous beliefs, including the use of Beecham's Pills as an abortificient, going immediately to the lavatory, and the idea that 'going steady' made one safe, for only bad, promiscuous girls get pregnant.

Secondly, knowledge about contraception may not mean ability to manage it. Fransella and Frost (1977, p. 148) quote a study of 500 pregnant London women in which, although nearly all knew where to go for advice, only 20 per cent used contraception regularly, 40 per cent irregularly and a further 40 per cent used none. Yet, as Ann Cartwright's work shows, by no means all of these women who do not want children but do not use contraceptives regularly are irrational. Some faced appalling difficulties (p. 48):

'I'm not allowed the pill and they won't fit the cap or the coil ... and I don't like Durex ... and we don't get on with the withdrawal method ...

Many of the women who were using contraception were also having problems with various methods, which could lead to further unwanted pregnancies, and others were receiving conflicting or unhelpful medical advice. Thus one woman said, about having an IUD (p. 63):

The doctor advised against it. I had actually made out to have it fitted at hospital . . . I cancelled the appointment after seeing my GP.

This leads to the third point, the medical control over access to legal methods of contraception and, more important still, abortion. If a married woman who rejects motherhood wants a legal abortion she is totally in the hands of a medical profession with strong ideas about women's fertility and its control. Ann Cartwright (1976) found that 6 per cent of her sample had considered abortion for their most recent pregnancy, and 17 per cent of those who considered the pregnancy 'unwanted'. Two-thirds of those considering abortion appealed to doctors, while one-third tried to abort themselves. Sally Macintyre (1976a) shows that doctors and nurses are likely to dismiss any negative feelings expressed by pregnant married women as unreal, and related to hormone changes. Hostile feelings are denied and married women are told they will change their minds during pregnancy and come to want the baby. Abortion requests, unless there are serious problems, are unlikely to be treated seriously. Cartwright (1976, p. 69) found one woman who, when pregnant with her second child, wanted an abortion, but was told by her female GP that wanting an only child was 'selfish', and was prevented from having a termination. The GP said 'she believed every family should have more than one'. In a parallel case Sally Macintyre describes a woman of 24, pregnant with her fourth child and awaiting divorce, who was told that discussion of future contraception was not appropriate. 'As you're marrying, your husband will be wanting two children.' The patient denied this, but the doctor was convinced that, to quote Macintyre, 'however many children a woman already has, a new husband will want her to provide some more, of his, and she should want to do this'.

Thus the medical professions, and their adherence to the conventional ideology of fertility, conspire with other forces in society to encourage married women towards attaining the 'ideal' family. With luck, the pressures turn the 'unwilling' into a willing mother, the subject of the next section.

WILLING MOTHERS

In contrast to those women who have motherhood thrust upon them are those who want motherhood from their wedding day, those initially hostile who change their minds and those awkward single women who want babies. Married women who always wanted children, and those initially hostile who change their minds, come to share similar views about children completing a relationship. Cartwright (1976, p. 21) quotes women who changed their minds:

I found with both of us working there was no family life without children.

Our life was getting a bit humdrum – both working, getting a bit fed up with each other.

I think once you are married you feel differently.

Those married women who want children and cannot have them are, as Sally Macintyre (1976a, 1976b and 1977) has shown, legitimately able to solicit help from the medical profession, after a 'reasonable' period. Thus a woman of 28 married seven years was considered 'reasonable' in her request for conception, and the gynaecologist agreed to her having an operation, but a woman of 19 who wanted treatment for infertility was seen as 'fussing'. At the other end of the scale, women with 'enough' children are allowed to seek medical help to stop conceiving, and sterilisation was agreed for a woman of 35 with three children, and one of 23 with one child and an alcoholic husband who forbade contraception. Among the 'reasonable' requests for gynaecological help, Macintyre found, were unmarried women who wanted abortions, while among the 'unreasonable' were single women who wanted to have babies but not get married.

Sally Macintyre has examined the trajectories of a sample of pregnant women in Aberdeen, with particular emphasis on what she calls their 'moral careers' and how these related to their inter-actions with medical personnel (Macintyre, 1976a, 1976b and 1977). She has found three distinct 'moral careers' for the single woman who presents herself pregnant to the world: the bad girl, the good girl who made one mistake and the 'normal' woman, who is some-one about-to-be-married whose conception occurred too soon. The doctors her sample visited were likely to discover *first* whether a pregnant single woman was going to regularise her position by marriage and, if so, abortion, adoption and single parenthood were not considered. The deliberately pregnant single woman was not considered to be a possibility, except if the woman concerned was mentally disturbed. This seems to be a common reaction. In an article in *Mother* (July 1978) Leslie Kenton tells how she always wanted to have a baby but 'never considered getting married'. She became pregnant, and told her father she intended to keep her baby. She goes on:

My poor father ... horrified ... He wrote back saying that there was no possibility of my being a *mother* without being a *wife*, too. Either I got married or I gave up the baby.

Macintyre's sample included several young women who wanted to be mothers outside wedlock, and all came under considerable pres-sure of these kinds. The maternal instincts of these women are stigmatised. They can remove the stigma by marriage, by abortion or by adoption. If they carry the baby and keep it, they are likely to bear the stigma of irresponsibility for a long time, as well as facing considerable maternal hardship.

Both married and single women, once a pregnancy is being con-tinued to full term, face the usual route to motherhood: child-birth. (Motherhood can be attained by marriage and by adoption, but for a minority of women.) The next section looks at childbirth and child-rearing in modern Britain, the former being experienced only by 'natural' mothers, but the latter by all 'social' mothers however the children were acquired.

CHILDBIRTH

As the quotations at the chapter head show, conception, pregnancy and childbirth were both a major focus of married women's lives and a threat to their financial and bodily well-being at the turn of the century. Llewelyn Davies (1915) collected a large number of accounts of numerous pregnancies, stillbirths, miscarriages and painful labours from women in the Co-operative Movement. Today childbearing is firmly controlled by the male-dominated medical profession (Oakley, 1976) but we know relatively little about how it is experienced by women. Jane Hubert's (1974) sample of fifty-four first pregnancies in London attending an antenatal clinic (and we know that the most 'unhealthy' women are least likely to attend such clinics) is one of the few studies we have, and it makes dispiriting reading.

During their pregnancies, Hubert says, 'these women had very little idea of what was happening to them, and often suffered because they did not realise medical help was available'. Hubert says there were 'women enduring such symptoms as severe back pains, vomiting through pregnancy etc., who did not think to ask for help, partly because they thought that their symptoms were probably usual and therefore ought not to be complained about and partly because they had no idea that anything could be done about them anyway'. Hubert attributes this to the conflicting attitudes to pregnancy of the women's mothers and the antenatal clinic staff. While the staff treated pregnancy as a state of health, the mothers treated them as if they were ill. Because pregnancy was 'normal' for clinic staff, but not for the young women, there was a serious communication gap between them. Most had gone into labour unprepared for the rigours of childbirth, as well as badly prepared for the baby itself, as we shall see later.

Lack of communication with the medical professions during pregnancy was also reported by Barbara Moyes (*New Society*, 10 November 1977) from a sample of women in Scotland. Also working class and pregnant, Moyes found her sample highly ambivalent about the role of medical professionals in their pregnancies. In particular, the internal examination, normal at the hospital, was, for many of the women, both mysterious and embarrassing. Because these women had no knowledge of why an internal was done, they could only interpret it as a sexual encounter. They made comments like 'Just the thought of anyone touching me there just made me squirm'. Some women found the encounter easier with a woman gynaecologist, but others felt that close to perversion: 'I dinna like women poking me, I mean, that sounds stupid, but I'd rather have a man than a woman.' Moyes argued that, had the internal been explained, the embarrassment would have been lessened. Hubert and Moyes were both reporting data from working-class women. However, ignorance of childbirth and reproductive biology is not confined to the poorly educated. Interviewed in the *Sunday Times* (2 October 1977) Claire Rayner said:

It's not uneducated people either – I had a girl, an arts graduate, very clever, eight months pregnant, who ... said she wanted to breast feed her baby but would it hurt when the doctors made the holes in her nipples to let the milk out.

Childbirth itself is the subject of controversy in Britain, with exponents of hospitalised, highly technological childbirth opposed to various groups wanting more 'natural' deliveries. A systematic sociological research project on how women relate to these various forms of childbirth is yet to be published. The Newsons (1965, pp. 27–31) report that many women found giving birth a 'deep joy', although the majority thought 'it was all right' and 10 per cent were negative. When the Newsons were beginning their research, a large number of births were still at home, and 43 per cent of women who gave birth at home had a neighbour or relative present. The Newsons found that women were more likely to have recalled the birth as pleasant if their husband had been present, and they found some enthusiastic men. One miner said:

I've seen everything: I've seen a breech birth, I've seen a normal birth, and now I just want to see a sincerian (*sic*) birth, and I *shall*, I'm *determined*.

A thorough study of different women's perceptions and experiences in various kinds of childbirth is needed to illuminate all the mass media controversies. We do, however, know a little more about how the women react to children when they have them, and this is the subject of the next section.

MOTHERHOOD

Once the baby is born, or acquired in some other way, the role of mother becomes a pervasive and time-consuming one. Even those women who report enjoyment of motherhood (Oakley, 1974a; Newson and Newson, 1965) find the tasks tiring and repetitive, particularly because they are usually carried out in isolation from other adults. Susan Chesters (*Mother*, August 1978), for example, says she 'felt severely the strain of being "on duty" round the clock', had 'no resources from which I could recharge my own emotional batteries', and says she could 'no longer sew, garden, read, cook, listen to a radio play, decorate the house or wash the floor without being interrupted'. These are the common plaints of the full-time mothers. It is clear that the negative sides of mother-hood catch many women unprepared; the question is whether the joys of motherhood outweigh the exhaustion and pain. The evidence from the Newsons' study of child-rearing in Nottingham suggests that there are joys in childbearing, but Jane Hubert's (1974) sample was totally unprepared for the actual demands of a new baby. They found infants exhausting and

> instead of a quiet, undemanding, doll-like baby, the new mother is often presented with a squalling, starving animal whose needs are both unpredictable and apparently insatiable.

Educated women may be equally unprepared for physical exhaustion and equally ignorant of the needs of a baby. Leslie Kenton (*Mother*, July 1978) was a university student, but in the nursing home she was brought her baby four times after it was born, and merely cuddled him. The fourth time he not unnaturally cried, and she rang for the nurse:

> 'He's crying,' I said. 'What should I do?'
> 'Have you burped him?'
> 'No.'
> 'You *have* fed him, of course.'
> 'Fed him? Am I supposed to feed him?'

The Newsons (1965) have argued that the mother in modern Britain is faced with problems over child-rearing because of the large number of different 'experts' and sources of advice. The young mother has her own family, her GP, a health visitor, the clinic doctor(s) and numerous books and magazines. Among recent developments have been glossy magazines devoted to motherhood: *Mother*, *Mother and Baby* and *Parents*. These are very interesting for the image of the 'ideal' modern mother which they seek to perpetrate, and the line they take on controversial issues. All three have medically qualified writers, and offer a good deal of medical information, together with more general articles on cooking, knitting and gardening. The general tone of all three is suffused with a glorification of conventional motherhood, with no toleration of role-reversals, abortion or even an unwilling mother. Indeed, no suggestion is ever made that mothers might want to continue with a career, and full-time motherhood is the only possible role offered. While much of the medical information is clearly presented, and would bridge gaps between women and doctors, the overall tone of the magazine would be off-putting for young women who are ambivalent about or resentful of their impending motherhood. These magazines support the medical dominance of women, and neglect any ideas hostile to motherhood as submissive martyrdom. Typically in *Mother and Baby* (August 1978) we read how watching Daniel come to life at two months 'is one of the richest and most rewarding experiences I have ever had . . . I am responding to him with intense

... love'. The realities of motherhood are more complex and less glorious.

Ann Oakley (1974a, p. 166) points out that motherhood and housewifery are inextricably linked for most women, and the roles cannot easily be separated. 'The majority of housewives have children, and virtually all mothers are housewives.' Yet there is a conflict between the two roles, for children constantly interrupt housework and create mess and chaos. Thus Oakley found that the birth of the first child 'appeared to induce a discontent with routine housekeeping chores' (p. 170) because it was harder to maintain the same standards or work uninterrupted. Oakley suggests that some women separate the roles of mother and housewife, while others do not, and these latter tend to stress the need to keep children clean and tidy. While none of the women expressed negative attitudes to motherhood, it was middle-class ones who emphasised the unique experience with another individual, and made comments like this (p. 173):

> I'd rather be at home with the child than at work – or doing anything else I could think of ... I expected to find it rewarding, but not quite as much as it is.

Overall, however, the feelings of most women were summarised by a mother who said 'You're all for the children, never for yourself' (p. 177). In other words, the constant responsibility, together with the social isolation, were the worst aspects of motherhood.

The sense of responsibility is also stressed by the Newsons in their study of 700 Nottingham mothers. They say (1976, p. 399) that:

> Parents of every social stratum and every level of adequacy have in common the basic knowledge that, because they have produced this child from their own bodies, society requires them to see the job through, and judges them accordingly.

This responsibility is accepted even by parents who feel they are falling down on their task, and only diminishes as the child grows older and other social forces come into play. The Newsons stress that parental responsibility has no fixed hours, but is continuous, and that because children combine their heredity and their environment, they are a walking testimony for their parents. They are, however, careful to point out that mothers are more vulnerable to social criticism, because they are primarily responsible (p. 401):

> Fathers are not expected to take public responsibility for either the behaviour or the appearance of very young children.

The other major finding of the Newsons' researches is the extent to which parenthood, and especially motherhood, is an *adaptive* process. They comment that 'mothers find themselves adapting beyond their own expectations to meet their children's personalities' (1976, p. 37). In so far as mothers do this, they are actually following a typical female pattern in which women are expected to adapt to others. However, unlike the picture portrayed by Hubert (1974) and Oakley (1974*a*), the Newsons do show mothers reaping some of the benefits of motherhood hymned in the mass media. Thus they quote a clerical worker's wife saying that her 7-year-old daughter 'can make you feel like a million dollars' (1976, p. 44) and a working-class woman saying of her son (p. 43):

> It wouldn't matter what you did for Nicholas, he appreciates everything – if you knitted him a sweater he'd be thrilled – ever such an appreciative child, he really is, and you love to do things for him.

It is for such positive feelings that motherhood is lauded in modern Britain, and such relationships make for the widely acclaimed 'proper family'. In the next section the idea of the proper family, and the role of women in it, is examined in more detail.

GRANNY AND THE PROPER FAMILY

The previous section showed that most British people believe children are necessary to turn a married couple into a proper family, and that there is widespread support for the idea that women have a maternal instinct and that motherhood is the most fulfilling role women can have in society. Sociologists have been uncritical of these beliefs, and have not, with the exception of Sally Macintyre, subjected them to a proper scrutiny. In this section and the following one the focus changes to two further roles women play in modern Britain about which myths abound: the grandmother and the widow. This section deals with the grandmother, that is, the woman with grandchildren, and focuses particularly on the women with married children who have legitimate children themselves. The final section looks at the role of the widow and the old woman in modern Britain.

The woman with married children occupies three roles, with very different connotations. She is both mother and mother-in-law, as well as granny. While popular belief has the mother-in-law painted as a harridan, sociologists have frequently been enthused by the mother/granny role in traditional working-class communities at least. Paeans of praise have been lavished on the working-class matriarch who rules her daughters, grand-daughters and great-grand-daughters while finding them houses and generally running their lives. Ever since Young and Willmott 'discovered' the working-class 'Mum' in Bethnal Green, she has been a powerful figure in sociological writing. In this section I want to examine the social roles of mother, mother-in-law and granny.

The lives of older women in Britain now have two quite distinct stages which did not exist until longer life expectancy and smaller families gave them a space between completion of childbearing and death. The majority of women can now expect a period in which they have independent children but are still active and relatively healthy, before old age and its associated poverty and ill-health set in. Some women may have twenty years at work after childbearing, and then twenty years of retirement.

Sociologists have not undertaken any systematic research into the lives of women between 40 and 60, but there are two quite distinct stereotypes which emerge from the popular writing on the subject. One school of thought is that these women can work, enjoy themselves, and by so doing are no longer available to help their married children; the other argues that working-class women at least are still available to take an active part in the everyday lives of their children and grandchildren. Thus Mary Loughton writing in *New Society* (11 September 1969) talks of:

present-day grandmothers – bustling women in their forties, fifties and sixties – are well-dressed and groomed, often earning, and spending as much as teenagers ... If her marriage is happy, then she is settling down into a time of considerable prosperity and freedom; if it is unhappy, she no longer has to endure it ... Healthy, energetic grandmothers can find suitable employment ... a young wife ... can no longer expect her mother to take over.

In complete contrast, Peter Willmott writing in *New Society* (13 June 1968), argued that 'there's nobody like Mum'. Using data collected by a market research organisation on housewives, he argued that his own earlier findings in Bethnal Green were supported by this new evidence. Between half and two-thirds of the women studied were living near their parents, and the majority saw their parents often, especially their mothers. This was almost as true of middle-class women (47 per cent saw their mother once a week) as of working-class ones (53 per cent). Married women without children were more likely to visit their mothers, while those with children were more likely to receive visits. However, Willmott argued that the most important finding of the survey was the deference of women to their mothers' advice and their dependence on her practical help. The grandmother was:

the most frequent adviser over bringing up the first baby ... she was overwhelmingly the person who looked after the first child when the second was born. She was the person most often consulted about child-care, cooking and shopping. And the 'brand-loyalty' of the younger women to the products their mothers favoured was impressive . . .

Here we have two opposed views about the grandmother–daughter–grandchild in modern Britain. Sociological evidence on this opposition is sparse, but it looks very much as though most women get little benefit from the earlier end of childbearing in so far as they have replaced care of small children with continued 'mothering' of adult offspring, married and single, and with care of grandchildren. Diana Barker (1972) showed that the older women in the Swansea area were happily undertaking large amounts of domestic work for adult children: that is, 'spoiling' them.

Although this research is now ten years old, and confined to a small area of South Wales, there is evidence in the mass media that other women all over Britain are still engaged in such 'spoiling'. Thus a woman wrote to *Woman* (15 July 1978) asking for advice because

After being a widow for a short time I'm thinking of remarrying – my friend is divorced, with two teenage boys at home. I also have a teenage son, and two others, one 24 and the other 25 – both still at home but with good jobs. My problem is that I can't take the two older boys to my new married home, nor can I leave them in my present home. They're both undomesticated and always out . . .

Here two adult men are receiving domestic care long after the woman might reasonably have been free of responsibility for them. Claire Rayner was concerned enough about the problem of 'spoiling' to write a major article in *Woman's Realm* (29 July 1978), warning women not to become slaves to their children. Case studies were cited which showed the problem:

Mrs B. goes out to work. She has a son, Nick, aged 21, who lives with her and gives her £8 a week for his keep. After she's cooked the evening meal, he goes out and does not return until bed time. At weekends, Mrs B. brings him breakfast in bed, as she doesn't like him milling around while she's catching up with the chores.

Mrs A. is a farmer's wife. She has two daughters, aged 17 and 18, who work in office jobs in the nearest town, where they have digs, 30 miles away. Most weekends, the girls come home, bringing all their laundry with them.

Claire Rayner argues that both these women are being exploited, and should refuse to subsidise their children financially, do their chores and wait upon them. Yet, as Diana Barker shows, these are precisely the ways in which mothers keep their children close.

In other words, there is a contradiction between the *positive* value placed by people, including sociologists, on the warmth and mutual support of the extended family, and the fact that families appear to be sustained by the continued domestic exploitation of women. If the working-class grandmother is the centre of the clan, cherished by all, it is largely because of her constant domestic labour and her financial support for its members.

This double-bind in the lives of the older women can be seen very clearly in the Swansea kinship study carried out by Rosser and Harris (1965). Rosser and Harris found that, despite new housing estates and increased affluence, the extended family was alive and flourishing in Swansea, centred on the women. Somehow the three- and four-generation family exists and 'the Mam holds them together' (1965, p. 12). The authors comment on how their first informant, a man of 74, used this evocative term 'the Mam' to refer both to his own mother, and to his wife, so that the *role* was always occupied: 'the Mam is dead, long live the Mam' (p. 13). Rosser and Harris traced a series of complex kinship networks across three and four generations, usually based on frequent visits and meetings. This geographical proximity has always been assumed to explain the 'close' working-class family, but a study of mobile middle-class families living far away from kin (Bell, 1968) showed that these people, too, had important family links which were used for advice and support as working-class ones were. The main difference lies in the means of maintaining the extended family, for while the working class relied more on frequent visits, the middle class made more use of the phone, letters and car travel to stay for longer periods, to maintain their familiar links. Thus, until we have data on the middle-class grandmother which shows she is less significant than her working-class counterpart, we must assume she too is highly salient in her married children's lives, although the discussion which follows is centred on working-class women.

The evidence produced by studies of working-class areas has shown that men and women are usually in closer contact with their own mother than their mother-in-law, unless their own mother is dead (Rosser and Harris, 1965; Willmott, 1968). Rosser and Harris showed that men may well be as assiduous in visiting their mothers as women are supposed to be, and as much in receipt of continuing domestic services. A not untypical case (p. 153) concerned

a railway clerk, aged 58... [who] told us that, apart from holidays, he has had his dinner every day for more than thirty years, since he married, at his mother's house ... 'I can say, with hardly any exceptions, that I saw her every day of my life until she died. Two other brothers besides myself used to go there for dinner every day.

Here a woman is protected from loneliness or isolation because she sees her sons every working day, but her freedom is severely curtailed by the necessity of providing meals. Elsewhere in Rosser and Harris we read of grandmothers caring for grandchildren, doing their married daughters' housework, cooking meals and babysitting for their extended families. It is clear that, in Swansea, 'marrying off' children does not mean that the domestic work and child care cease; rather, they begin again for the grandchildren.

Throughout Rosser and Harris's study, older women appear at the centre of kinship networks, surrounded by loving families, *but* they are also perpetually working. The *only* older woman who appears in the study not doing domestic work for her family is a cleaner married to a bricklayer who says (p. 83):

I put by the money I get cleaning and my husband and I go abroad for a holiday every August. Last year we went to Austria, and this year we're going on a coach tour of Spain. I really live for that now that the children have all married and left home. Let's enjoy ourselves while we can I say.

This woman does cleaning for a dentist, so even she has not escaped domesticity. The other women we see, however, are holding their families together by their labour. Thus we read (p. 153):

Mrs Ruth Anstey ... has one of her two married daughters next door. 'I see my daughter next door about a dozen times a day. I just knock on the wall if I want to call her, and she does the same if she wants me. I help her to get the children off to bed every night ... '

Another woman was giving her married son breakfast and lunch every working day. Later we read of a reconciliation between brothers after a twenty-year estrangement, which is resolved now because the widower 'comes down here ... and the wife gets him something to eat' (p. 225). In another family the son of a brother who had gone to Bolton appears on the doorstep because he is working in Swansea, and is reunited with his Welsh kin, because 'Auntie Rhoda' is prepared to put him up (p. 229). In such ways women hold their families together, and where such help is not offered, or not wanted, the kinship network lies dormant. The fact of *substitution*, where an adult who has lost his or her own parent may create a close relationship with the spouse's parent, is clearly documented by Rosser and Harris. However, it is clear that such substitutions work when the women undertake the labour for the *affines* (kin by marriage) as they might have done for their 'own'. Thus Mary Wood, who says 'My closest friend is my mother-in-law (p. 260), also reveals that her mother-in-law would do 'everything possible' for her, and 'came to help when I had the children'.

Thus the kinship system outside the nuclear family is sustained as an *active* unit by women engaging in domestic labour for each other within the kindred. The majority of women in Britain, lacking financial independence, and largely dependent on relations for company, must keep the kinship network alive if they are to avoid the fate which awaits many old women: loneliness. The extended family can mitigate the problems of widowhood, and of old age, only if it is kept active. The widow, like other single women in Britain, is in a position of isolation, especially in old age, unless she has an active extended family around her. The differences between the isolated old woman and the one surrounded by family will become clear in the next section.

WIDOWHOOD AND OLD AGE

The majority of women in Britain marry, and the majority of wives face widowhood because their husbands have a shorter life-expectancy than they do and most women are younger than their husbands. Yet not only is there ample evidence that being widowed catches most women unprepared, financially, socially and emotionally, the sociologists have neglected to study women in this predicament. There are studies of old people, many of whom are widows, but little recent data on widows who are not yet old. The best-known study was published twenty years ago (Marris, 1959) and there are no recent research reports on either organisations for widows such as Cruse and the National Association of Widows or on widows themselves. Again in this section, as in many other places in the book, we must turn to old studies and recent writing in the mass media. This section focuses first on the widow who is not old, and then turns to the old women of all marital statuses.

Hairy Spiders, Lonely Women
A widow wrote an article for the *Sunday Times* (23 July 1978) with this deliberately repellent title. She argued that

if there is one type of woman more superfluous, spurned and unsought than the rest, it is that synonym of dreariness, rootlessness, rightlessness, the widow.

Several of the correspondents the following week agreed with her points, arguing that widows are second-class citizens. Back in 1964 Celia Hobson studied forty younger widows in the English midlands (*New Society*, 24 September 1964) and her conclusions support these accusations of social ostracism. Hobson found, first, that nearly all the women had suffered physical symptoms after the death of their husband. Thirty-five of the forty had experienced insomnia, and loss of appetite, headaches, stomach upsets and other 'nervous' complaints were also common. There were mental symptoms as well as physical ones reported: feelings of indifference to life, detachment or remoteness from others, and a sense of unreality. In addition, over half the sample said they resented the happiness of other people, expressed hostility to the medical professionals who had dealt with their husbands, and admitted a loss of faith in God because he had taken their 'good' man while letting bad husbands live. Apart from these physical and mental symptoms of bereavement, the widows had to face major readjustments in their lives. Many were forced into financial dependence on the state for the first time in their lives, all were faced with financial problems, and most found themselves facing social isolation. Hobson said that most women abandoned all their social activities except the all-female clubs (e.g. WI) they had always belonged to. Most still saw relations, but those who took jobs found that they even saw less of their families than before. Hobson paints a picture of social isolation, financial hardship and ill-health which fulfil the popular stereotype of the old woman in society, and it may be that widows are, in effect, thrust prematurely into the life patterns of old age to which this chapter now turns.

Old and Alone?

Mary Chamberlain (1975, p. 176) has argued that old age makes little difference to the lives of the women in the fen countries because:

> Men retire, but a woman's work is never done. There's the spring cleaning and the shopping, the washing and the ironing, the cooking and the mending. There's making do on a pension . . . Once a week, there's the Evergreen Club for recreation. You've had to wait till you're old and grey for that, and even then, you help make the tea, if you're a woman.

In other words, old age still means domestic labour for women and, in this respect, is no different from other phases of life. In so far as this is true, the social differences between wife, widow and spinster may well become less significant. The real differences in the quality of life for old women seem from the research evidence

(Tunstall, 1966) to concern whether old people live alone, what kind of health they are in, how much money they have, and how socially isolated they are. None of these variables is necessarily related to marital status. For example, some of the old people who were alone when interviewed for Tunstall's (1966) research were widows from the First World War, who had been *socially* like spinsters for forty years. There is not room in this volume to discuss the lives of old women in different social situations in any detail, but one or two basic facts are presented, and then the stereotype of the neglected old woman, hungry, old and ill, is examined.

There are a great many people over retirement age in Britain, far more than in earlier periods of British history. In 1976 there were 6,504,000 women over 60 and 4,532,000 men over 65. The number of women over 60 had risen by 2 million since 1951, and an increasing number of old women are living to 75 and over. The majority of these old women were not living in 'homes', but in private accommodation of some kind. In 1975 about 90,000 old women were in some form of residential home, which is a tiny proportion of the $6\frac{1}{2}$ million in the country (*Social Trends, 1977*, pp. 65–7). Most of the old who were not living alone or with a spouse were with a sibling. In 1976 the average household with a head aged 65 or over had an income of £42·68 a week and expenditure of £35·51. Most old people are, therefore, poor; their income derives largely from social security benefits and pensions, and is spent on basics such as food, heat and housing. Although the actual figures presented in the research carried out by Tunstall (1966) are now out of date, the picture given there of poor housing, poor food and poor health has probably not changed. The life of the woman of 74 in Northampton (1966, pp. 29–34) is probably little different today.

Mrs Marshall is a widow living with her widowed sister, in a gas-lit terraced house with one married daughter nearby and grandchildren able to visit. She suffers from bronchitis and an ulcerated leg, cannot get upstairs and has poor sight. Her main problems are a damp and insanitary house, and a lack of money for fuel. She also suffers grief at the loss of her husband and claims that her children neglect her. None of the benefits of the welfare state, apart from her GP, reaches her: she has no home help, meals on wheels, optician or chiropodist, belongs to no clubs and never goes out.

This sounds like a classic pattern which, if one of the sisters died, would leave the other vulnerable to hypothermia, hunger, accidents in the home and squalor. Old people in such circumstances are frequently written up as neglected by their families. Old people frequently made such complaints to Tunstall (1966), Rosser and Harris (1965) and Chamberlain (1975). In fact, a study in Glasgow by Isaacs and others (1972) of old people living in filth, cold, danger and hunger casts doubt on the idea of neglectful families. They studied ninety-one severely neglected old people, and found that the majority (fifty-two) had no close families but *had* been receiving help from distant relations, neighbours, friends and the social services. The other thirty-nine old people had families in Glasgow but almost invariably these relatives were unable to care for the old person because they were facing equally pressing problems themselves. For example, some old people had relatives who were themselves chronically sick, or were nursing other relations, or had mentally subnormal children to care for. A further subgroup of the old who had relatives around were found to have refused all help from them. Isaacs himself argued that only 1 per cent of the sample were genuinely neglected by their families. If this pattern is true for other areas of Britain than Glasgow, then the stereotype of neglected old people has to be re-examined. The neglected old person is liable either to have no friends or relations alive and within reach, or to have friends or relations who face so many other problems they cannot offer help, or to have rejected all offers.

There may be an interesting research problem here. Children are believed to bring comfort in old age, and grandchildren likewise. However, if it is true that women need to engage in continued domestic labour to keep the extended family operative when they are still healthy and active, it may also be true that this is also their best insurance policy for a comfortable old age. In other words, only an *active* extended family will prevent loneliness and destitution in old age. Given that few women ever earn enough to insure their own financial security, it may be that endless domestic labour is their only insurance. Because women's work is not a subject of serious academic study yet, the answer to this question lies in further research into women's lives.

Chapter 10

Conclusions

Ann Oakley (1979) has written:

> men and women have separate positive valuations of their own
> spheres of activity. As a consequence, women believe that their
> own labour and resources (both productive and reproductive) have
> high social value, whereas male resources and labour (for example
> masculine ceremonial rituals) are relatively unimportant. Men
> believe the opposite.

The message of this book is that sociology has been too concerned
with the masculine view of the world, or with what Shirley Ardener
(1975) would call the dominant rather than the muted model. In
conclusion, then, the book calls for both a greater understanding
of the worldview of women and an incorporation of that worldview
into sociology. This involves more research into women's lives,
more female researchers, and a critical re-examination of all aspects
of sociological explanation, theory and methodology. If this book
has succeeded in inspiring some further research, or some critical
thinking about sex and gender in society, then it has done its job.
I hope that those who were convinced feminists before they read it,
the converts, and the sceptical will all use the further reading to
follow up the ideas that have been raised by the arguments.

Further Reading

There is an excellent annotated bibliography of material on women which makes an ideal starting point for anyone wishing to read about or do research on sex and gender in society. Six thousand entries are collected in the following:

Rosenberg, Marie B. and Bergstrom, L. V. (eds), *Women and Society* (New York: Sage, 1976).
Een, JoAnn Delores, and Rosenberg Dishman, Marie B. (eds), *Women and Society: Citations 3601 to 6000* (New York: Sage, 1978).

Also useful as a research starter is:

Evans, Mary, and Morgan, David, *Work on Women* (London: Tavistock, 1979).

There are several collections of papers which provide interesting reading and provocative ideas, namely,

Barker, Diana L., and Allen, Sheila (Eds), *Sexual Divisions and Society* (London: Tavistock, 1976).
Barker, Diana L., and Allen, Sheila (Eds), *Dependence and Exploitation in Work and Marriage* (London. Longman, 1976).
Chetwynd, Jane, and Hartnett, Oonagh (eds), *The Sex Role System* (London: Routledge & Kegan Paul, 1978).
Millman, Marcia, and Kanter, Rosabeth M. (eds), *Another Voice* (New York: Anchor/Doubleday, 1975).
Mitchell, Juliet, and Oakley, Ann (eds), *The Rights and Wrongs of Women* (Harmondsworth: Penguin, 1976).
Smart, Carol, and Smart, Barry (eds), *Women, Sexuality and Social Control* (London: Routledge & Kegan Paul, 1978).

Scholarship pertaining to women has, in the last decade, become increasingly polarised between Marxist-feminist writing and 'the rest'. Readers who wish to explore non-Marxist arguments can start from the following:

Ardener, Shirley (ed), *Perceiving Women* (London: Dent, 1975).
Ardener, Shirley (ed), *Defining Women* (London: Croom Helm, 1978).
Burman, Sandra (ed), *Fit Work for Women* (London: Croom Helm, 1979).
Delamont, Sara and Duffin, Lorna (eds), *The Nineteenth Century Woman* (London: Croom Helm, 1978).

The Marxist scholarship can be explored in:

Hamilton, Roberta, *The Liberation of Women* (London: Allen & Unwin, 1978).
Kuhn, Annette and Wolpe, Ann Marie (eds), *Feminism and Materialism* (London: Routledge & Kegan Paul, 1978).
Women's Studies Group (ed.), *Women Take Issue* (London: Hutchinson, 1978).

Finally, any of the titles in the Tavistock Women's Studies series makes provocative reading.

Bibliography

Abrams, Philip, and McCulloch, A. (1976), 'Men, women and communes', in Barker and Allen (1976a).

Acker, Joan (1973), 'Women and social stratification', in Joan Huber (ed), *Changing Women in a Changing Society* (Chicago: Chicago University Press).

Adelman, Clem (1979), unpublished material on nursery classes.

Alderson, Connie (1968), *Magazines Teenagers Read* (London: Pergamon).

Amir, M. (1971), *Patterns in Forcible Rape* (Chicago: Chicago University Press).

Anthony, Peter (1977), *The Ideology of Work* (London: Tavistock).

Ardener, Shirley (1975), *Perceiving Women* (London: Dent).

Arensberg, C. M., and Kimball, S. T. (1940), *Family and Community in Ireland* (London: Peter Smith).

Atkinson, Paul A. (1976), 'The clinical experience', unpublished PhD thesis, University of Edinburgh.

Atkinson, Paul A., *et al.* (1977), 'Medical mystique', *Sociology of Work and Occupations,* vol. 4, no. 3, August, pp. 243–80.

Austin, Rita (1977a), 'Sex and gender in the future of nursing I', *Nursing Times,* 25 August, pp. 113–16.

Austin, Rita (1977b), 'Sex and gender in the future of nursing II', *Nursing Times,* 1 September, pp. 117–19.

Ballard, Roger, and Ballard, Catherine (1977), 'The Sikhs', in Watson (1977).

Banks, Olive, and Finlayson, Douglas (1974), *Success and Failure in the Secondary School* (London: Methuen).

Barker, Diana L. (1972), 'Keeping close and spoiling', *Sociological Review,* vol. 20, no. 4, pp. 569–90.

Barker, Diana L., and Allen, Sheila (eds) (1976a), *Sexual Divisions and Society* (London: Tavistock).

Barker, Diana L., and Allen, Sheila (eds) (1976b), *Dependence and Exploitation in Work and Marriage* (London: Longman).

Barker, Paul (1979), *The Founding Fathers of Social Science* (London: Scola Press).

Barrett, Michele, and Roberts, Helen (1978), 'Doctors and their patients', in Smart and Smart (1978).

Baruch, Grace K. (1974), 'Sex-role attitudes of fifth-grade girls', in Judith Stacey *et al.* (1974).

Bell, Colin (1968), *Middle Class Families* (London: Routledge & Kegan Paul).

Bell, Colin (1974), review of Young and Willmott (1973), *Sociology,* vol. 8, no. 3, pp. 505–12.

Bell, Colin, and Newby, Howard (1971), *Community Studies* (London: Allen & Unwin).

Bell, Daniel (1961), *The End of Ideology* (New York: Collier).

Berger, P. L., and Berger, B. (1976), *Sociology* (Harmondsworth: Penguin).

Bergman, Jane (1974), 'Are little girls being harmed by "Sesame Street"?', in Judith Stacey *et al.* (1974).

Boslooper, T., and Hayes, Marcia (1973), *The Femininity Game* (New York: Stein & Day).

Brake, Mike (1976), 'I may be queer but at least I am a man', in Barker and Allen (1976*a*).

Braman, Olive (1977), 'Comics', in King and Stott (1977).

Brookes, Pamela (1967), *Women at Westminster* (London: Peter Davies).

Brophy, J. E. and Good, T. L. (1974), *Teacher–Student Relationships* (New York: Holt, Rinehart & Winston).

Broverman, T. K., *et al.* (1972), 'Sex-role stereotypes: a current appraisal', *Journal of Social Issues,* vol. 28, no. 22, pp. 59–78.

Brown, Gordon (ed), (1975), *The Red Paper on Scotland* (Edinburgh: EUSPB).

Brown, Richard (1976), 'Women as employees', in Barker and Allen (1976*b*).

Brown, Roger (1965), *Social Psychology* (London: Collier Macmillan).

Brownmiller, Susan (1975), *Against Our Will* (Harmondsworth: Penguin).

Busfield, Joan (1974), 'Ideologies and reproduction', in M. Richards (ed), *The Integration of a Child into a Social World* (Cambridge: Cambridge University Press).

Butler, David, and Stokes, D. (1974), *Political Change in Britain* (London: Macmillan).

Byrne, Eileen M. (1978), *Women and Education* (London: Tavistock).

Cartwright, Ann (1976), *How Many Children?* (London: Routledge & Kegan Paul).

Chamberlain, Mary (1975), *Fenwomen* (London: Virago).

Chiplin, B., and Sloane, P. J. (1976), *Sex Discrimination in the Labour Market* (London: Macmillan).

Ciarain, Mary (1973), unpublished undergraduate dissertation, Sociology Department, University of Leicester.

CIS (n.d.), *Crisis: Women Under Attack* (London: Counter Information Services).

Conran, Shirley (1975), *Superwoman* (Harmondsworth, Penguin).

Constantinides, Pamela (1977), 'The Greek Cypriots', in Watson (1977).

Cook, Robin (1975), 'Scotland's housing', in Gordon Brown (1975).

Coote, Anna (1976), 'Child's guide to male chauvinism', *Sunday Times Magazine,* 3 March, pp. 16–17.

Court Report (1976), *Fit for the Future* (London: HMSO).

Critcher, C. (1974), 'Women in sport', *Contemporary Cultural Studies,* vol. 5, Spring, pp. 3–13.

Currell, Melville (1974), *Political Women* (London: Croom Helm).

Dalla Costa, M., and James, Selma (1972), *The Power of Women and the Subversion of the Community* (Bristol: Falling Wall Press).

Davidoff, Leonore (1976), 'The rationalization of housework', in Barker and Allen (1976*b*).

Davidoff, Leonore, *et al.* (1976), 'Landscape with figures', in Mitchell and Oakley (1976).

Davie, R., *et al.* (1972), *From Birth to Seven* (London: Longman).

Davies, Ross (1975), *Women and Work* (London: Arrow).

Delamont, Sara (1978), 'The domestic ideology and women's education', in Delamont and Duffin (1978).

Delamont, Sara (1980), *Sex Roles and Social Structure* (London: Methuen).

Delamont, Sara, and Duffin, Lorna (1978), *The Nineteenth Century Woman* (London: Croom Helm).

Dennis, Norman, *et al.* (1957), *Coal Is Our Life* (London: Routledge & Kegan Paul).

Dobash, Rebecca, and Dobash, Russell (1977), 'Wife beating – still a common form of violence', *Social Work Today,* vol. 9, no. 12, 15 November.

Douglas, J. W. B. (1964), *The Home and the School* (London: MacGibbon & Kee).

Douglas, J. W. B., *et al.* (1968), *All Our Future* (London: Peter Davies).

Douglas, Mary (1966), *Purity and Danger* (London: Routledge & Kegan Paul).

Dove, Linda (1976), 'The hopes of immigrant schoolchildren', *New Society,* 10 April, pp. 63–5.

Dowse, Robert, and Hughes, John A. (1972), *Political Sociology* (Chichester: Wiley).

Duffin, Lorna (1978), 'The conspicuous consumptive', in Delamont and Duffin (1978).

Elyan, Olwen, *et al.* (1978), 'RP-accented female speech: the voice of perceived androgyny', in P. Trudgill (ed.), *Sociolinguistic Patterns in British English* (London: Edward Arnold).

Emmett, Isabel (1964), *A North Wales Parish* (London: Routledge & Kegan Paul).

Eppel, E. M., and Eppel, M. (1966), *Adolescent Values* (London: Routledge & Kegan Paul).

Epstein, Cynthia (1970), *Woman's Place* (Berkeley, Calif.: University of California Press).

Farrell, Christine (1978), *My Mother Said* (London: Routledge & Kegan Paul).

Firth, R. (1974), review of Young and Willmott (1973), *Sociology,* vol. 8, no. 3, pp. 505–12.

Firestone, Shulamith (1972), *The Dialectic of Sex* (London: Paladin).

Fisher, Elizabeth (1974), 'Children's books', in Judith Stacey (1974).

Fogarty, Michael, *et al.* (1971), *Women in Top Jobs* (London: Allen & Unwin).

Fogelman, Ken (1976), *Britain's Sixteen-Year-Olds* (London: National Children's Bureau).

Frankenberg, R. (1957), *Village on the Border* (London: Cohen & West).

Frankenberg, R. (1966), *Communities in Britain* (Harmondsworth, Penguin).

Frankenberg, R. (1976), 'In the production of their lives, men (?) sex and gender in British community studies', in Barker and Allen (1976a).

Fransella, Fay, and Frost, Kay (1977), *On Being a Woman* (London: Tavistock).

French, Peter, and McClure, Margaret (1979), 'Getting the right answer', *Research in Education,* May.

Friedan, Betty (1963), *The Feminine Mystique* (Harmondsworth, Penguin).

Galloway, H. Margo (1973), 'Female students and their aspirations', unpublished M.Sc. thesis, University of Edinburgh.

Galton, Maurice (1979), personal communication.

Gardiner, Jean (1976), 'Political economy of domestic labour in capitalist society', in Barker and Allen (1976b).

Gavron, Hannah (1966), *The Captive Wife* (Harmondsworth: Penguin).

Gayford, John J. (1975), 'Wife battering', *British Medical Journal,* vol. 1, pp. 194–7.

Giddens, A. (1973), *The Class Structure of the Advanced Societies* (London: Hutchinson).

Giddens, A. (1974), 'Elites in the British class structure', in Stanworth and Giddens (1974).

Giddens, A. (1976), 'The rich', *New Society,* 14 October, pp. 63–6.

Gill, Derek (1977), *Illegitimacy, Sexuality and the Status of Women* (Oxford: Blackwell).

Goffman, E. (1968), *Stigma* (Harmondsworth: Penguin).

Goldberg, Philip (1974), 'Are women prejudiced against women?', in Judith Stacey *et al.* (1974).

Goode, W. J. (1964), *The Family* (Englewood Cliffs, NJ: Prentice-Hall).

Goodman, L. W., *et al.* (1974), 'A report on children's toys', in Judith Stacey *et al.* (1974).

Goody, Esther N., and Groothues, C. M. (1977), 'The West Africans', in J. Watson (1977).

Goot, M., and Reid, E. (1975), *Women and Voting Studies* (London: Sage).

Greer, Germaine (1971), *The Female Eunuch* (London: Paladin).

Hall, Stuart, and Jefferson, T. (1975), *Resistance Through Rituals* (London: Hutchinson).

Hamilton, David (1977), *In Search of Structure* (London: Hodder & Stoughton).

Hanmer, Jalna (1977), 'Community action, women's aid and the women's liberation movement', in M. Mayo (ed.), *Women in the Community* (London: Routledge & Kegan Paul).

Harbury, C. D., and McMahon, P. C., 'Intergenerational wealth transmission', in Stanworth and Giddens (1974).

Hargreaves, David (1967), *Social Relations in a Secondary School* (London: Routledge & Kegan Paul).

Harris, C. (1974), review of Young and Willmott (1973), *Sociology,* vol. 8, no. 3, pp. 505–12.

Harrison, P. (1975), 'Growing up ordinary', *New Society,* 18 September, pp. 630–3.

Hart, Nicky (1976), *When Marriage Ends* (London: Tavistock).

Hart, Roger (1979), *Children's Experience of Place* (New York: Irvington Press).

Henning, Clara M. (1974), 'Canon law and the battle of the sexes', in R. R. Ruether (ed.), *Religion and Sexism* (New York: Simon & Shuster).

Hill, Stephen (1977), *The Dockers* (London: Heinemann).

Hobson, Celia (1964), 'Widows of Blacktown', *New Society* 24 September, pp. 13–16.

Hobson, Dorothy (1978), 'Housewives: isolation as oppression', in *Women Take Issue*, Women's Studies Group, Centre for Contemporary Cultural Studies (London: Hutchinson).

Hope, Emily, *et al.* (1976), 'Homeworkers in north London', in Barker and Allen (1976b).

Horner, Martha S. (1971), 'Femininity and successful achievement', in M. H. Garskof (ed.), *Roles Women Play* (California: Brooks/Cole).

Horobin, Gordon (1973), *Experiences with Abortion* (Cambridge: Cambridge University Press).

Hubert, Jane (1974), 'Belief and reality', in M. Richards (ed.), *The Integration of a Child into a Social World* (Cambridge: Cambridge University Press).

Humphrey, Michael (1969), 'The enigma of childlessness', *New Society*, 13 March, pp. 399–402.

Hunt, Audrey (1975), *Management Attitudes and Practice towards Women at Work* (London: HMSO).

Hutchinson, G., and McPherson, Andrew (1976), 'Competing inequalities', *Sociology*, vol. 10, no. 1, pp. 111–16.

Ingelby, J. D. and Cooper, E. (1974), 'How teachers perceive first-year schoolchildren', *Sociology*, vol. 8, no. 3, pp. 463–73.

Isaacs, Bernard, *et al.* (1972), *Survival of the Unfittest* (London: Routledge & Kegan Paul).

Jackson, P. W., and Lahaderne, H. M. (1967), 'Inequalities of teacher–pupil contacts', *Psychology in the Schools*, vol. 4, pp. 204–11.

James, Selma (1975), 'Wageless of the world', in W. Edmond and S. Fleming (eds), *All Work and No Pay* (Bristol: Falling Wall Press).

Jaquette, Jane S. (1974), *Women in Politics* (New York: Wiley).

Jeffery, Patricia (1976), *Migrants and Refugees* (Cambridge: Cambridge University Press).

Joffe, C. (1971), 'Sex role socialization and the nursery school', *Journal of Marriage and the Family*, vol. 33, no. 3.

Johnson, B. D. (1972), 'Durkheim on women', in N. Glazer-Malbin and H. Y. Waehrer (eds), *Woman in a Man-Made World* (Chicago: Rand McNally).

Johnson, Terence (1972), *Professions and Power* (London: Macmillan).

Jones, Irene (1974), unpublished dissertation, School of Education, University of Leicester.

Kanter, Rosabeth Moss (1975), 'Women and the structure of organizations', in Millman and Kanter (1975).

Kerr, Madeline (1958), *The People of Ship Street* (London: Routledge & Kegan Paul).

Kessler, Suzanne J., and McKenna, Wendy (1978), *Gender: An Ethnomethodological Account* (New York: Wiley).

Khan, Verity Saifullah (1976), 'Purdah in the British situation', in Barker and Allen (1976*b*).

Khan, Verity Saifullah (1977), 'The Pakistanis', in Watson (1977).

King, J., and Stott, Mary (eds) (1977), *Is This Your Life?* (London: Virago).

King, R. A. (1971), 'Unequal access in education – sex and social class', *Social and Economic Administration,* vol. 5, no. 3, July, pp. 167–74.

Koerber, Carmel (1977), 'Television', in King and Stott (1977).

Komorovsky, Mirra (1946), 'Cultural contradictions and sex roles', *American Journal of Sociology,* vol. 52, pp. 182–9.

Komorovsky, Mirra (1973), 'Cultural contradictions and sex roles: the masculine case', in J. Huber (ed.), *Changing Women in a Changing Society* (Chicago: Chicago University Press).

Kraditor, Aileen (1968), *Up From the Pedestal* (New York: Quadrangle).

Kroll, Una (1975), *Flesh of my Flesh* (London: Darton, Longman & Todd).

Lacey, Colin (1970), *Hightown Grammar* (Manchester: Manchester University Press).

Ladbury, Sarah (1977), 'The Turkish Cypriots', in Watson (1977).

Lakoff, Robin (1973), *Language and Women's Place* (New York: Harper Colophan).

Lambert, R., *et al.* (1977), *The Chance of a Lifetime?* (London: Weidenfeld & Nicolson).

Leeson, Joyce, and Gray, Judith (1978), *Women and Medicine* (London: Tavistock.

Levitt, Ian (1975), 'Poverty in Scotland', in Gordon Brown (1975).

Leibow, E. (1967), *Tally's Corner* (Boston, Mass.: Little, Brown).

Littlejohn, John (1964), *Westrigg* (London: Routledge & Kegan Paul).

Llewelyn Davies, Margaret (1915), *Maternity: Letters from Working Women* (London: repr. Virago, 1978).

Lloyd, Leonora (n.d.), *Women Workers in Britain: A Handbook* (London: Socialist Women Publications).

Lobban, Glenys (1974), 'Presentation of sex-roles in British reading schemes', *Forum,* Vol. 16, no. 3, pp. 57–60.

Lobban, Glenys (1975), 'Sex roles in reading schemes', *Educational Review,* vol. 27, no. 3, pp. 202–10.

Lofland, Lyn H. (1975), 'The "thereness" of women: a selective review of urban sociology', in Millman and Kanter (1975).

Lopata, H. Z. (1971), *Occupation Housewife* (New York: Oxford University Press).

Lorber, Judith (1975), 'Women and medical sociology', in Millman and Kanter (1975).

Loughton, Mary (1969), 'The young mothers', *New Society* 11 September, p. 386.

Lupton, Tom, and Wilson, Shirley (1973), 'The kinship connections of "top decision makers" ', in Urry and Wakeford (1973).

Maccia, E. S., *et al.* (1975), *Women and Education* (New York: C. C. Thomas).

Macintyre, Sally (1976a), 'Who wants babies?', in Barker and Allen (1976a).

Macintyre, Sally (1976b), 'To have or have not', in M. Stacey (ed.), *The Sociology of the NHS*, Sociological Review Monograph, No. 22 (1976).

Macintyre, Sally (1977), *Single and Pregnant* (London: Croom Helm).

Mackie, L. and Pattullo, P. (1977), *Women at Work* (London: Tavistock).

Madgwick, P. J., *et al.* (1973), *The Politics of Rural Wales* (London: Hutchinson).

Mann, Jean (1962), *Woman in Parliament* (London: Odhams).

Mann, Michael (1973), *Consciousness and Action among the Western Working Class* (London: Macmillan).

Manton, Jo (1965), *Elizabeth Garrett Anderson* (London: Methuen).

Marris, P. (1959), *Widows and their Families* (London: Routledge & Kegan Paul).

Marsden, D. (1973), *Mothers Alone* (Harmondsworth: Penguin).

Martindale, Hilda (1938), *Women Servants of the State* (London: George Allen).

Mathieson, Margaret (1975), *The Preachers of Culture* (London: Allen & Unwin).

McEwan, John (1975), 'Highland landlordism', in Gordon Brown (1975).

McKay, Ann, Wilding, Paul, and George, Vic (1972), 'Stereotypes of male and female roles and the influence on people's attitudes to one parent families', *Sociological Review*, vol. 20, no. 1, pp. 79–92.

McRobbie, Angela (1978), 'Working class girls and the culture of femininity', in *Women Take Issue*, Women's Studies Group, Centre for Contemporary Cultural Studies (London: Hutchinson).

McRobbie, Angela, and Garber, J. (1975), 'Girls and subcultures', in Hall and Jefferson (1975).

Mellors, Colin (1978), *The British MP* (Farnborough: Saxon House).

Middleton, C. (1974), 'Sexual Inequality and Stratification Theory', in F. Parkin (ed.), *The Social Analysis of Class Structure* (London: Tavistock).

Millet, Kate (1972), *Sexual Politics* (London: Abacus).

Millman, Marcia (1975), 'She did it all for love', in Millman and Kanter (1975).

Millman, Marcia, and Kanter, Rosabeth Moss (eds) (1975) *Another Voice* (New York: Anchor Books).

Mitchell, Juliet, and Oakley, Ann (eds) (1976), *The Rights and Wrongs of Women* (Harmondsworth: Penguin).

Mitchison, Naomi (1975), *All Change Here* (London: Bodley Head).

Moberly Bell, E. (1953), *Storming the Citadel* (London: Constable).

Moody, Eileen (1968), 'Right in front of everybody', *New Society,* 26 December, pp. 952–3.

Moyes, B. (1977), 'A doctor is a doctor', *New Society,* 10 November, pp. 289–91.

Mungham, G. (1976), 'Youth in pursuit of itself', in Mungham and Pearson (1976).

Mungham, G. and Pearson, G. (1976), *Working Class Youth Culture* (London: Routledge & Kegan Paul).

Murcott, Anne (1980), 'The social construction of teenage pregnancy', *Sociology of Health and Illness,* vol. 2, no. 1.

Murdock, Graham, and McCron, Robin (1976), 'Youth and class', in Mungham & Pearson (1976).

Murdock, Graham, and Phelps, G. (1973), *Mass Media and the Secondary School* (London: Macmillan).

Newby, Howard (1977*a*), 'In the field', in Colin Bell and Howard Newby (eds), *Doing Sociological Research* (London: Allen & Unwin, 1977).

Newby, Howard (1976*b*). *The Deferential Worker* (London: Allen Lane, 1977).

Newson, John, and Newson, Elizabeth (1965), *Patterns of Infant Care* (Harmondsworth: Penguin).

Newson, John, and Newson, Elizabeth (1970), *Four Years Old in an Urban Community* (Harmondsworth, Penguin).

Newson, John, and Newson, Elizabeth (1976), *Seven Years Old in the Home Environment* (London: Allen & Unwin).

Newson, John, Newson, Elizabeth, Richardson, Diane, and Scaife Joyce (1978), 'Perspectives in sex role stereotyping' in Jane Chetwynd and Oonagh Hartnett (eds), *The Sex Role System* (London: Routledge & Kegan Paul).

Nilsen, A. P. (1975), 'Women in children's literature', in E. Maccia *et al.,* (1975).

Oakley, Ann (1972), *Sex, Gender and Society* (London: Temple Smith).

Oakley, Ann (1974*a*) *The Sociology of Housework* (London: Martin Robertson).

Oakley, Ann (1974*b*), *Housewife* (London: Allen Lane).

Oakley, Ann (1976), 'Wisewoman and medicine man', in Mitchell and Oakley (1976).

Oakley, Ann (1979), 'The failure of the movement for women's equality', *New Society,* 23 August, pp. 392–4.

Otley, C. B. (1973), 'The public schools and the Army', in Urry and Wakeford (1973).

Owens, D. J., and Read, M. (1979), *The Provision, Use and Evaluation of Medical Services for the Subfertile*, SRU Working Paper, No. 6, University College, Cardiff.

Pahl, R. E. and Winkler, J. (1974), 'The economic elite', in Stanworth and Giddens (1974).

Paneth, Marie (1944), *Branch Street* (London: Allen & Unwin).

Parker, Howard (1974), *View from the Boys* (Newton Abbot: David & Charles).

Parkin, F. (1971), *Class Inequality and Political Order* (London: MacGibbon & Kee).

Parkin, F. (1979), *Marxism and Class Theory* (London: Tavistock).

Parsons, Talcott (1948), 'The family in urban-industrial America', in Michael Anderson (ed.), *Sociology of the Family* (Harmondsworth: Penguin. 1971).

Partington, G. (1976), *Women Teachers in the 20th Century* (Slough: NFER).

Perman, David (1977), *Changes and the Churches* (London: Bodley Head).

Pollak, Otto (1961), *The Criminality of Women* (Pennsylvania: University of Pennsylvania Press).

Powell, Rachel, and Clarke, John (1975), 'A note on marginality', in Hall and Jefferson (1975).

Proops, Marjorie (1977), *Dear Marje* (London: Coronet).

Quine, W., and Quine, L. (1966), 'Boys, girls and leisure', *New Society,* 18 June, pp. 258–60.

Raison, T. (1969), *The Founding Fathers of Social Science* (Harmondsworth: Penguin).

Rapoport, R., and Rapoport, R. (1976), *Dual-Career Families Re-Examined* (London: Martin Robertson).

Rees, A. D. (1950), *Life in a Welsh Countryside* (Cardiff: University of Wales Press).

Rees, A., and Davies, E. (eds) (1960), *Welsh Rural Communities* (Cardiff: University of Wales Press).

Rigby, Andrew (1974), *Communes in Britain* (London: Routledge & Kegan Paul).

Roby, Pamela (1975), 'Sociology and women in working-class jobs', in Millman and Kanter (1975).

Rosser, C., and Harris, C. (1965), *The Family and Social Change* (London: Routledge & Kegan Paul).

Rubinstein, W. D. (1974), 'Men of property', in Stanworth and Giddens (1974).

Runciman, G. (1973), review of Young and Willmott (1973), *Listener,* 25 October, and correspondence, *Listener* 1 and 8 November 1973.

Rushton, W. (1976), *Superpig* (Harmondsworth: Penguin).

Sachs, A., and Wilson, J. H. (1978), *Sexism and the Law* (Oxford: Martin Robertson).

Sayre, Anne (1975), *Rosalind Franklin and DNA* (New York: Norton).

Schofield, Michael (1965), *The Sexual Behaviour of Young People* (Harmondsworth: Penguin).

Schwendinger, J., and Schwendinger, H. (1971), 'Sociology's founding fathers: sexists to a man', *Journal of Marriage and the Family,* vol. 33, no. 4.

Scott, John, and Hughes, M. (1975), 'Finance capital and the Scottish upper class', in Gordon Brown (1975).

Scott, John, and Hughes, M. (1976a), 'Patterns of ownership in top Scottish companies', *Scottish Journal of Sociology,* vol. 1, no. 1, pp. 15–28.

Scott, John, and Hughes, M. (1976b), 'Ownership and control in a satellite economy', *Sociology,* vol. 10, no. 1, pp. 21–42.

SCRE (1970), *A Study of Fifteen-year Olds* (London: University of London Press).

Sharpe, Sue (1976), *Just Like a Girl* (Harmondsworth: Penguin).

Shaw, Jenny (1976), 'Finishing school', in Barker and Allen (1976a).

Smart, Carol (1976), *Women, Crime and Criminology* (London: Routledge & Kegan Paul).

Smart, Carol, and Smart, Barry (eds) (1978), *Women, Sexuality and Social Control* (London: Routledge & Kegan Paul).

Smith, Cyril (1973), 'Adolescence', in M. Smith *et al.* (eds), *Leisure and Society in Britain* (London: Allen Lane).

Smith, Dorothy (1973), 'Women, the family and corporate capitalism', in Marylee Stephenson (ed.), *Women in Canada* (Toronto: The New Press).

Smith, Lesley Shacklady (1978), 'Sexist assumptions and female delinquency', in Smart and Smart (1978).

Smith, Roger (1976), 'Sex and occupational role in Fleet Street', in Barker and Allen (1976*b*).

Stacey, Judith, *et al.* (eds) (1974), *And Jill Came Tumbling After* (New York: Dell).

Stacey, Margaret (1960), *Tradition and Change* (London: Oxford University Press).

Stacey, Margaret, *et al.* (1975), *Power, Persistence and Change* (London: Routledge & Kegan Paul).

Stanworth, P. and Giddens, A. (eds) (1974), *Elites and Power in British Society* (Cambridge: Cambridge University Press).

Stubbs, Michael (1976), *Language, Schools and Classrooms* (London: Methuen).

Stott, Mary (1978), *Organization Women* (London: Heinemann).

Thorne, Barrie, and Henley, Nancy (eds) (1975), *Language and Sex* (Rowley, Mass.: Newbury House).

Toner, Barbara (1977), *The Facts of Rape* (London: Arrow).

Trudgill, Peter (1974), *Sociolinguistics* (Harmondsworth: Penguin).

Tunstall, Jeremy (1966), *Old and Alone* (London: Routledge & Kegan Paul).

Tunstall, Jeremy (1972), *The Fisherman*, 3rd edn (London: MacGibbon & Kee).

Urry, J., and Wakeford, J. (eds) (1973), *Power in Britain* (London: Heinemann).

Wallis, Roy (1976), 'Moral indignation and the media', *Sociology*, vol. 10, pp. 271–95.

Walum, L. R. (1977), *The Dynamics of Sex and Gender* (New York: Rand McNally).

Walton, R. G. (1975), *Women in Social Work* (London: Routledge & Kegan Paul).

Wandor, M. (ed.) (1972), *The Body Politic* (London: Stage One).

Ward, J. (n.d.), *Social Reality for the Adolescent Girl* (Swansea: Faculty of Education, University College, Swansea).

Watson, James (1968), *The Double Helix* (London: Weidenfeld & Nicolson).

Watson, James (ed.) (1977), *Between Two Cultures* (Oxford: Blackwell).

Wedge, P., and Prosser, H. (1973), *Born to Fail?* (London: Arrow).

Weeks, J. (1977), *Coming Out* (London: Quartet).

Weitzman, L. J., *et al.* (1972), 'Sex role socialization in picture books for pre-school children', *American Journal of Sociology*, vol. 77, no. 6, pp. 1125–50.

Westergaard, John, and Resler, Henrietta (1975), *Class in a Capitalist Society* (London: Heinemann).

Whitehead, Annie (1976), 'Sexual antagonism in Herefordshire', in Barker and Allen (1976b).

Whitley, R. (1974), 'The City and industry', in Stanworth and Giddens (1974).

Whyte, W. F. (1955), *Street Corner Society*, 2nd edn (Chicago: Chicago University Press).

Wilding, Paul (1977), *Poverty: The Facts in Wales* (London: CPAG).

Williams, Glyn (ed.) (1978), *Social and Cultural Change in Contemporary Wales* (London: Routledge & Kegan Paul).

Williams, Raymond (1973), *The Country and the City* (London: Chatto & Windus).

Williams, Raymond (1976), *Keywords* (London: Fontana/Croom Helm).

Williams, W. M. (1956), *The Sociology of an English Village* (London: Routledge & Kegan Paul).

Williams, W. M. (1963), *A West Country Village* (London: Routledge & Kegan Paul).

Willis, Paul (1977), *Learning to Labour* (Farnborough: Saxon House).

Willmott, P. (1968), 'There's nobody like Mum', *New Society*, 13 June, p. 373.

Wilson, Deirdre (1978), 'Sexual codes and conduct', in Smart and Smart (1978).

Young, M., and Willmott, P. (1957), *Family and Kinship in East London* (London: Routledge & Kegan Paul).

Young, M., and Willmott, P. (1975), *The Symmetrical Family* (Harmondsworth: Penguin; 1st edn, London: Routledge & Kegan Paul, 1973).

Index of Authors

Index of Subjects